Praise for *The Smart Negotiator*

"Having worked with negotiation for many years, I've read a fair number of books on the subject. What makes *The Smart Negotiator* by Keld Jensen stand out is its grounded approach and the way it brings AI into the conversation—not as hype, but as a practical tool that negotiators can actually use."

"Jensen has contributed to developing negotiation as a professional field for a long time, and this book continues that effort with clarity and relevance. He manages to show how human judgment and technological insight can work together to improve outcomes—without overcomplicating the process."

"One thing I appreciated in particular was the use of real-world examples. They make it clear how AI can reduce bias, surface important data, and help uncover overlooked areas of value—something that's highly relevant whether you're negotiating in business, academia, or public leadership."

"The book builds on the SMARTnership concept and extends it with strategic tools that help shift the focus from win-lose to joint value creation. It's a sober, well-organized read with takeaways you can apply in real-life settings."

"For professionals who want to sharpen their negotiation skills in step with today's challenges—this is a book worth reading."

—**Lars Krull**
Professor, Aalborg University

"You can't go to a conference or read an article without mention of the importance of AI. Yet no one explains how human insight is just as critical or how the two connect, especially in deal making. Thankfully, we are now able to find those answers through the wisdom of Dr. Keld Jensen in his latest work, *The Smart Negotiator*."

—**Linda Swindling, JD, CSP, CPAE**
Negotiation expert and Hall of Fame speaker; author of *Ask Outrageously: The Secret to Getting What You Really Want*

"Keld Jensen's newest book on the intersection of AI and negotiation is a timely and crucial contribution to the field. Building upon his established expertise and unwavering commitment to fair play, this work thoughtfully explores the exciting new opportunities that artificial intelligence presents in business negotiations. While Keld's previous books have consistently championed ethical practices and the powerful concept of SMARTnership—where mutual benefit and long-term relationships are prioritized—this latest offering delves into how we can strategically leverage AI tools to enhance these very principles. The integration of AI offers unprecedented potential for greater efficiency and more informed decision-making on both sides of the negotiating table. From sophisticated data analysis that can reveal hidden value and potential synergies, to AI-powered tools that can facilitate clearer communication and identify areas of common ground, this book illuminates how we can move beyond traditional adversarial approaches. Keld expertly guides us on how to harness these technological advancements not only to optimize our own outcomes but also to foster environments where all parties can gain more. By understanding and ethically deploying AI, we can unlock new levels of efficiency, uncover previously unseen opportunities for mutual benefit, and ultimately build stronger, more sustainable business relationships rooted in the principles of SMARTnership. This book is an essential read for any business professional seeking to navigate the future of negotiation with intelligence, integrity, and a focus on creating value for all involved."

"Keld Jensen's latest book is a vital guide to the future of negotiation, revealing how AI can elevate fairness, efficiency, and mutual value. Building on his SMARTnership philosophy, he shows how technology can uncover hidden potential, improve decision-making, and strengthen relationships. A must-read for professionals ready to negotiate smarter—with both strategy and integrity."

—**Werner Valeur**
Successful serial entrepreneur with million-dollar exits

THE
SMART
NEGOTIATOR

THE SMART NEGOTIATOR

UNLOCKING THE POWER OF AI AND HUMAN INSIGHT IN EFFECTIVE DEAL-MAKING

KELD JENSEN

WILEY

Copyright © 2025 by Keld Jensen. All rights reserved.

Published by John Wiley & Sons, Inc., Hoboken, New Jersey.
Published simultaneously in Canada.

No part of this publication may be reproduced, stored in a retrieval system, or transmitted in any form or by any means, electronic, mechanical, photocopying, recording, scanning, or otherwise, except as permitted under Section 107 or 108 of the 1976 United States Copyright Act, without either the prior written permission of the Publisher, or authorization through payment of the appropriate per-copy fee to the Copyright Clearance Center, Inc., 222 Rosewood Drive, Danvers, MA 01923, (978) 750-8400, fax (978) 750-4470, or on the web at www.copyright.com. Requests to the Publisher for permission should be addressed to the Permissions Department, John Wiley & Sons, Inc., 111 River Street, Hoboken, NJ 07030, (201) 748-6011, fax (201) 748-6008, or online at http://www.wiley.com/go/permission.

The manufacturer's authorized representative according to the EU General Product Safety Regulation is Wiley-VCH GmbH, Boschstr. 12, 69469 Weinheim, Germany, e-mail: Product_Safety@wiley.com.

Trademarks: Wiley and the Wiley logo are trademarks or registered trademarks of John Wiley & Sons, Inc. and/or its affiliates in the United States and other countries and may not be used without written permission. All other trademarks are the property of their respective owners. John Wiley & Sons, Inc. is not associated with any product or vendor mentioned in this book.

Limit of Liability/Disclaimer of Warranty: While the publisher and author have used their best efforts in preparing this book, they make no representations or warranties with respect to the accuracy or completeness of the contents of this book and specifically disclaim any implied warranties of merchantability or fitness for a particular purpose. No warranty may be created or extended by sales representatives or written sales materials. The advice and strategies contained herein may not be suitable for your situation. You should consult with a professional where appropriate. Further, readers should be aware that websites listed in this work may have changed or disappeared between when this work was written and when it is read. Neither the publisher nor authors shall be liable for any loss of profit or any other commercial damages, including but not limited to special, incidental, consequential, or other damages.

For general information on our other products and services or for technical support, please contact our Customer Care Department within the United States at (800) 762-2974, outside the United States at (317) 572-3993 or fax (317) 572-4002.

Wiley also publishes its books in a variety of electronic formats. Some content that appears in print may not be available in electronic formats. For more information about Wiley products, visit our web site at www.wiley.com.

Library of Congress Cataloging-in-Publication Data is Available:

ISBN 9781394255696 (Cloth)
ISBN 9781394255726 (ePub)
ISBN 9781394255740 (ePDF)

Cover Design: Wiley
Cover Image: © Tang Yan Song/Shutterstock
Author Photo: Courtesy of Keld Jensen, DBA

SKY10122331_071825

This book is dedicated to my late mother and father, Laura and Elmo. Their love and wisdom continue to guide and inspire me every day. Their legacy lives on in all that I do.

Contents

Introduction: The Evolving World of Negotiation   1
  A Forgotten Potential in Negotiation   2
    Capitalizing on Potential   2
    Is Negotiation a Science or an Art?   2
  Introduction to a New Era: Negotiation in a World of Sharks—and AI   3
    The New Negotiator at the Table: Artificial Intelligence   4
    The Evolution of Negotiation: From Zero-Sum to AI-Enhanced Value Creation   4
    Understanding AI's Role in Modern Negotiation   5
    The SMARTnership AI Framework   6
    Challenges and Ethical Considerations   6
    Practical Implementation: Getting Started with AI-Enhanced Negotiation   7
    Looking Ahead: The Future of AI in Negotiation   8
  Conclusion: A New Era of Value Creation   8

Part I   The Foundations of Negotiation: Strategy, Value, and AI   9

1   **The History of Negotiation**   11
  How AI Is Shaping Negotiation   13
    Data-Driven Preparation   13
    Enhanced Decision-Making   13
    Real-Time Assistance   13
    Cross-Cultural Negotiation   14
    Efficiency and Scalability   14
  Challenges and Ethical Considerations with AI   14
  A New Era of Negotiation   15

2   **Compelling Reasons to Focus on AI for Negotiations**   17
  The New Attendee at the Negotiation Table: AI   18
    The AI Edge: Enhancing Negotiation Capabilities   19
    The Human Advantage: Why People Still Drive Negotiation   20
    Better Together: The Human-AI Alliance   20
    The Three A's: Your Guide to Mastery in AI-Enhanced Negotiation   21

CONTENTS

3 Revolutionizing Commercial Relationships: The SMARTnership Approach 23
   The Roadmap for SMARTnership 24
      The $3.25 Trillion Opportunity You're Ignoring 24
      What Is NegoEconomics? 25
      Enter SMARTnership 27
      Distributive Negotiations Generates Poor Economics for All 27
      A Bigger Pie Means More for Everyone 28
   SMARTnerships, Partnerships, or Zero-Sum Games 29
      Do You Actually Have a Negotiation Strategy? 29
      SMARTnership in Action 30
      The SMARTnership Advantage 31
      Lessons for SMART Negotiators 32
   Ten Landmark Negotiations: Mastering the Art of Strategic Deal-Making 32
      Tesla and Panasonic: Powering the Future 32
      Disney and Pixar: Creativity Meets Corporate Strategy 32
      IBM and Lenovo: Strategic Global Shift 33
      The Camp David Accords: Peace in the Middle East 33
      Google's Acquisition of YouTube: Scaling Digital Content 33
      Microsoft's Acquisition of LinkedIn: Building a Professional Network 34
      The Paris Climate Agreement: Global Cooperation for a Common Goal 34
      Amazon's Purchase of Whole Foods: Revolutionizing Retail 35
      Sony and Marvel Studios: The Spider-Man Deal 35
      PayPal and eBay: Merging for Mutual Growth 35
   The Art of Strategic Deal-Making 36

4 Defining the Rules of the Game and Creating a Strategy 37
   Discussing Negotiation Before Negotiating 37
   Articulating a Negotiation Strategy for the Organization 38
   The Negotiation Code of Conduct 39
      Crafting Your Own Code of Conduct 40
   Conscious and Unconscious Negotiation with Yourself 41
      Preconceived Notions 41
      Time Is Negotiable 42
      Reschedule and Take Control 42
   Thinking Through the Transaction Ahead of Time 44
   Working with an Agenda 44

Understanding the Other Party's Intentions 44
The Advantage of Preparing an Agenda 45
Collaborating on an Agenda 45
Advantages of Using an Agenda 45
- Taking the Initiative 45
- Controlling the Other Party 45
- Becoming More Prepared 46

When an Agenda May Not Be Suitable 46
Understanding the Other Party's Requirements 46
Integrating AI to Define the "Rules of the Game" and Develop a Negotiation Strategy 47
Leveraging AI to Define the Rules of Engagement 47
AI-Enhanced Negotiation Strategy Development 47
Suggested Prompts for AI Integration 48

5 Prerequisites for a Successful Collaboration Agreement 49

Requirements for Success 49
- The Chemistry Must Be Right 49
- Both Parties Must Believe in the Collaboration Model 50
- You Must Have Rational and Knowledgeable Negotiators 50
- You Must Have Communication Proficiency 51
- You Need a Spirit of Generosity 51
- Creativity Must Be a Priority 51

How AI Can Help Craft and Execute Successful Collaboration Agreements 51
- Ensuring Compatibility: The Role of Human Chemistry 52
- Encouraging Belief in the Collaboration Model 52
- Enhancing Rationality and Knowledge in Negotiations 53
- Improving Communication Proficiency 53
- Fostering Generosity 54
- Encouraging Creativity in Solutions 54
- Supporting Managerial Tasks 54

6 Unveiling Value: The Hunt for NegoEconomics in Every Deal 57

Key Principles of NegoEconomics 57
- Example: Selling a Gaming Console 58
- Example: Car Dealership Negotiation 58
- Benefits of Focusing on NegoEconomics 59
- The Room for Negotiation 59
- Simple Model to Locate NegoEconomics 59
- Locating NegoEconomics in a Project 61

Examples of NegoEconomics 62

From Public Authority to Commercial Enterprise   63
Buying a Table in the 1950s: A Detailed Process   63
  Understanding the Shift in Furniture Packaging
    and Industry Transformation   64
  Lessons from the Furniture Industry's Evolution   66
Benchmarking and Applying NegoEconomics   66
  Financial Variables as NegoEconomic Opportunities   67
    Terms of Payment   67
    Ownership Models   68
    Pricing and Budgeting   68
  Currency Management: Money, Goods, or Services   71
  Initial Payments and Royalties   72
A Strategic Approach to Balancing Requirements,
    Costs, and Negotiation   73
  Economies of Scale   75
  Time in Agreements   76
  Purchasing Patterns and Modern Commerce   77
  Rights   78
  Example: Tesla and Rivian Collaboration   78
Leveraging AI in NegoEconomics   79
  Example: AI in Action for Tesla and Rivian   81
  AI Prompt Examples for NegoEconomics   81

Part II   Mastering the Art of Strategy   85

7 **The Power of Generosity in Negotiation**   87
   Rethinking Negotiation: A "Giver" Mindset   87
   Generosity as Strategic Capital   88
     SMARTnership and Generosity   88
     Overcoming the Myth: Why Generosity Isn't a Weakness   88
   Tru$tCurrency and the "Giver Advantage"   89
   The Giver as the Ultimate Negotiator   89
   The Real Cost of Cheap   90
     Negotiation as the Antidote to Price Frenzy   91
     A New Paradigm for Negotiation   91

8 **Success Is Based on Trust and Openness**   93
   Building a Relationship with Your Counterpart   93
     Two-Way Communication   94
     Participate in an Open Dialogue   94
     Listen Actively   95

Be Clear on What You Want 96
Say What You Mean—Clearly and Directly 96
Use Open Calculations 98
Conflict Destroys Relationships 99
A Third Party Can Help Build Rapport 99
Informal Contacts Can Offer Valuable Insights 100
Backdoor Selling 100
A Tour of the Production Plant 101
Understand Your Counterpart 102
Using Alternatives to Strength Your Position 104
Use Alternatives as a Trial Balloon 104
Handling Trial Balloons Effectively 105
Preventing Negotiations from Becoming Deadlocked 105
Breaking a Deadlock in Negotiation 106
Moving Past a Deadlock 107
Breaking the Stalemate 108
Avoiding Imbalance in the Information Flow 110
Don't Let the Counterpart Define the
   Playing Field 110
Use Questions as a Negotiation Technique 111
Using Hypothetical Questions Strategically 113
How AI Can Assist in Creating a Culture of Trust and
   Openness in Negotiations 114
Analyzing Human Chemistry and Compatibility 114
Enhancing Communication Proficiency 114
Facilitating Two-Way Communication 115
Building Trust Through Open Calculations 115
Improving Rapport Through Informal Interactions 115
Enhancing the Use of Visuals and Demonstrations 116
Breaking Deadlock with Data 116
Using AI to Manage Information Flow 117

9 **Valuing Trust** 119
How Can You Value Trust? 119
Creating Trust 120
Apple iTunes 120
Amazon's "Customer Obsession" and AI Integration 120
Netflix's "Continue Watching" Feature 121
How AI Can Enhance Trust in Business 122
AI-Driven Insights for Building a Trust Strategy 122
Why AI Matters in Trust-Building 124

10   The Different Negotiation Styles   125
    The Five Main Negotiation Styles   125
    DISC Styles in Negotiation: Adapting to Achieve Better Outcomes   126
      What Is DISC?   127
      Negotiating with the Four DISC Styles   127
        Dominance (D): The Results-Driven Negotiator   127
        Influence (I): The Relationship-Oriented Negotiator   128
        Steadiness (S): The Harmonious Negotiator   129
        Compliance (C): The Analytical Negotiator   129
      DISC Styles in Negotiation Teams   130
        Dominance (D): The Natural Leader   130
        Influence (I): The Engaging Communicator   130
        Steadiness (S): The Dependable Anchor   130
        Compliance (C): The Analytical Expert   131
      Balancing DISC Styles for Success   131
    How AI Can Assist in Leveraging Negotiation Styles and DISC Framework   131
      AI's Role in Supporting Negotiation Styles   132
        Behavior Analysis   132
        Dynamic Strategy Recommendations   132
      AI's Role in DISC-Based Negotiations   132
        DISC Profiling   132
        Team Optimization   133
        Simulating DISC Scenarios   133
        Real-Time Feedback   133
      Additional Prompts for AI Assistance   134
      Benefits of Using AI for Identifying Negotiation Styles   134

11   Masters of the Deal: What Sets Great Negotiators Apart   135
    Over 35,000 Negotiators Tested   135
      How Much Do All the Mistakes Cost?   136
      The Ketchup Effect   136
    Common Traits of Successful Negotiators   137
      They Analyze the Negotiation and the Negotiation Variables   138
      They Prioritize Important over Less Important Factors   138
      They Make a Decision and Put a Price on the Soft Variables   139
      They Embrace AI and Understand How to Prompt It Effectively   139
      They Often Outline the Negotiation on a Board to Get an Overview   139
      They Incorporate the Message of NegoEconomics   140
      They Take the Initiative During Negotiations   140

They Are Good at Communicating   140
They Have High But Realistic Goals   141
They Quickly Start Negotiating   141
They Try to Avoid Problems by Suggesting Alternatives   141
They Create a Positive Negotiation Climate   142
They Actively Present Offers and Counteroffers   142
They Have a Strategy   142
They Distribute the Roles Within the Group and Are Disciplined   143
They Work Methodically   143
They Do Not Dig Themselves into Foxholes and Fight About Details   143
They Start Bargaining in Good Time   143
They Take One Last Break Before Entering into an Agreement   144
They Make a Point of Behaving in a Credible Manner   144
Common Mistakes of Failing Negotiators   144
They Only See Half the Negotiation   145
They Aim Too Low   145
They Do Not Actively Search for the NegoEconomics   147
They Throw Themselves into Traditional Negotiation Fights   147
Price Is More Important Than the Overall Costs   148
The Concept of NegoEconomics Is Vague to Them   149
They Overlook the Totality   150
They Don't Understand That the Partner Also Has to Make Money   151
They Are Afraid of Opening Up   152
They Work Unstructured   153
They Have Not Distributed the Roles Within the Group   154
They Are Afraid of Bargaining   155
They Do Not Set Up a Strategy   156
They Lose Their Grip on the Economy   157
They Make Insultingly Low Offers   158
They Do Not Accept That the Opponent Makes Money   159
They Seek "Fair" Solutions   160
They Are Not Good at Listening   160
Preparing to Avoid Failure   160
Other Common Mistakes in Negotiation   161
The Personal Contact Is Forgotten   161
They Do Not Understand the Opponent   162
They Insult the Opponent   163
They Forget the Other Interested Parties   164

Cost Savings Within One Link Are Eaten
  Up by Problems in Another 164
Exaggerated Suspiciousness Is Present 165
There Is a Sense of Stinginess 165
They Guard Preserves 165
Political Value Norms Influence the Situation 166
Envy Impacts the Process 166
Cultural Differences Affect the Situation 167
The "We-versus-Them" Feeling Hinders the Negotiation 167
Leveraging AI for Negotiation Insights 168

PART III The Future of Negotiation: AI, Psychology, and Advanced 169

12 Creating AI Prompts for Negotiation-Specific Tasks 171

13 AI in Negotiation: Amplifying Human Insight for SMARTnership Success 177
Refining AI to Reflect Your Voice in Negotiation 177
Overcoming Challenges in Negotiation Using AI Prompts 178
  Leveraging Emotion-Focused Prompts in Negotiation 179
  Building Empathy into Negotiation Messages 179
  Key Takeaways for Effective AI-Assisted Negotiation Writing 180
The Irreplaceable Human Touch 180
  The Four Pillars of Human-AI Synergy in Negotiation 180
    Emotional Intelligence (EQ) in the Digital Age 180
    Cultural Intelligence (CQ) in a Connected World 181
    Relationship Architecture in the AI Era 181
    Creative Problem-Solving: The Human Advantage 182
  Practical Integration: The Human-AI Balance 182
  The Future of Human-AI Collaboration in Negotiation 183
  Conclusion: The Human Advantage 184

14 AI as the Negotiator's New Ally 185
Preparation: Building a Solid Foundation 185
Strategy: Designing Your Path to Success 186
During the Negotiation: Real-Time Assistance 187
Emotional Intelligence: Understanding and Responding 187
Simulation: Practicing for Excellence 188
Crafting Your Next Best Alternative (NBA) 188
Communication: Streamlining Dialogues 189

  Review: Learning from the Process **189**
  Conclusion: Your AI-Powered Negotiation Partner **190**

15 AI in Contracting: Redefining How to Write and Read Contracts **191**
  The Challenges of Traditional Contracting **191**
  How AI Transforms Contract Writing **192**
   Automating Repetitive Tasks **192**
   Simplifying Language **192**
   Customizing Templates **193**
   Embedding Goals and Values **193**
  Enhancing Contract Reading with AI **193**
   Simplifying Document Navigation **193**
   Identifying Risk **193**
   Providing Contextual Insights **194**
   Providing Real-Time Explanations **194**
  The Ethical Dimension of AI in Contracting **194**
  The Future of AI in Contracting **195**
  Contract Writing Prompts **195**
   General Drafting Prompts **195**
   Clause Suggestions **195**
   Formatting and Structure **196**
   Customization **196**
   Scenario-Specific Drafting **196**
   Clause Summarization **196**
   Risk Identification **196**
   Comparison **196**
   Regulatory Compliance **197**
   Quick Navigation **197**
   Rewriting and Simplification **197**
   Executive Summaries **197**
   Creating FAQs **197**
   Real-Time Questions **197**
   Document Improvement **198**
   Ethical Review **198**
   SMARTnership Optimization **198**
  Embracing AI for Better Contracts **198**

16 Lessons from the Field: Harnessing Artificial Intelligence in Negotiation **199**
  A Case Study in AI-Driven Negotiation **200**
   Key Details of the Experiment **200**
   The Results: Unpacking the Experiment's Findings **200**

Efficiency and Resolution 200
Enhanced Preparation 201
Behavioral Dynamics 201
Challenges and Lessons from Integration 201
Asymmetric Usage 201
Learning Curve 202
Employing AI as a Strategic Partner 202
Standardization and Best Practices 202
Ethical Considerations 202
Machine-to-Machine Negotiation 202
The Future of Negotiation in an AI-Driven World 203
A New Paradigm for Negotiation 203

17 Revolutionizing Negotiation with Real-Time AI Feedback 205
The Power of Real-Time Data Analysis 205
Emotion and Sentiment Analysis: The Empathy Engine 206
Tactical Assistance on the Fly 207
Simulating Scenarios for Better Outcomes 207
Balancing Technology and Human Intuition 208
Overcoming Challenges in AI-Driven Negotiation 208
The Future of Real-Time AI Feedback 209

18 Defining Authority Bias and Mitigating the Risk 211
Origins of Authority Bias 211
Modern Manifestations of Authority Bias 212
How to Avoid Authority Bias 212
Comparison to Anthropomorphism 213
Beware of AI Solutions Searching for Problems 213

19 The Power of Prompts in Negotiation 215
Prompts to Prepare for Negotiations 216
Prompts for Building Relationships and Rapport 216
Prompts for Negotiation Strategies 218
Prompts for Negotiation Tactics 219
Prompts for Negotiation Scripts 219
Prompts for Risk Management 219
Prompts for Scenario Planning 220
Prompts for Advanced Techniques 220
Prompts for Metrics and Analysis 220
Prompts for AI and Negotiation 220
Prompts for Training and Development 221
Prompts for Sustainability in Negotiations 221

Prompts to Close the Deal 221
Prompts for Conflict Resolution 221
Prompts for Continuous Improvement 222
Prompts for Leveraging Tru$tCurrency 222
Scenario-Specific Prompts 222
Prompts for Innovation in Negotiation 222
Prompts for Ethical Considerations 223
Prompts for Adding Final Touches 223

20 The Role of Artificial Intelligence in Modern Negotiation Dynamics 225

Efficiency: The New Paradigm 225
The Power and Pitfalls of Information Asymmetry 226
Challenges of AI-Driven Negotiation 226
AI and SMARTnership: A Collaborative Approach 227
Ethical and Regulatory Considerations 227
The Future of Negotiation 228
Implementing AI-Enhanced SMARTnership Strategies 229
   Measuring ROI: Quantifying the Impact of AI-Enhanced Strategies 229
   Financial Metrics 229
   Performance Metrics 230
   Relationship Value Metrics 230
Change Management: Navigating the Transition to AI-Enhanced Negotiation 230
   Stakeholder Analysis and Engagement 230
   Implementation Roadmap 231
   Resistance Management 231
Team Training: Building Competence in AI-Enhanced SMARTnership 231
   Core Competency Development 231
   Training Program Structure 232
   Certification Program 232

CONCLUSION THE STARTING POINT IS YOU 233
ACKNOWLEDGMENTS 235
ABOUT THE AUTHOR 237
INDEX 239

INTRODUCTION

The Evolving World of Negotiation

I claimed in a recent article that negotiation as a science hasn't truly progressed since 1776, the year the Scottish philosopher Adam Smith published *The Wealth of Nations*.

Walking the Scottish Highlands, Smith envisioned how nations could trade collaboratively, laying the foundation for negotiation as a discipline.

Fast-forward to 1976, when Mr. Iwar Unt, founder of the organization I head today, published his first book in Sweden, or jump to 1981 and the world's best-selling negotiation book, *Getting to Yes*, by Roger Fisher and William Ury—negotiation had remained relatively unexplored as a professional science. Since then, hundreds of books have advocated collaboration over zero-sum tactics. However, the win-lose approach still dominates, leaving much value untapped.

Do we need more books on negotiation?

The short answer is no. The challenge isn't a lack of knowledge about effective negotiation but a failure to apply it. If more books equaled better negotiators, every industry would have mastered the science by now.

New negotiation books emerge monthly, promising fresh perspectives, yet the issue persists. Effective negotiation already has well-established principles—creating long-term value for both sides. What's missing isn't theory or tools but a change in mindset and practice.

You might find this message strange, coming from someone who has written 27 books on negotiation. But I believe the focus must shift from piling on techniques to understanding what negotiation is—and what it isn't. Successful negotiation isn't about clever tricks but about creating and distributing value, a process requiring consistency, context awareness, and a deep understanding of the people involved.

A Forgotten Potential in Negotiation

Negotiation is one of humanity's oldest tools for resolving conflict and creating opportunities. From bartering in ancient marketplaces to today's complex multinational deals, its essence remains unchanged: finding common ground. Yet, despite advances in technology and behavioral science, negotiators still fall into predictable traps, leaving significant value on the table. Why? Because traditional models focus on claiming value rather than creating it.

This book challenges these outdated notions. By integrating the SMARTnership framework, the revolutionary concept of NegoEconomics, and the transformative potential of AI, it lays the groundwork for moving negotiation from a transactional practice to a transformational one.

Capitalizing on Potential

A critical aspect of successful negotiation is identifying and capitalizing on untapped potential. Research shows that up to 42 percent of the potential value in negotiations remains unutilized. This gap is the basis of *NegoEconomics* (negotiation economics).

This "lost" value stems from the asymmetry in each party's costs and benefits for negotiation variables. Consider transportation costs. You know it costs your business $20,000, but you might be unaware of your counterpart's cost—say, $15,000. In traditional, zero-sum negotiation, this information remains hidden. However, in an interest-based SMARTnership approach, utilizing NegoEconomics, you and your counterpart would share these details, uncovering a $5,000 negotiable advantage. This is NegoEconomics in action.

Is Negotiation a Science or an Art?

We often hear terms like "the art of negotiation" or "the science of negotiation," but what do these actually mean? If negotiation were purely an art, perhaps some would be born with a talent for it, like painters or musicians. If it were purely a science, it would rely entirely on structured methods and practice. In reality, negotiation is both—a skillset blending intuition, experience, and practice.

Some naturally enjoy negotiating, but not due to an inherent talent; they appreciate the process and rewards. Yet enjoyment alone doesn't make one a skilled negotiator. To truly excel, we must study, refine, and continuously adapt our approach, just as with any evolving field.

Reflecting on my first book, published in 1998, I was struck by how much negotiation practices have changed. People negotiate differently today than they did 30 years ago. In fact, studies show that 20 percent of professional negotiators are not particularly skilled, often because they dislike negotiating.

Ask yourself, "Do I enjoy negotiation?" If so, that's a solid start. If not, there's still room to develop and, potentially, to find enjoyment through mastery. That's where this book can help.

Introduction to a New Era: Negotiation in a World of Sharks—and AI

"Execution trumps talent."

—Robert Herjavec, Shark Tank

Millions tune in weekly to watch the sharks of *Shark Tank* negotiate high-stakes deals. Adapted globally from the original Japanese *Dragons' Den*, the show simplifies negotiation for entertainment while dealing with real stakes: millions of dollars and entrepreneurs' dreams.

While entertaining, *Shark Tank* reinforces a narrative that negotiation is a zero-sum game, where one party wins and the other loses. Hollywood often amplifies this perspective, portraying negotiation as a battlefield rather than a collaborative opportunity. This portrayal has led many professionals to view negotiation as inherently adversarial—a mindset that undermines the potential for creating mutual value.

The sharks are often called the best negotiators in the world. This book briefly examines that claim, looking at their methods and tactics. But it doesn't stop there. Beyond *Shark Tank*, this book explores successful negotiations in various domains, analyzing what we can learn from those who excel at creating value, fostering trust, and achieving mutually beneficial agreements.

Studying these examples highlights principles and practices that elevate negotiation from mere transactions to strategic collaborations.

Experience alone does not guarantee expertise in negotiation. Too often, individuals claim decades of experience without realizing they may have been repeating the same flawed approach year after year. Twenty-three years of negotiation does not equate to growth if those years are built on the repetition of ineffective strategies. True mastery comes not from the length of time spent negotiating but from the continuous refinement of skills, thoughtful reflection on outcomes, and the willingness to evolve methods based on proven principles and new insights. Without this, what appears to be 23 years of experience is, in reality, one year of poor negotiation repeated 23 times. This book challenges that mindset, providing the tools to break that cycle and achieve measurable progress.

While *Shark Tank* simplifies negotiation for TV, its lessons are invaluable. The show's format mirrors real challenges negotiators face, offering insights into creating value under pressure. However, it is equally important to unlearn the adversarial mindset and embrace a more collaborative approach—one that this book guides you through.

The New Negotiator at the Table: Artificial Intelligence

In the spring of 2022, a mid-sized manufacturing company faced a critical supplier negotiation that would determine its future. The traditional approach would have been to squeeze the supplier on price, potentially damaging a long-term relationship. Instead, they employed an AI-enhanced SMARTnership approach. The AI analyzed years of transaction data, numerous variables, existing contracts, market trends, and supply chain patterns, revealing opportunities for value creation that neither party had considered. The result? A deal that increased profits for both parties by 27 percent and strengthened their strategic partnership.

This is not a unique story. Across industries and cultures, AI and SMARTnership negotiation are transforming how we negotiate, not by replacing human negotiators, but by augmenting their capabilities in ways that align perfectly with the principles of SMARTnership negotiation.

The Evolution of Negotiation: From Zero-Sum to AI-Enhanced Value Creation

For centuries, negotiation has been viewed as a battlefield where one party's gain must come at another's expense. This mindset, deeply rooted in the traditional "win-lose" approach, has led to countless missed opportunities and destroyed relationships. Even after groundbreaking works like *Getting to Yes* were published in 1981, the fundamental approach to negotiation remained largely unchanged.

Consider these sobering statistics:

- 42 percent of the values in a negotiation are never capitalized.
- 33 percent of negotiations beneficial for both parties fail to reach an agreement.
- 35 percent more profit is achieved in high-trust negotiations compared to those with low trust.
- 84 percent of negotiators believe they are negotiating the wrong variables in a negotiation.

The SMARTnership approach was developed to address these challenges by emphasizing trust, transparency, and mutual gain. Now, with the advent of AI, we have the tools to implement these principles more effectively than ever before.

Understanding AI's Role in Modern Negotiation

AI is not just another tool in the negotiator's toolkit—it represents a fundamental shift in how we approach value creation and distribution. The following sections explain how AI transforms key aspects of negotiation.

Data Analysis and Pattern Recognition
AI can analyze data and recognize patterns in several ways:

- **Market intelligence:** AI systems can analyze vast amounts of market data to identify trends and opportunities that human negotiators might miss. For example, an AI system might notice that your counterpart's business experiences seasonal fluctuations that create opportunities for asymmetric value creation.
- **Behavioral analysis:** Advanced AI can analyze negotiation patterns across thousands of deals to identify successful strategies and potential pitfalls.
- **Risk assessment:** AI can simulate countless scenarios to help negotiators understand and mitigate risks in complex deals.

Value Creation Through Asymmetric Discovery
One of the most powerful applications of AI in SMARTnership negotiation is its ability to uncover asymmetric values—situations where an asset or condition has different values for different parties. As an example, consider the following case study.

Case Study

A real estate developer used AI to analyze property usage patterns and discovered that a seemingly worthless parking restriction had significant value to the neighboring business. This insight led to a creative solution that increased the deal's total value by 40 percent.

Trust-Building Through Transparency
AI can enhance trust-building in several ways:

- **Objective data analysis:** By providing unbiased, data-driven insights, AI helps create a foundation of shared understanding.
- **Real-time validation:** AI systems can verify claims and commitments during negotiations, reducing uncertainty and building confidence.

- **Transparent decision-making:** When properly designed, AI systems can explain their recommendations, making the negotiation process more transparent.

The SMARTnership AI Framework

To effectively integrate AI into negotiation, we need a structured approach that aligns technology with human expertise. The SMARTnership AI Framework consists of four key elements:

1. Preparation Phase
   - AI-driven market analysis
   - Stakeholder mapping and relationship assessment
   - Value opportunity identification
   - Risk analysis and mitigation planning
2. Engagement Phase
   - Real-time data analysis and insight generation
   - Behavioral pattern recognition
   - Cultural and communication alignment
   - Trust-building opportunity identification
3. Value Creation Phase
   - Asymmetric value discovery
   - Creative solution generation
   - Impact simulation and optimization
   - Stakeholder benefit analysis
4. Implementation Phase
   - Agreement monitoring and compliance
   - Performance tracking and optimization
   - Relationship strengthening
   - Continuous learning and improvement

Challenges and Ethical Considerations

While AI offers tremendous potential, its integration into negotiation presents several challenges that must be addressed.

The Trust Paradox How do we ensure that AI systems enhance rather than diminish trust between negotiating parties? The solution lies in:

- Transparent AI systems that explain their recommendations
- Clear governance frameworks for AI use in negotiations
- Balanced integration of human judgment and AI insights

The Digital Divide Not all parties have equal access to advanced AI tools, which could create unfair advantages. We must consider:

- Ways to democratize access to AI negotiation tools
- Standards for AI use in negotiations
- Ethical guidelines for AI-enhanced negotiation

The Human Element Negotiation is fundamentally about human relationships. AI must enhance, not replace, the human elements of negotiation:

- Emotional intelligence
- Cultural sensitivity
- Relationship building
- Creative problem-solving

Practical Implementation: Getting Started with AI-Enhanced Negotiation

To begin implementing AI in your negotiations, consider these steps:

1. **Assessment:** Evaluate your current negotiation processes and identify areas where AI could add value.
2. **Tool selection:** Choose AI tools that align with your needs and capabilities. Consider:
   - Data analysis requirements
   - Integration capabilities
   - User-friendliness
   - Cost-effectiveness

3. **Team Development:** Train your team to effectively use AI tools while maintaining focus on human relationships and value creation.
4. **Process Integration:** Gradually integrate AI tools into your negotiation process, starting with simple applications and progressing to more complex ones.

Looking Ahead: The Future of AI in Negotiation

The integration of AI into negotiation is not just about improving efficiency—it's about transforming how we create and distribute value. As AI technology continues to evolve, we can expect to see:

- More sophisticated pattern recognition capabilities
- Better prediction of negotiation outcomes
- Enhanced ability to identify value creation opportunities
- Improved support for cross-cultural negotiations

Conclusion: A New Era of Value Creation

The combination of AI and SMARTnership principles represents a powerful opportunity to transform negotiation from a zero-sum game into a collaborative value-creation process. By embracing this approach, negotiators can:

- Create more value for all parties
- Build stronger, more sustainable relationships
- Achieve better outcomes more consistently
- Drive innovation in deal-making

The following chapters explore specific applications of AI in different aspects of negotiation, from preparation to implementation, always focusing on the core principles of SMARTnership: trust, transparency, and mutual value creation.

Remember: AI is not here to replace human negotiators but to enhance their capabilities and help them create more value for all parties involved. The future of negotiation lies not in choosing between human expertise and artificial intelligence, but in finding ways to combine them effectively to achieve superior outcomes.

—Dr. Keld Jensen
Laguna Niguel, California

PART I

The Foundations of Negotiation: Strategy, Value, and AI

This section, covering Chapters 1–6, lays the groundwork for a deeper understanding of modern negotiation. From historical perspectives to cutting-edge AI integration, these chapters explore how negotiation has evolved and why mastering it is essential for success in any field.

Chapter 1 traces the history of negotiation from ancient barter systems to modern strategic deal-making. Understanding how negotiation has developed over centuries provides critical insights into why certain tactics work and how negotiation strategies have been shaped by economic, political, and technological forces.

Chapter 2 explores the growing role of AI in negotiation. AI is not replacing human negotiators—it's augmenting their abilities. From data-driven preparation to real-time analysis, AI enables negotiators to uncover asymmetric value, optimize outcomes, and create stronger partnerships.

Chapter 3 introduces the *SMARTnership approach*, a game-changing strategy that moves beyond traditional zero-sum bargaining. By focusing on trust, transparency, and NegoEconomics, negotiators can unlock untapped value, transforming deals into high-value, long-term collaborations.

Chapter 4 defines the *Rules of the Game*—a critical step that too many negotiators overlook. Before entering discussions, it's essential to establish a structured approach, agree on ethical guidelines, and align expectations. This chapter also highlights how AI can assist in setting clear negotiation parameters.

Chapter 5 outlines the prerequisites for a successful collaboration agreement. Success isn't just about numbers—it's about chemistry, trust, and communication. The right people, mindset, and approach can make the difference between a deal that thrives and one that collapses.

Finally, Chapter 6 explores the powerful concept of *NegoEconomics*—the hidden value in every deal. By identifying asymmetric costs and benefits, negotiators can create value that wasn't initially on the table, leading to better outcomes for all parties involved.

Together, these six chapters provide a solid foundation for mastering negotiation in today's complex and rapidly evolving landscape. Whether you're negotiating contracts, partnerships, or deals of any kind, the principles in Part I will equip you with the mindset, strategies, and tools to excel.

CHAPTER 1

The History of Negotiation

Before we dive into the present and future, let's take a look back in time. How old is the negotiation as a science?
Negotiation is as old as human interaction, evolving from basic barter systems in ancient societies to complex, multifaceted processes in modern times. The following table outlines a more concise history.

Era	Characteristics and Location
Ancient times	Barter systems: Early humans engaged in simple negotiations through barter, exchanging goods and services directly.
	Mesopotamia and ancient Egypt: Evidence of early written contracts and treaties, such as the clay tablets from Mesopotamia, shows formalized negotiation processes.
Classical antiquity	Ancient Greece and Rome: Greek city-states and Roman provinces used negotiation for trade and diplomacy. Philosophers like Aristotle discussed principles of rhetoric and persuasion, influencing negotiation tactics.
	China: Sun Tzu's *The Art of War* (5th century BCE) offered strategic negotiation insights applicable to both warfare and diplomatic negotiations.
Middle Ages	Feudal Europe: Negotiations focused on land, vassalage, and marriage alliances. The *Magna Carta* (1215) was a landmark in negotiated agreements between monarchs and subjects.
	Islamic golden age: Islamic scholars like Al-Ghazali contributed to negotiation theory through works on ethics and commerce.

12 CHAPTER 1 The History of Negotiation

Era	Characteristics and Location
Early modern period	Renaissance Europe: Trade expansion led to more sophisticated negotiation tactics, with Italian city-states like Venice excelling in diplomatic and commercial negotiations.
	Colonial era: European powers negotiated treaties and trade agreements, often exploiting indigenous populations.
19th century	Industrial Revolution: Rapid industrialization and globalization necessitated complex labor negotiations, leading to the rise of labor unions and collective bargaining.
	Diplomacy: The Congress of Vienna (1814–1815) exemplified sophisticated diplomatic negotiations to establish a balance of power in Europe post–Napoleonic Wars.
20th century	World Wars: Postwar negotiations, like the Treaty of Versailles (1919) and the formation of the United Nations (1945), highlighted the importance of international negotiation to maintain peace.
	Cold War: The era saw strategic negotiations like the Strategic Arms Limitation Treaties (SALT; 1972, 1979) to control arms proliferation between the United States and the USSR.
	Business negotiations: The rise of multinational corporations led to advanced negotiation strategies in mergers, acquisitions, and international trade agreements.
	Academic contributions: Negotiation was first systematically described and explained academically in the early 20th century, with foundational works like Mary Parker Follett's writings on conflict resolution and collaborative problem-solving in the 1920s.
Contemporary period	Technological influence: Digital communication has transformed negotiation practices, enabling real-time global negotiations.
	Theory and practice: Modern theories like game theory, pioneered by John Nash, and integrative negotiation models focus on win-win outcomes and mutual gains.
	Cross-cultural negotiation: Globalization necessitates understanding cultural differences in negotiation styles and practices.

How AI Is Shaping Negotiation

As negotiation evolves into the 21st century, artificial intelligence (AI) is poised to revolutionize the field, introducing unprecedented levels of efficiency, adaptability, and precision. While negotiation has historically relied on human intuition, strategy, and psychology, AI adds a new layer of data-driven decision-making, dynamic modeling, and enhanced communication tools.

Data-Driven Preparation

AI can analyze vast datasets—financial models, industry benchmarks, and competitor strategies—providing negotiators with deeper insights than ever before. This enables precise preparation tailored to counterpart priorities.

What it changes: Negotiators can move beyond intuition to rely on concrete data to craft arguments and predict outcomes.

Example: AI can identify patterns in counterpart behavior from past negotiations, suggesting tailored strategies to align with their priorities and style.

Enhanced Decision-Making

AI excels at evaluating complex scenarios in real time, simulating outcomes based on various negotiation strategies. It provides decision-makers with immediate feedback on the likely consequences of their choices.

What it changes: Negotiators gain access to predictive models that optimize deal structures, pricing strategies, and concession plans.

Example: During a business merger, AI could simulate financial impacts under multiple offer scenarios, helping both parties find the most mutually beneficial outcome.

Real-Time Assistance

AI-powered negotiation assistants provide live feedback and strategy adjustments during discussions. These tools analyze language, tone, and emotional cues to guide the negotiator's responses.

What it changes: Negotiators receive actionable insights mid-conversation, enabling them to adapt dynamically.

Example: If the counterpart begins showing signs of disengagement, AI could suggest shifting the focus of discussion or adjusting tone to reengage them.

Cross-Cultural Negotiation

AI can interpret cultural differences in negotiation styles and practices, ensuring that negotiators avoid missteps and build stronger relationships with counterparts from diverse backgrounds.
   What it changes: Global negotiations become smoother and more effective, reducing misunderstandings and fostering trust.
   Example: In a negotiation with a Japanese counterpart, AI might recommend prioritizing harmony and group consensus over aggressive tactics, aligning with cultural norms.

Efficiency and Scalability

AI automates repetitive tasks like drafting contracts, analyzing clauses, and managing negotiation workflows, freeing up negotiators to focus on strategic decision-making.
   What it changes: Negotiators can handle more complex, high-volume negotiations without sacrificing quality.
   Example: AI tools could analyze hundreds of contract drafts in minutes, identifying potential risks or opportunities for improvement.

Challenges and Ethical Considerations with AI

While AI offers tremendous potential, it also raises important questions:

   Ethical use: Ensuring transparency and fairness in AI-driven negotiations is critical. AI must not manipulate or deceive counterparts.

   Human oversight: Negotiation will always involve human judgment, especially in high-stakes situations where emotional intelligence and relationship-building are essential.

   Bias in data: AI systems are only as good as the data they're trained on. Poor data can lead to flawed recommendations, reinforcing existing biases.

A New Era of Negotiation

AI is not replacing human negotiators but augmenting their capabilities. By combining AI's analytical power with human creativity and emotional intelligence, negotiators can achieve:

- **Better outcomes:** Data-driven insights create more equitable and efficient deals.
- **Faster processes:** Automation and real-time feedback reduce the time needed to finalize agreements.
- **Stronger relationships:** AI ensures clearer communication and greater cultural understanding.

The history of negotiation has shown an evolution from bartering to diplomacy to corporate deal-making. With the rise of AI, the field is entering a new phase where technology empowers negotiators to achieve unparalleled precision and effectiveness. The future of negotiation is not just about strategy—it's about integrating intelligence, both human and artificial, for mutual success.

Negotiation has evolved from simple exchanges to sophisticated strategies involving psychology, economics, and international relations. Understanding its history provides valuable insights into its current practices and future trends.

CHAPTER 2

Compelling Reasons to Focus on AI for Negotiations

Regardless of your job, career, or industry, mastering negotiation is crucial. This might surprise some—or it could confirm what you've suspected all along. Among essential skills like critical thinking, managing people, and solving complex problems, negotiation stands out as a skill that demands deliberate cultivation. The World Economic Forum ranks negotiation among the top 10 skills for success in any role. Moreover, a recent survey by Speakers Gold placed negotiation among the 25 most requested keynote topics in North America.

Many envision negotiation as a high-stakes boardroom activity for executives in suits, but that's only one type. Anyone engaged in interpersonal relationships—professional or personal—participates in negotiations daily. Studies estimate that an individual engages in 8,000–10,000 negotiations each year, often without consciously realizing it.

In my experience, professionals in varied fields negotiate frequently, sometimes over contracts worth millions, often without formal negotiation training. Many simply rely on experience or by observing colleagues, with some claiming "decades of experience." Yet, as I've observed, they may have one year of experience, repeated multiple times. Ultimately, the idea of a "born negotiator" is a myth.

The New Attendee at the Negotiation Table: AI

We are at the dawn of a transformative period in which artificial intelligence (AI) is reshaping not just the way we negotiate but the entire landscape of strategic collaboration. This book serves as a guide to integrating AI into your negotiation processes, helping you save time, build stronger agreements, and redefine the art of deal-making.

As the first generation of negotiators, managers, and leaders to harness AI, we face an unprecedented inflection point. Ignoring AI's role in negotiation is a strategic misstep. Embracing AI is not just prudent; it is essential for effective negotiation in the modern landscape.

The shift ahead is irreversible, setting us on a path where future negotiators will seamlessly blend AI into their strategies, as will your counterparts across the table. The question is not if but how you will incorporate these tools into your approach.

AI is already proving its value by automating repetitive tasks, such as compiling data, analyzing patterns, and tracking deal progress in real time. This is just the beginning. The challenge lies in using AI to strengthen negotiation tactics—complementing human insight and skill rather than replacing it. While some may mistakenly attempt to automate the entire negotiation process, only those who combine AI with human ingenuity will truly unlock its potential.

Our early studies on the influence of AI in negotiation indicate clear benefits: AI enhances efficiency, helps capture more value, and drives better outcomes. Surprisingly, AI also has the potential to foster trust, transparency, and collaboration among parties. By analyzing vast amounts of data and detecting patterns and opportunities humans might miss, AI creates pathways for mutually beneficial solutions that might otherwise remain unseen.

AI's ability to generate and analyze alternative solutions—often in real time—boosts the effectiveness of negotiation by focusing on interests rather than positions, a cornerstone of the SMARTnership approach. In fact, AI has proven effective in supporting NegoEconomics by identifying and capitalizing on asymmetric value potentials, empowering both parties to uncover added value they may not have anticipated.

McKinsey Global Institute's research suggests that as automation and AI reshape industries, demand for high-level cognitive skills—like negotiation—will only increase. As technology advances, negotiation skills will evolve alongside it, amplifying the need for adaptability, insight, and strategic foresight. Developing these skills isn't just an advantage; it's essential for thriving in the future of work.

The AI Edge: Enhancing Negotiation Capabilities

At its core, generative AI is powered by a large language model (LLM) that predicts what you need based on statistical probabilities and the prompts you provide. When you interact with AI, it pulls from a vast database to create content that matches the context of your input. The accuracy and depth of its output depend on how clear and precise your instructions are.

In essence, the better your guidance, the better the results. AI can achieve astonishing things, but its effectiveness is tied to your ability to steer it. Ultimately, the outcomes it generates are yours to own—not the machine's.

The true magic of AI goes far beyond mastering grammar. Its real power lies in its training. These models absorb immense amounts of data from a wide variety of sources, including books, websites, articles, and more. This expansive foundation allows AI to produce responses that are not only grammatically correct but also contextually insightful and highly relevant.

Everything AI creates is based on its ability to predict the next step, whether it's a word, a sound, or an image. This precision is a result of the structured rules of language—grammar and syntax—that guide its understanding. These rules enable AI to analyze patterns and respond intelligently based on what it has learned.

Note: To fully leverage AI's potential, you must learn how to direct it effectively. This requires patience, experimentation, and a willingness to invest time—and often, resources. Mastering AI is not instant, but the possibilities it unlocks make the journey worthwhile.

AI is poised to elevate negotiation, streamlining complex tasks and delivering insights that amplify your effectiveness. Here are key ways AI will redefine negotiation:

- **Data-driven preparation:** AI can process vast datasets to provide you with detailed profiles, historical patterns, and predictive insights on your counterparts, allowing you to approach negotiations with an informed strategy.
- **Dynamic proposal creation:** AI can instantly generate proposals and counteroffers tailored to each negotiation's unique demands, increasing your adaptability and response time.
- **Enhanced stakeholder analysis:** AI tools can analyze body language, tone, and text sentiment during discussions, helping you gain a deeper understanding of your counterpart's motivations and emotions.
- **Advanced scenario planning:** By simulating different negotiation outcomes, AI can help you refine strategies, anticipate objections, and identify potential win-win scenarios.

- **Automated follow-ups:** AI can ensure timely and relevant post-negotiation communications by automating follow-up messages that align with agreements and previous discussions.

These capabilities make you faster, more informed, and better equipped to negotiate effectively. But AI is a tool, not a replacement for human intelligence. The real power lies in your ability to use it to deepen understanding, identify creative solutions, and forge stronger partnerships.

The Human Advantage: Why People Still Drive Negotiation

Despite the buzz around AI's potential, the art of negotiation remains deeply human. AI is not here to replace the negotiator but to enhance their role. With AI handling data analysis and logistical tasks, you are free to focus on what's truly essential: building trust, fostering relationships, and crafting mutually beneficial solutions.

Exceptional negotiators excel at interpreting human behavior—reading subtle cues, responding empathetically, and adapting to shifting dynamics. These qualities are irreplaceable. AI cannot replicate the intuition and adaptability that skilled negotiators bring to the table. Complex negotiations hinge on emotional intelligence, the ability to manage nuance, and the skill to guide parties through ambiguity toward a shared goal.

Negotiation, at its core, is a dialogue. AI may assist, but only a human can truly understand the unspoken nuances, empathize with diverse perspectives, and build trust over the course of complex deal-making. Your ability to connect authentically remains your ultimate asset.

Better Together: The Human-AI Alliance

The combination of human insight and AI capabilities creates a formidable advantage. Together, they become a force that is faster, smarter, and more agile than either alone. By allowing AI to handle data-centric tasks, you gain more time to focus on relationship-building, strategy, and decision-making.

Navigating this new landscape requires an "evolve-or-die" mindset. Embrace AI's potential while sharpening the human skills that machines cannot replicate—empathy, creativity, critical thinking, and adaptability. Cultivate a sense of curiosity, a willingness to experiment, and a commitment to lifelong learning.

The Three A's: Your Guide to Mastery in AI-Enhanced Negotiation

To fully leverage AI in negotiation, focus on these three principles:

- **Adopt:** Embrace AI tools early to stay ahead of the curve. Use these technologies to gain a competitive edge and expand your capabilities.
- **Adapt:** Tailor AI applications to your unique negotiation style. Remember, AI is not a one-size-fits-all solution; it should complement your strategy, not dictate it.
- **Adept:** Integrate AI incrementally into your process, using it, refining it, and practicing until it becomes a natural extension of your negotiation skillset.

Mastery takes time, patience, and experimentation. Start by using AI in one or two areas, measure its impact, and refine your approach. The rewards are worth the effort.

This is your opportunity to lead the next generation of negotiators and reimagine the possibilities of collaboration. As the first generation at this intersection of human insight and artificial intelligence, the future of negotiation is yours to shape. Embrace the journey—this new era belongs to those bold enough to evolve.

CHAPTER 3

Revolutionizing Commercial Relationships

The SMARTnership Approach

As you sit down across from your counterpart, you know they hold something of value—cash, services, or products. Based on past experience, you already anticipate the likely outcome. You have a fixed idea of what you'll walk away with—within a narrow range.

Now double that expectation. Triple it.

Your initial vision is too small. The conventional rules of commercial negotiation no longer serve you. Sticking to what's familiar means leaving millions on the table—not because of higher costs, but because of missed opportunities. The real potential of the deal lies hidden, only revealed when you leave the well-trodden path and choose the third alternative: **SMARTnership**.

This third road is not free. It's a toll road, and the toll is paid in **trust, transparency, and NegoEconomics**.

Tru$tCurrency is the critical enabler of SMARTnership. It's a blend of trust, transparency, integrity, and the willingness to ensure that the other party benefits fully. It shifts the negotiation dynamic from adversarial to collaborative. This environment of openness is where hidden value is unlocked.

In a SMARTnership, both parties agree to be governed by the **Trust Factor**—to share relevant information, align on mutual interests, and explore value creation together. When trust becomes the operating system, **NegoEconomics** kicks in, revealing asymmetries in cost and value that can be converted into gains for both sides.

Negotiating with openness and creativity reveals benefits that weren't even on the table at the outset. A SMARTnership is not about compromise—it's about expansion. It's where real value lives.

The Roadmap for SMARTnership

Here is the roadmap to SMARTnership:

- Creating a negotiation strategy, based on zero-sum, partnership, or SMARTnership, or perhaps a combination
- Tru$tCurrency, negotiating constructively, using open transparent, two-way communication
- Rules of the game, agreeing on how to negotiate before negotiating
- NegoEconomics, harnessing the asymmetric values between the parties

These elements sound simple, but they make serious demands on the delegates, and failure to follow them has enormous costs. According to my studies at the Copenhagen Business School, businesses are forfeiting as much as 42 percent of the total value of the transaction because both sides fail to bargain for hidden variables—variables that may allow for an alternate solution that enhances the relative value of the transaction for both parties.

The $3.25 Trillion Opportunity You're Ignoring

Billions are left on the table every year because most business negotiations still follow a win-lose, zero-sum mindset. Success is measured by who gets the bigger slice, not whether the pie itself can grow. This outdated model is costing the global economy—big time.

If organizations shifted to a SMARTnership/NegoEconomics approach, the value hidden inside everyday commercial transactions could be unlocked and activated. The SMARTnership model expands what's possible, moving beyond price and into mutual value creation. The potential isn't hypothetical—it's measurable.

By analyzing the total revenue of the 1,000 largest US companies and isolating the portion tied directly to negotiation activities (procurement, sales, etc.), I estimate that **42 percent of the value is lost** due to inefficiencies, poor collaboration, and missed opportunities. That translates to **$3.25 trillion** in unrealized value.

Think that's too high?

Let's assume, just for argument's sake, the researchers behind this number weren't brilliant. Maybe they were average. That still leaves **$2.5 trillion** in missed opportunity. Still too high? Let's pretend they did the math over drinks—cut the number to **$1.5 trillion**.

Even at that lowest estimate, that's **$1.5 billion in additional profit per company** in the top 1,000 per year.

Still not worth exploring?

If even a fraction of this potential is real, ignoring it is not just costly—it's irresponsible. SMARTnership isn't about theory. It's about transforming the way business is done—through trust, transparency, and the economics of collaboration. The numbers speak for themselves.

What Is NegoEconomics?

Money is a commodity—no different from a book, a computer, a car, or a house. It has a price, and that price reflects its value in a given context.

Just look at your credit card statement. Are you paying 13 percent? 21 percent? More? That interest rate isn't just a number—it's the cost of accessing someone else's capital. It quantifies the value of using American Express's financial leverage to buy what you couldn't otherwise afford immediately.

We assign value to money the same way we assign value to people, organizations, and products. Money is not free—and every percentage point tells you exactly how much it's worth.

Example: Sophia runs a small tech startup, EdgeTech, with limited cash reserves. She secures a $15 million contract with a major e-commerce company, Velocity, which is well funded and cash-rich. Velocity's negotiators refuse to provide Sophia with an upfront payment and insist on paying the full amount upon delivery, scheduled eight months from now.

This creates a significant problem for Sophia. Her key suppliers, who provide critical components for her products, require a 40 percent upfront payment totaling $6 million to fulfill their part of the deal. Unfortunately, Sophia doesn't have the $6 million.

Sophia has two options:

- She can approach a venture capital firm for a bridge loan to cover the $6 million.
- She can request that Velocity pays $6 million upfront.

Sophia chooses the second option and asks Velocity for the upfront payment. Velocity's lead negotiator dismisses the request, stating that upfront payments are not part of their policy and threatens to cancel the contract if Sophia insists.

26 CHAPTER 3 Revolutionizing Commercial Relationships

Sophia is left with no choice but to approach a venture capital firm for the $6 million loan. The firm agrees but charges her $400,000 in fees and interest, which significantly cuts into her profit margin.

For Velocity, the cost of providing Sophia with the $6 million upfront would have been just $120,000 due to their lower cost of capital.

Velocity's negotiator believes they achieved a strong victory by not paying anything upfront. Sophia knows the deal's financial strain could have been avoided, and in reality, both parties missed out on maximizing value. By failing to negotiate on payment terms, they lost the opportunity to leverage the cost of capital differences.

What NegoEconomics value was lost?

The difference between Sophia's borrowing cost and Velocity's cost of capital:

$$\begin{array}{r}\$400,000 \\ -\$120,000 \\ \hline \$280,000 \end{array}$$ was lost between the two parties

What should Sophia and Velocity have done?

By identifying their respective costs of capital, they could have created $280,000 of shared value to split.

For example, if Sophia reduced her price by $200,000, Velocity would gain an extra $80,000, and Sophia would save $120,000 in financing costs. A mutually beneficial outcome, with the venture capital firm left out of the equation entirely.

When I present this simplified example of NegoEconomics to executives, I often hear the same objection: "We're working on a $10 million deal. I don't have time to focus on $150,000."

So I ask, "Do you personally earn more than $150,000 an hour?"

The answer is almost always no.

Then I point out that in a $10 million negotiation, there are easily **200 to 300 variables**—each with the potential to deliver $150,000 in NegoEconomic value. That's not small change. That's millions in value hiding in plain sight.

NegoEconomics is the value created when one party's extra effort or cost results in a disproportionately higher gain for the other. For example, if a supplier shortens delivery time at minimal cost, and the buyer gains significantly through earlier revenue generation, both win. The net gain is greater than the net cost—that's NegoEconomic value.

But here's the problem: Too many large companies miss this because they're locked in old thinking.

Take the current trend in procurement. Large corporations increasingly demand extended payment terms—moving from 30 days to 60 or even 90. The goal? Improve their own cash flow. But at whose expense?

Let's be honest: Who has the lower cost of capital—a multinational corporation with an investment-grade credit rating or a small supplier with 50 employees? The answer is obvious. The smaller company ends up subsidizing the larger one. It's inefficient. It's unfair. And it's economically irrational.

Enter SMARTnership

Whether you're negotiating for yourself, your employer, or a client, SMARTnership is the way out of the zero-sum trap. It's not about squeezing the other side. It's about **unlocking asymmetric value**—value that can't be seen unless both sides are willing to be open, transparent, and creative.

Negotiation is no longer about winning slices. It's about baking a bigger pie.

Distributive Negotiations Generates Poor Economics for All

Distributive negotiations—also known as zero-sum games—continue to dominate the negotiation landscape because of a deep-rooted survival mindset, where the strongest take the largest share of limited resources. At the table, this approach is driven by shortsighted strategies, fear of vulnerability, lack of preparation, and a poor understanding of what genuine collaboration can achieve.

This mindset often leads to unnecessarily expensive solutions. When negotiators are driven by emotion—stress, insecurity, or threats—they fall into a fight-or-flight response. Rational thinking is replaced by reflex. As a result, potential value vanishes. Resources are left untapped, and both sides lose the opportunity to benefit.

In a typical zero-sum game, negotiators rely on four flawed strategies: **combat, concession, stalling, and compromise**. Alongside these, the pattern includes:

- Withholding key information
- Bluffing to gain advantage
- Power plays to create imbalance
- Tactics designed to stress or intimidate
- Dishonest or unclear communication
- High-risk decisions made in uncertainty

- Obsession with short-term wins
- Status maneuvers that reject partnership
- Overt manipulation

The result? A dysfunctional process where neither party reaches the full potential of the deal. Zero-sum isn't just outdated—it's expensive, inefficient, and self-defeating.

A Bigger Pie Means More for Everyone

Picture the total value of a commercial transaction as a cherry pie—fresh out of the oven. You see the golden crust, smell the warm cherries, and, naturally, you want the biggest slice. Maybe even the whole thing. That's how most people approach negotiation. They focus on how much they can carve out for themselves.

But here's what most negotiators miss: there's a way for both parties to get *more* pie.

You can split a small pie 50/50, or 30/70. Fine. But if both parties commit to uncovering hidden value in the deal—if they actively cooperate to expand it—the pie gets bigger. And suddenly, your share is worth more than your original half.

That's what NegoEconomics is about. It's the disciplined pursuit of *additional* value—value that doesn't exist until both sides collaborate to find it. That value can take many forms: financial gain, reduced risk, increased stock, shared knowledge, stronger brand positioning—you name it.

Once the extra value is unlocked, the only thing left is deciding how to divide it. And that's a far more productive conversation than fighting over a fixed slice. NegoEconomics creates the conditions for smarter, more profitable deals—for both sides.

EXAMPLE | Negotiating to Build a Wall

Jordan and Mia have partnered on a construction project. They have been hired to build a wall. Jordan's cost is $60 per foot, while Mia's cost is $40. If Mia builds the entire wall, the partnership will save $20 per foot. If Jordan builds the entire wall, instead of splitting the task 50–50, they will save $10 per foot.

In a zero-sum scenario, conflict arises over who will take on the work. If the partners collaborate, however, they can assign the task to the person with the lowest cost, maximizing efficiency. Then the added value can be shared, with Mia being paid $45 per foot.

> While this solution seems straightforward, it is often difficult to achieve because negotiators frequently approach such situations as zero-sum games. In these cases, the party with the higher cost may end up doing all the work due to manipulation, threats, or coercive tactics.
>
> For instance, Jordan might say:
>
> - "This wall is straightforward to build—you won't have to work hard."
> - "It's not very long, just a few hundred feet."
> - "If you want to get paid, you'd better finish the wall by the end of the day!"
>
> Without trust and openness, such negotiations waste energy on conflict rather than focusing on value creation. Zero-sum thinking leads to inefficient outcomes, where decisions are made based on pressure rather than logic.
>
> By fostering collaboration, Jordan and Mia could have avoided unnecessary conflict and shared the added value. Instead of fighting over the work, they could have worked together to maximize efficiency and profits, creating a win-win scenario.

SMARTnerships, Partnerships, or Zero-Sum Games

The three main negotiation approaches are zero-sum games, partnerships, and SMARTnerships. The question to consider is not always: *How can I use one of these methods to get the best possible result?* A qualified negotiator could combine SMARTnership, partnership, and zero-sum games and use each strategically to improve the negotiation outcome. They use collaborative negotiation (SMARTnership or partnership) to improve relationships and increase Tru$tCurrency. Zero-sum games are implemented to negotiate the split of the asymmetrical value that materializes during the NegoEconomics process. The way in which these three approaches are combined varies from negotiation to negotiation, depending on the industry, circumstances of the transaction, and the personal relationship.

Do You Actually Have a Negotiation Strategy?

Open a blank document right now and describe your company's negotiation strategy—not your sales policy, not your supplier policy. I mean your actual approach to building cooperation with trading partners—short term or long term, domestic or international.

Chances are, you're staring at the screen, unsure what to write. You're not alone. Over 96 percent of companies, governments, and organizations operating globally have no defined negotiation strategy. None.

So why does this matter?

Because if you don't know what you want from a trading relationship, how can you achieve it? Are you aiming for a **zero-sum outcome**, a **partnership**, or a **SMARTnership**?

In my experience, when asked this question, most people claim they aim for partnerships. But when we examine their tactics, what we find is pure zero-sum behavior—win-lose thinking masked as collaboration.

Most organizations run their negotiations on autopilot. They use zero-sum strategies not by choice but by habit. They are unconsciously incompetent—simply unaware that there's a better way.

The solution? Define your strategy. Choose your model intentionally. And if your goal is real cooperation, mutual value creation, and long-term success, SMARTnership isn't just an option—it's the standard.

SMARTnership in Action

The following stories are great examples of real SMARTnerships in action.

Disney and Pixar: A Masterclass in NegoEconomics and SMARTnership

One of the most powerful real-world examples of NegoEconomics and SMARTnership in action is the merger between Disney and Pixar.

This deal was far more than a business transaction—it was a strategic alliance rooted in mutual respect and shared purpose. Instead of enforcing control, Disney allowed Pixar to retain its creative autonomy. Just two years into the merger, the results spoke for themselves: Hits like *WALL-E* and *Cars* rolled out, marking a new era in animation excellence.

Before the deal, skepticism ran high. Critics doubted whether Disney could handle Pixar's bold, independent culture. Inside Pixar, there were fears of losing creative freedom under a corporate giant. But when both sides came to the table, they focused on a single, unifying goal: producing world-class animation for future generations.

What followed was textbook SMARTnership. Two seemingly opposing cultures—Pixar's relaxed, quality-focused pace versus Disney's high-output model—didn't clash. They complemented each other. Pixar saw a boost in productivity, while Disney expanded its creative reach and captured a new market segment.

By recognizing and leveraging each other's strengths, Disney and Pixar didn't just split the pie—they *grew* it. This merger didn't succeed in spite of their differences; it succeeded *because* they negotiated through them, applying trust, transparency, and the principles of NegoEconomics to create something bigger than either company could have achieved alone.

The AI Supercomputer   In a groundbreaking alliance, three distinct forces—NVIDIA, Novo Nordisk (the pharma company behind Wegovy), and the Danish monarchy—joined to build a revolutionary supercomputer, pushing the boundaries of innovation and research. This SMARTnership exemplifies collaboration at its finest, where mutual strengths converge for transformative global impact.

The project aimed to create a computational powerhouse to address pressing global challenges. NVIDIA provided cutting-edge AI chips, Novo Nordisk brought its expertise and funding to accelerate healthcare research, and Denmark's Export and Investment Fund, with royal endorsement, ensured political and logistical backing to establish the supercomputer on Danish soil.

Each partner played a critical role:

- NVIDIA supplied the AI technology to process massive datasets, enabling advancements in genetic research, climate modeling, and more.
- Novo Nordisk, seeking breakthroughs in healthcare, invested heavily and guided the supercomputer's design to support personalized medicine and drug development.
- The Danish government provided infrastructure, regulatory navigation, and talent development, making Denmark a global hub for innovation.

The supercomputer, now operational, is a marvel of modern engineering. It accelerates healthcare research by analyzing genetic data at unprecedented speeds, enabling faster identification of drug targets. In green energy, it advances wind energy optimization and grid management, reinforcing Denmark's leadership in sustainability. By integrating a tech giant, a healthcare leader, and a national government, this alliance became a model for tackling global issues through shared expertise.

The SMARTnership Advantage

These collaborations demonstrate SMARTnership principles—transparency, respect, and shared goals. Each partner leveraged unique strengths, creating value unattainable in isolation.

Lessons for SMART Negotiators

- **Leverage asymmetrical value:** Each partner brought essential resources that were less costly or more accessible to them than to the others.
- **Align on shared outcomes:** Commitment to a common vision transcended individual goals, enabling a world-class research hub.
- **Build trust:** Open communication and transparency ensured confidence and long-term collaboration.

Ten Landmark Negotiations: Mastering the Art of Strategic Deal-Making

Successful negotiations are built on vision, creativity, and a willingness to collaborate, where both parties benefit and the outcomes reshape industries. This section explores 10 iconic negotiations that exemplify how strategic thinking, trust, and a collaborative mindset can lead to transformative results across various sectors.

Tesla and Panasonic: Powering the Future

Elon Musk and Kazuhiro Tsuga led a groundbreaking partnership between Tesla and Panasonic, essential for Tesla's growth in the electric vehicle (EV) market. In the early 2010s, Musk recognized the critical need for reliable battery production to meet Tesla's ambitious goals. Panasonic was a global leader in lithium-ion battery production, and Musk saw a mutual opportunity.

The negotiations resulted in Panasonic co-investing billions with Tesla to build the Gigafactory, a massive battery production facility. Instead of a simple supplier agreement, this deal represented a shared risk-and-reward model, where both companies would benefit from scaling EV production. This collaboration has been a cornerstone of Tesla's success, highlighting the importance of aligning long-term strategic goals in negotiations.

Disney and Pixar: Creativity Meets Corporate Strategy

As mentioned earlier in the chapter, Disney's acquisition of Pixar in 2006 for $7.4 billion revitalized Disney's animation division. Bob Iger, Disney's CEO, saw the declining creativity within Disney and recognized that Pixar, led by Steve Jobs, was the future of animation. However, Jobs was protective of Pixar's culture and autonomy, which had been the driving force behind its success.

Negotiations centered on preserving Pixar's creative control while allowing Disney to handle distribution and marketing. The agreement ensured that Pixar's John Lasseter would lead Disney Animation, maintaining the studio's creative vision. This successful negotiation balanced corporate needs with creative integrity, leading to a new era of blockbuster films for Disney and a lucrative partnership for both companies.

IBM and Lenovo: Strategic Global Shift

IBM's decision to sell its PC division to Lenovo in 2005 was a strategic move to exit the low-margin hardware business and focus on services and software. Lenovo, under CEO Yang Yuanqing, sought to expand globally and saw acquiring IBM's ThinkPad brand as the key.

Samuel Palmisano, CEO of IBM, negotiated a $1.25 billion deal, ensuring that IBM could shift its focus, while Lenovo gained credibility and global presence. Lenovo successfully maintained IBM's brand identity while using the acquisition to grow into one of the world's leading PC manufacturers. This negotiation illustrates how divestitures can create new opportunities for both parties when long-term goals align.

The Camp David Accords: Peace in the Middle East

The Camp David Accords of 1978, brokered by the US president at the time, Jimmy Carter, are a landmark in diplomatic negotiations. Egyptian President Anwar Sadat and Israeli Prime Minister Menachem Begin sat down for direct negotiations, facilitated by Carter, to resolve decades of conflict.

The negotiation centered on Israel's withdrawal from the Sinai Peninsula in exchange for Egypt's formal recognition of Israel. Carter's role was pivotal in mediating the personal and political tensions between the two leaders. The result was a peace treaty that has endured for over four decades, showcasing the power of diplomacy and compromise in high-stakes negotiations.

Google's Acquisition of YouTube: Scaling Digital Content

In 2006, Google recognized the explosive growth potential of YouTube as a video-sharing platform but also saw its challenges, including legal battles over copyrighted content and the need for scaling infrastructure. Eric Schmidt, Google's CEO, led negotiations with YouTube founders Chad Hurley and Steve Chen.

The $1.65 billion deal in stock allowed YouTube to retain its brand and leadership while benefiting from Google's resources to handle technological challenges. Google's expertise in advertising and infrastructure positioned YouTube to become the dominant platform for digital video. This negotiation succeeded by combining YouTube's user growth with Google's operational strength, creating a mutually beneficial outcome.

Microsoft's Acquisition of LinkedIn: Building a Professional Network

Satya Nadella, CEO of Microsoft, and Jeff Weiner, CEO of LinkedIn, forged one of the most significant tech acquisitions in 2016 when Microsoft purchased LinkedIn for $26.2 billion. Nadella's vision was to integrate LinkedIn's professional network with Microsoft's software ecosystem, enhancing services like Office 365 and Dynamics.

Weiner was focused on maintaining LinkedIn's culture and growth trajectory, which led to negotiations ensuring LinkedIn's operational autonomy post-acquisition. The success of this deal lay in aligning both companies' goals—Microsoft gained a vast professional network, while LinkedIn accelerated its growth with Microsoft's resources. This strategic acquisition expanded Microsoft's influence in enterprise services and cloud computing.

The Paris Climate Agreement: Global Cooperation for a Common Goal

In 2015, representatives from 196 countries came together in Paris to negotiate a global framework for addressing climate change. The Paris Climate Agreement was groundbreaking because it managed to unite countries with vastly different economic conditions and priorities around a shared goal of reducing greenhouse gas emissions.

Laurent Fabius, France's foreign minister, played a key role in brokering compromises, particularly through the creation of nationally determined contributions (NDCs), which allowed each country to set its own targets. This flexibility made the agreement possible, allowing developed and developing nations to participate on terms suited to their capacities. The negotiation succeeded by balancing global environmental responsibility with national interests.

Amazon's Purchase of Whole Foods: Revolutionizing Retail

Jeff Bezos, CEO of Amazon, and John Mackey, CEO of Whole Foods, came together in 2017 to negotiate a deal that would reshape the retail and grocery sectors. Amazon's $13.7 billion acquisition of Whole Foods was driven by Bezos's vision to integrate technology into brick-and-mortar retail, while Mackey saw Amazon as a lifeline for his company, which had been facing declining growth.

A key element of the negotiation was Bezos's assurance that Whole Foods would maintain its brand identity and focus on organic products while benefiting from Amazon's technological and logistical expertise. The deal successfully combined Amazon's efficiency and reach with Whole Foods' loyal customer base, leading to innovations like cashier-less stores and transformed shopping experiences.

Sony and Marvel Studios: The Spider-Man Deal

Sony's ownership of Spider-Man's film rights created a unique challenge for Marvel Studios, which wanted to integrate the character into its Marvel Cinematic Universe (MCU). In 2015, Amy Pascal of Sony and Kevin Feige, president of Marvel Studios, negotiated a groundbreaking deal that allowed Spider-Man to appear in the MCU while Sony retained creative control and distribution rights.

This collaboration was beneficial for both studios—Marvel gained a beloved character to enhance its film slate, and Sony reaped the financial rewards of Spider-Man's integration into the MCU. The negotiation's success was based on mutual recognition of the character's value and the potential for shared profits without diminishing either studio's control.

PayPal and eBay: Merging for Mutual Growth

In 2002, eBay was struggling with its payment system, Billpoint, while PayPal had become the preferred payment platform for eBay users. Meg Whitman, CEO of eBay, recognized the opportunity to streamline the user experience by acquiring PayPal. Peter Thiel and Elon Musk, PayPal's leaders, were negotiating to maintain PayPal's autonomy and brand post-acquisition.

The $1.5 billion deal allowed PayPal to expand its presence beyond eBay while providing a seamless payment solution for the auction site. This negotiation was successful because both sides prioritized long-term growth over immediate control, resulting in PayPal becoming one of the world's leading payment platforms.

The Art of Strategic Deal-Making

These 10 landmark negotiations highlight a common theme—success lies in collaboration, strategic vision, and trust. Whether it's forging global peace, revolutionizing industries, or securing a competitive edge, the best negotiators focus on creating long-term value rather than short-term wins. By understanding the motivations and needs of both parties, they find solutions that transcend mere transactions and lay the foundation for enduring partnerships. These case studies serve as powerful reminders of how thoughtful negotiation can reshape industries, countries, and even the future itself.

I have numerous lesser-known success stories of organizations that have utilized the concepts of SMARTnership and NegoEconomics to create mutual value—value that would have otherwise remained hidden beneath the surface. The encouraging news is that this isn't rocket science. It simply requires a shift in how we perceive and approach collaboration.

This SMARTnership concept and negotiating in collaboration proves that when negotiators unite with trust and shared purpose, they can harness diverse strengths to create a transformative impact. It's a pathway to sustainable innovation, addressing the world's most complex challenges.

There was a time when a deal was sealed with a handshake—a gentleman's agreement built on mutual respect and trust. No employment contracts, NDAs, or armies of lawyers carrying boxes of documents. Yes, today's legal frameworks protect our interests—but they can't create trust. They can't enforce ethics. And they certainly can't replace personal integrity.

What follows will challenge how you think about negotiation and success. If you're willing to shift your mindset and move beyond traditional deal-making, you'll not only achieve better business outcomes—you'll elevate your personal effectiveness.

But it starts with one thing: the **Trust Factor**.

Trust isn't a tactic. It's the foundation. Without it, the rest of your strategy is just noise. The beauty of the Trust Factor is that it doesn't require anything external—no forms, no systems, no permission. Just a decision.

The shift begins with you.

CHAPTER 4

Defining the Rules of the Game and Creating a Strategy

The international standards for negotiation have yet to be clearly established. The UN has not provided guidance on how negotiations should take place, making it crucial to discuss and define the negotiation process before engaging in negotiations. That's the goal of this chapter.

Discussing Negotiation Before Negotiating

Imagine you're heading to a tennis match, your racket ready in your bag, excited for some rallying, volleying, and serving. To your surprise, when you arrive at the court, your opponent has set up two chairs and a table on one side of the net, complete with a chessboard and pieces. Looking at you expectantly, they ask, "Are you ready to play?"

This scenario mirrors countless negotiation situations worldwide. One party arrives with a clear understanding of the rules, while the other has entirely different assumptions. Many clients have been taken aback when I begin with this question: "Shall we discuss how we're going to negotiate?"

The first step in any negotiation should be for both parties to agree on the negotiation process itself. The "Rules of the Game" must be clearly defined before delving into the specifics of the issues or the deal at hand. Key questions include these: Who are the stakeholders? What are the rules of engagement? What conditions will terminate the negotiation? While this foundational work can be time-consuming—sometimes taking longer than the negotiation itself—establishing these ground rules up front helps prevent misunderstandings, saves time later, and fosters a cooperative atmosphere.

The Rules of the Game should cover several key elements, including an agreed-upon agenda, the negotiation strategy, and a code of conduct:

- Should we negotiate in a zero-sum framework, in a partnership, or via a SMARTnership?
- How do we created an agenda everyone can agree on?
- How will we share the NegoEconomic value if we choose partnership or SMARTnership (collaborative negotiation)?
- Who will initiate the exchange of information?
- How will we build trust?
- How will we present all relevant variables, and who will compile them?
- Who will manage the visual aids and blackboard?
- What are the agreed-upon break times, if any?
- Do all participants have a mandate, and what is it?
- Should we openly acknowledge any lack of trust?

Failing to define the Rules of the Game is akin to allowing a football team to play without a common set of rules. It may be an exciting game, but no one understands how to score, and the players are left unsure of how to win.

Articulating a Negotiation Strategy for the Organization

Successful businesses have strategies for nearly every aspect of their operations. They invest significant resources in crafting and refining marketing, product development, HR, communication, and R&D strategies. It's hard to imagine a company like Apple or Toyota functioning without clearly defined strategies or budgets.

When I pose the question of negotiation strategy to various audiences of business leaders across different cultures, generations, and genders, the answer remains consistent: very few have a clear negotiation approach guiding their interactions with partners, suppliers, customers, or other stakeholders. Most negotiators lack strategic awareness and often rely on intuition and emotions to drive their demands. This makes it challenging to foster open, honest, and transparent partnerships that create added value.

Despite the fact that "all business is human," there is rarely a policy that instructs employees on how to engage with strategic partners—an oversight comparable to not having a communication, legal, or marketing strategy. This gap results in suboptimal relationships characterized by limited openness, trust, and profitability.

So why establish a negotiation strategy? It's essential to determine what you seek from a trading partner. Are you aiming for a win-lose, zero-sum relationship with little long-term potential? Do you want a partnership that functions on minimal sharing while maintaining some distance? Or do you aspire to a SMARTnership, where both parties openly share needs and desires to cultivate a lasting relationship that can withstand the inevitable fluctuations of business?

Note: Interestingly, neither the United Nations nor any other organization has ever defined a universal standard for negotiation, leading to vastly different interpretations of negotiation from one delegate to another.

In my experience, most negotiators claim to be seeking partnerships but often engage in behaviors that yield zero-sum outcomes. Many organizations, through their ingrained culture, unknowingly adopt a zero-sum negotiation strategy. Leaders in these companies often remain unaware of their options, falling into the trap of unconscious incompetence.

By developing a well-structured negotiation strategy, organizations can foster relationships built on informed cooperation. Effectively managing personal dynamics and enhancing communication allows negotiators to find common ground, making problem-solving more appealing than conflict. This approach creates added value, promotes co-innovation, and supports long-term relationship stability.

Starting negotiations effectively can lead to suppliers actively supporting your objectives. However, it's crucial to recognize your power position—understanding how the other party may exert control and how you can assert your influence by presenting compelling arguments.

The Negotiation Code of Conduct

This code outlines the behavioral standards that guide a company through even the toughest negotiations. It specifies what employees will and will not do to maintain the honesty and integrity of any internal or external negotiation. Every staff member, regardless of their position, should sign this code.

In my practice, I take this commitment a step further. When negotiating with a partner, I ask them to sign the code as well. This fosters an atmosphere of open communication and establishes a positive environment.

I've created a Negotiation Code of Conduct to help you and your business partners navigate challenging situations. This code includes explicit statements of acceptable behavior to ensure the integrity of the negotiation process. Use this list as a foundation for your own code, share it with your partners, and refer back to it when tensions rise:

We Will Not:
- Lie or bluff
- Intentionally pressure the counterparty, including through time constraints
- Make inflated offers
- Engage in emotional manipulation
- Use aggressive or hostile negotiation tactics
- Withhold information

We Will:
- Strive to maintain high levels of trust throughout the negotiation
- Refrain from spying, bribery, or infiltration
- Uphold our agreements if they are reached
- Be transparent about variables and values, sharing information equally
- Aim for fairness and equitable distribution of any added value

We Believe:
- Collaborative efforts yield better outcomes than winning at the expense of others
- Ethical behavior and morality are vital in negotiations

Please notify us immediately if you notice any breaches of our Negotiation Code of Conduct.

Ultimately, consistently adhering to a shared set of ethical guidelines boosts company morale and assures your business partners that you are a fair negotiator.

Crafting Your Own Code of Conduct

When you and your colleagues collaboratively develop your own code of conduct, it becomes easier to uphold your commitments and approach negotiations—regardless of their difficulty—with a focus on productivity and integrity. Encourage your employees and trading partners to embrace this code and highlight its significance, especially during challenging transactions. This shared commitment will help foster a culture of honesty and accountability in all your negotiations.

Conscious and Unconscious Negotiation with Yourself

As soon as you recognize that you're entering a negotiation, you initiate a mental preparation process—part of which is conscious and part unconscious. It's crucial to be aware of the irrational behaviors that can influence your decisions.

When gearing up to make a deal, internal negotiations occur between your conscious and subconscious minds. Many people are unaware of the extent to which their subconscious affects their negotiation approach, often denying its impact altogether.

Without your awareness, your conscious and subconscious minds start to work together, leading you to rationalize your thoughts. While focusing on your goals, you might convince yourself of how easy or difficult the upcoming negotiation will be. You weigh the opportunities and constraints before you and assess your power position, considering thoughts like:

- "There's no point in asking for a raise; the budget is tight this year."
- "They won't give me a discount; this model is brand new and in high demand."
- "I probably shouldn't ask her out; she doesn't date guys like me."

Ultimately, only you can decide if you're viewing the negotiation through an overly optimistic or pessimistic lens. Being aware of this dynamic can significantly influence your approach and outcomes.

Preconceived Notions

It's essential to recognize that you can fall victim to your own preconceived notions. Sometimes you may not set your expectations high enough, limiting your perspective and preventing yourself from gaining potential benefits.

Entering negotiations with negative expectations is counterproductive:

- "They'll never agree to this."
- "Cooperation is pointless."
- "The other side is ready for a fight."

If you're anxious and carry negative expectations, those feelings will likely surface during the negotiation, impacting the outcome. Remember, as long as the negotiation is ongoing, anything is possible.

Your assessment of the negotiation circumstances is based on incomplete information, which you often fill with preconceived notions about the other party, shaped by past experiences and expectations. However, the reality you encounter at the negotiating table will rarely align with your initial assessment.

> **EXAMPLE** | Ambushed by the Buyer
>
> Elger receives a call from Biyu, a key customer, who wants to discuss details for the upcoming year. As the head of production, Elger expects the conversation to focus on technical aspects, as it has in previous years. However, when they meet, Biyu wants to discuss terms, delivery, and financing—topics Elger hasn't prepared for. Consequently, he agrees to terms he's unhappy with.
>
> Afterward, when Elger's boss inquires about the meeting, Elger expresses frustration, saying he couldn't have anticipated Biyu's shift in focus. He believes Biyu caught him off guard by deviating from her usual agenda.
>
> In hindsight, Elger should have asked Biyu what the meeting would cover and who would attend. Had he done so, he could have prepared for the relevant variables.
>
> Importantly, remember that time is negotiable. Elger could have requested additional time to gather his thoughts and suggested a follow-up call the next day, allowing him to prepare effectively.

Time Is Negotiable

Avoid starting a negotiation when you lack sufficient time to see it through—such as right before a vacation. It's better to postpone finalizing the negotiation than to rush to a conclusion that doesn't reflect your best efforts. Remember, you can negotiate the timing and location of meetings. If you find yourself short on time, suggest a new time frame to allow for adequate preparation. If you must negotiate without preparation, take a measured approach: Focus on listening, refrain from making on-the-spot decisions, gather information, and give yourself time to reflect.

Reschedule and Take Control

Imagine you receive a last-minute call to participate in a negotiation. You arrange your travel, book a hotel, and pack your important documents, hoping to prepare while on the move or the night before your meeting. Deep down, you know this plan is unlikely to work, but you feel you have no other choice.

If the other party dictates the schedule, you can still negotiate the timing. You might say, "I'd love to attend, but I can't make it until Wednesday."

It's wise to avoid making significant decisions or signing important documents within the first 24 hours after a long journey. The stress and jet lag can impair your decision-making abilities.

> **EXAMPLE | The Cruise Ship Leaves Tomorrow, But There Is No Deal in Sight**
>
> Picture this: You're negotiating in a foreign country, and discussions are dragging on without a resolution. You have a family vacation cruise booked and are eager to return home. The day of your scheduled flight arrives, and the agreement is still pending. You have several options:
>
> - **Cancel your family holiday** and continue negotiating without a deadline.
> - **Lower your expectations** and rush to reach an agreement by the end of the day.
> - **Acknowledge that success is unlikely** and head home.
> - **Engage with the other party's concerns,** but postpone any decisions, requesting a follow-up meeting to finalize the agreement.
> - **Do not accept any deadlines** imposed by the other party. Keep your return flight details private; if they know you're pressed for time, they may intentionally delay negotiations to create pressure.
> - **If pressured by a deadline**, consider pushing back. You could say, "I'm not sure how we can resolve this. Let's pause for now to see how you respond." This might prompt the other party, who may also be under pressure, to accelerate the process. Maintain your composure and test their urgency: "If you need an answer today, it will have to be a no, but if you give me another day, I might be able to provide a positive response."
>
> By managing your time and expectations, you can navigate negotiations more effectively, ensuring you're not rushed into unfavorable agreements.

Thinking Through the Transaction Ahead of Time

Preparation is a crucial component of a successful negotiation strategy. Before entering any negotiation, consider the following questions:

- **What are the negotiation variables?** Identify the times, prices, performance metrics, and payment plans that will be discussed.
- **What is the scope of the negotiation?** Define the boundaries for all points of discussion and determine your threshold of pain.
- **Are we willing to accept greater risk for the potential of higher returns?** Assess your risk tolerance in relation to potential rewards.
- **What are the consequences of making concessions?** Determine what you might concede and what you will ask for in return.

Taking these factors into account during the preparation stage is essential. Additionally, estimate how the other party may respond to your proposals. Depending on the specific aspects of the negotiation, there may be further questions to address to ensure you are fully prepared.

Working with an Agenda

An agenda is a powerful tool for organizing and structuring negotiations. By outlining your ideas in a clear manner, you can enhance the efficiency and orderliness of discussions. It's essential to address one issue at a time and avoid making decisions until you have a comprehensive understanding of the overall situation and the other party's requirements.

Understanding the Other Party's Intentions

Before the negotiation, examine what the other party hopes to achieve, anticipate potential questions, and identify who will be involved. If you enter the negotiation without this knowledge, you risk losing initiative and control, which can undermine your confidence and the success of the negotiation. Misreading the situation may even lead to a deadlock.

The Advantage of Preparing an Agenda

When you prepare the agenda, you gain a tactical advantage. You control which issues will be discussed and in what order, shaping the expectations and preparations of the other party. This proactive approach allows you to steer the negotiation in a way that aligns with your objectives.

If the other party provides the agenda, request a copy in advance. This will give you insight into their perspective and allow you to prepare your team accordingly, minimizing surprises. Your bargaining strategy should be informed by an understanding of what the other side aims to gain.

Collaborating on an Agenda

Whenever possible, reach out to a representative from the other party a few days prior to the meeting to collaborate on the agenda. This ensures that both parties are aligned on key discussion points, reducing the likelihood of unexpected terms and pressure during the meeting.

Advantages of Using an Agenda

The advantages of using an agenda are myriad and are outlined in this section.

Taking the Initiative If the other party surprises you with their own agenda, take a break to review it. Proceeding without adjustments can lead to several issues:

- You may lose the initiative and find yourself on an unexpected negotiation platform.
- You could be drawn into discussions for which you are unprepared.
- The other party may control the sequence of agenda items.
- They might gather information while minimizing their own disclosures.
- Unwanted topics may be strategically omitted or postponed.
- "Any other business" could conceal unexpected surprises.

Controlling the Other Party Even with a pre-sent agenda, several dynamics can affect your negotiation:

- It may shape your expectations positively or negatively.
- It can dictate your preparation regarding necessary documentation.

- It influences the makeup of your negotiation team.
- You might feel pressured to provide all necessary information to meet the objectives outlined by the other party.

Becoming More Prepared Discussing the agenda internally ensures your negotiation remains structured, helping avoid confusion over roles. Each member can stick to their responsibilities, preventing the chaos that often arises from ill-prepared negotiations.

Using an agenda not only keeps the negotiation organized but also enhances your strategic positioning, making it an invaluable asset in the negotiation process.

When an Agenda May Not Be Suitable

It's important to recognize that some negotiators may feel uncomfortable when presented with an agenda. This discomfort can create a negative atmosphere and make the other party feel manipulated. In certain situations, an agenda can inadvertently hinder the negotiation process, locking both parties into a rigid framework.

Some negotiators may resist the use of an agenda entirely. If you encounter this reluctance, it's often best to set the agenda aside and proceed without one. Even in the absence of a formal agenda, both parties will likely have their own objectives and can navigate the discussion in their own styles.

Additionally, an agenda can sometimes stifle the creativity necessary for effective negotiations. If the person who prepared the agenda fails to adhere to it, its value diminishes significantly. In these cases, flexibility and openness may prove more beneficial than a strict agenda.

Understanding the Other Party's Requirements

Before advocating for your own needs in a negotiation, it's essential to fully understand the requirements of the other party. Don't assume that their initial position statement captures all their needs. While it may outline technical and financial requirements, it often lacks the context and underlying motivations behind those needs.

Personal and psychological needs, which are critical to the negotiation, are rarely expressed in initial bids. To ensure that the solutions and arguments you present are persuasive, they must resonate with the other party's specific needs and concerns.

By grasping what the other party truly wants, you can tailor your proposals to be more relevant and impactful, increasing the likelihood of a successful outcome.

Integrating AI to Define the "Rules of the Game" and Develop a Negotiation Strategy

AI can significantly enhance the process of establishing the Rules of the Game and crafting a comprehensive negotiation strategy for your organization. The following sections explain how.

Leveraging AI to Define the Rules of Engagement

AI tools can simulate negotiation scenarios, allowing teams to identify potential pitfalls and opportunities before actual discussions. These simulations help refine the process of defining key variables, such as:

- Stakeholders and their interests
- Optimal negotiation frameworks (e.g., zero-sum, partnership, or SMARTnership)
- Trust-building measures and transparency requirements

AI can also assist in drafting agendas, codes of conduct, and decision trees, ensuring that the negotiation process is structured and consistent.

AI-Enhanced Negotiation Strategy Development

AI-driven analytics enable organizations to:

- **Assess historical data:** Analyze past negotiations to identify successful strategies and avoid pitfalls.
- **Predict outcomes:** Use machine learning to forecast potential outcomes based on available data.
- **Optimize variables:** Determine the best combinations of terms, pricing, and conditions for maximum value creation.
- **Benchmark performance:** Compare organizational practices against industry standards to identify areas for improvement.

Suggested Prompts for AI Integration

To effectively use AI in defining the rules and strategy, consider the following prompts:

- **Scenario planning:** "Simulate a negotiation scenario with [specific variables] and identify potential challenges."
- **Data analysis:** "Analyze historical negotiation outcomes to identify patterns of success and failure."
- **Strategy optimization:** "Suggest an optimal negotiation strategy for [context], focusing on trust-building and long-term partnerships."
- **Agenda creation:** "Draft an agenda for a negotiation involving [specific stakeholders] with [defined objectives]."
- **Stakeholder insights:** "Provide an analysis of stakeholder interests and their potential impact on negotiation dynamics."
- **Code of conduct drafting:** "Generate a draft negotiation code of conduct based on [organizational values and goals]."

These steps and prompts can streamline preparation and ensure your organization approaches all negotiations with a clear, effective strategy.

CHAPTER 5

Prerequisites for a Successful Collaboration Agreement

The experiences I have told you about so far in this book speak for themselves. Cooperating is not easy, and it is often made impossible because the wrong people are assigned to the project.

Requirements for Success

There are a number of basic prerequisites that must be fulfilled if the parties are to have the chance of success, each discussed in this section.

The Chemistry Must Be Right

If there is no human chemistry characterized by mutual respect, trust, and openness, the collaboration agreement is doomed to fail. It is people who do business with each other, not computers, and it is people who are assigned to find the optimal prerequisites of the project. Human beings have feelings.

Openness, humility, and respect are not always sufficient ingredients. Enthusiasm and a positive basic view can be equally important. I have met people at the negotiation table who completely lack personal magnetism, which may be needed. All attempts to communicate with them fail. They are silent; there is no repartee. People do perceive the words they are saying, but in spite of that they do not understand what they want to tell them. All the signals people are used to, such as eye contact, gesture, intonation, are absent.

These people can function very well indeed when they communicate with computers and other machines, but when it comes to associating with other people, they have a problem.

Lack of sympathy, understanding, and respect for the existing cultural differences can also destroy meetings between people.

Both Parties Must Believe in the Collaboration Model

Being motivated and sacrificing the time it takes, running the risks always present, pushing their own value norms aside, and adjusting to the surroundings require that the parties believe in the advantages of collaboration. They are totally familiar with the theories. They realize that the collaboration model is not for "soft men" and that it can make equally tough demands as in the traditional fighting model. They do not need to be "machos."

You Must Have Rational and Knowledgeable Negotiators

The knowledge of the things we negotiate about is greatly lacking. In today's slim organizations, employees must cope with bigger and bigger demands. People who have never negotiated before end up in jobs where negotiating is one of their most important duties. You may meet a technician who is expected to be able to handle the business side of negotiations. Their lack of business experience and knowledge of economy makes it impossible for them to see the deal. They see the technical requirement specifications as a challenge. The costs, the time, and the risks that the demands result in become vague and a general view of the business is missing. Their decisions will not be businesslike.

Knowledge of how different people function and think is missing. Life experience is not sufficient for the necessary humility to be present. The rationale can become unattainable if prestige and personal value norms become too important.

The companies' bookkeeping must take into consideration the total effect of an agreement. It must not be possible for a negotiator to conceal or transfer costs to a "wrong" account.

You Must Have Communication Proficiency

Heavy demands are made on communicative competence. This includes personal magnetism, enthusiasm, the ability to persuade others, being able to sell one's ideas, listening to others, and understanding them. I see many negotiators here who fail just before the finishing line. Their attributes may well be first class, but they do not succeed in getting their message across. They talk at cross-purposes and there is no offer of a new chance. One of the big problems I have experienced is the lack of good communicators.

You Need a Spirit of Generosity

Many people find it difficult to be generous. Their envy is too strong. Your own assessment of what makes fair compensation is nonnegotiable. This is influenced by the who-do-you think-you-are attitude. If you try to eliminate the opponent's possibilities of achieving a profit, you are, in reality, cutting off your nose to spite your face.

Creativity Must Be a Priority

Added value can only arise if you change what is given. The necessary creative forces are up against:

- The conservative person who opposes any change
- The person who settles and thinks that everything is fine the way it is
- The person who perceives change as a threat

Note: It is management's job to make sure that the right people are assigned to negotiations and projects. Knowledge and skills can be developed. Organizational problems, distribution of responsibility, reward systems, and bookkeeping problems that make a general view impossible can be eliminated.

How AI Can Help Craft and Execute Successful Collaboration Agreements

AI is an invaluable tool for navigating the complexities of collaboration agreements. It can enhance communication, foster mutual understanding, and streamline processes by addressing each of the prerequisites. AI can empower organizations to approach collaboration agreements with greater precision, creativity, and confidence. By addressing challenges in communication, preparation, and execution, AI can enhance every stage of the process, ensuring that agreements are not only successful but also mutually rewarding.

This section looks at how AI can assist you in achieving a successful collaboration agreement.

Ensuring Compatibility: The Role of Human Chemistry

AI tools can analyze communication patterns, sentiment, and tone to identify potential mismatches or alignment in interpersonal dynamics.
How AI helps:

- It can assess whether team members' communication styles align, using tools like sentiment analysis and behavioral profiling.
- It can recommend adjustments to tone or approach to foster mutual respect and trust.

Example: AI-powered collaboration platforms might suggest phrasing changes in emails to reduce potential misunderstandings.
Prompt example: "Analyze recent communication between teams and identify areas where tone or style might be improved to enhance rapport and mutual understanding."

Encouraging Belief in the Collaboration Model

AI can provide data-backed insights into the benefits of collaboration, quantifying the potential value of collaboration versus traditional competition.
How AI helps:

- It can generate case studies or scenarios where similar agreements led to measurable success.
- It can simulate potential outcomes to demonstrate the advantages of collaborative models.

Example: AI might create a comparative analysis showing how collaboration could improve revenue by 15 percent versus pursuing independent strategies.

Prompt example: "Generate a report comparing collaborative versus competitive approaches in similar industries, highlighting potential risks and benefits."

Enhancing Rationality and Knowledge in Negotiations

AI tools can fill knowledge gaps by providing real-time access to data, insights, and analysis.

How it helps:

- It can offer detailed reports on technical, financial, and operational considerations, ensuring negotiators have a comprehensive view.
- It can identify areas where negotiators might need additional training or support.

Example: AI-powered dashboards could display the long-term financial impacts of specific clauses during contract drafting.

Prompt example: "Provide a summary of key technical and financial implications for the proposed agreement, highlighting areas requiring further clarification."

Improving Communication Proficiency

AI enhances communication by analyzing and improving how messages are conveyed. It can simulate conversations and provide feedback on clarity and tone.

How AI helps:

- It can suggest optimized phrasing and structuring of proposals to make them more persuasive and relatable.
- It can analyze cross-cultural nuances to avoid misunderstandings in global agreements.

Example: AI tools could flag overly complex sentences in a contract draft and propose simpler alternatives.

Prompt example: "Analyze this draft proposal and recommend changes to make it more concise, persuasive, and culturally appropriate for an international audience."

Fostering Generosity

AI can identify opportunities where giving slightly more can yield greater overall benefits, fostering goodwill without excessive cost.
How AI helps:

- It can recommend small concessions that provide significant perceived value to the other party.
- It can model scenarios to show how generosity could lead to long-term gains.

Example: AI might suggest offering a slightly extended warranty period, which is low-cost for the provider but highly valued by the client.
Prompt example: "Identify low-cost, high-impact concessions we could offer to strengthen the collaboration agreement."

Encouraging Creativity in Solutions

AI-driven brainstorming tools can generate innovative solutions by analyzing past agreements, market trends, and industry benchmarks.
How AI helps:

- It can provide alternative approaches to address challenges and create additional value.
- It can simulate creative "what-if" scenarios to explore new possibilities.

Example: AI could propose bundling complementary services into the agreement to enhance its value proposition.
Prompt example: "Suggest innovative ways to structure the collaboration agreement that maximize value for both parties while minimizing risk."

Supporting Managerial Tasks

AI can streamline the process of selecting the right people for negotiations and projects, using behavioral analysis and performance metrics.
How AI helps:

- It can identify team members with the necessary skills and traits for successful negotiation.
- It can highlight potential gaps in the team and suggest training programs or resources.

How AI Can Help Craft and Execute Successful Collaboration Agreements 55

Example: AI tools could recommend DISC-profiled team members for specific roles in the negotiation process.

The DISC personality profiling model categorizes behavior into four primary styles:

- Dominance (D) focuses on results, assertiveness, and control.
- Influence (I) emphasizes communication, persuasion, and relationships.
- Steadiness (S) prioritizes stability, cooperation, and dependability.
- Conscientiousness (C) values accuracy, organization, and adherence to standards.

DISC helps individuals understand their behavioral tendencies and how they interact with others, fostering improved communication and teamwork.

Prompt example: "Analyze team profiles and recommend individuals best suited for leading the negotiation based on their skills and DISC traits."

CHAPTER 6

Unveiling Value: The Hunt for NegoEconomics in Every Deal

If there is motivation, an open mind, and enough freedom for individuals in an organization to look for and find new paths, considerable NegoEconomics can be created if only negotiators know where to look. NegoEconomics increases the room for negotiation and the cake that can be divided.

NegoEconomics is more crucial than ever. According to a recent study by World Commerce & Contracting, only 16 percent of respondents believed they were negotiating the right variables to create value in their contracts. Another World Commerce & Contracting study sheds light on the issue: Among the top 10 most negotiated items, only 2 contribute to generating NegoEconomics. The takeaway is clear: Success in negotiation depends not only on how you negotiate but also on focusing on the right variables that drive value.

Key Principles of NegoEconomics

Here are the key principles of NegoEconomics:

- **Asymmetric value:** Identify that something may cost one party less than it is worth to the other, creating leverage (e.g., a low-cost service for the seller that is highly valuable to the buyer).

- **Value creation:** Find ways to add value creatively to a deal without significantly increasing costs, such as offering extra services or flexible payment options.
- **Win-win outcomes:** Prioritize collaborative agreements where both parties benefit more than in traditional competitive negotiation.
- **Expanding the room for negotiation:** Broaden negotiation beyond price to include services, time, resources, and risks for additional value creation.
- **Cost-benefit analysis:** Understand opportunities for mutual gain by assessing costs and benefits for both parties.

Example: Selling a Gaming Console

Suppose you're selling a gaming console for $200, and a buyer offers $180. Instead of accepting or rejecting the lower price, you enhance the deal by adding two games that you no longer play. While these games are worth only $10 to you, they hold a $40 value to the buyer. The buyer agrees to pay the full $200 due to the added value.

Outcome:

- You maintained your desired price without a discount.
- The buyer gained more value for the same amount.
- Both sides felt satisfied, achieving a win-win outcome.

Example: Car Dealership Negotiation

A dealership lists a car for $30,000. The buyer offers $28,000. Rather than dropping the price, the dealership includes a premium service package (oil changes, tire rotations) valued at $2,500 to the buyer but costing the dealership only $500.

Outcome:

- **Dealership:** Maintains profit margin with minimal expense
- **Buyer:** Gains more perceived value, justifying the original price
- **Result:** Beneficial outcome for both sides, building trust for future sales

Benefits of Focusing on NegoEconomics

NegoEconomics shifts the mindset of negotiation from a competitive win-lose dynamic to one of collaboration and creative problem-solving. This approach enhances outcomes for all parties involved.

- **Stronger, long-term relationships:** Fosters trust and partnerships
- **Discovery of hidden opportunities:** Identifies new ways to create value
- **Improved outcomes:** Achieves better results while controlling costs and minimizing risks

NegoEconomics is particularly valuable in complex or high-stakes negotiations, where traditional methods may overlook opportunities for shared benefits.

The Room for Negotiation

Traditionally, the room for negotiation is the range between the highest price a buyer will pay and the lowest price a seller will accept. A deal can only be made if the buyer's maximum is higher than the seller's minimum, creating a positive space for agreement. For example, if the buyer's limit is $14,000 and the seller's minimum is $12,000, the $2,000 difference is the room for negotiation.

However, the real room for negotiation often exceeds this range. It includes both the traditional negotiation space and the additional value created through NegoEconomics. This expanded approach can enable agreements even when the buyer's maximum is below the seller's minimum, by finding added value that benefits both sides.

Simple Model to Locate NegoEconomics

Effective preparation is essential for finding NegoEconomics opportunities. Traditional preparation for negotiations often involves determining the offer:

- How are you going to submit and explain your offer?
- What questions and objections are the other party likely to put forward?
- What terms, conditions, and price should you open with?
- Where lies the threshold of pain?

CHAPTER 6 Unveiling Value: The Hunt for NegoEconomics in Every Deal

For example, if you start with an offer of $118,000 and your minimum acceptable price (threshold of pain) is $103,000, the room for negotiation is $15,000. Typically, the goal is to secure a deal while conceding as little as possible of that $15,000.

However, defining objectives this way risks a zero-sum perspective where gains are made at the expense of the other party. Reducing your price by $5,000 lowers your profit by the same amount and benefits the other party equally, making it a 1:1 trade-off.

To avoid this, broaden your approach during preparation. Aim to create value beyond just price concessions, enabling negotiations where both parties can win without simply trading concessions.

Consider this four-step model for NegoEconomics:

1. **Make your offer:** Identify your room for negotiation (e.g., $15,000) and focus on how to leverage that value creatively, rather than simply lowering the price.
2. **Determine what else you can offer:** Think beyond money and consider adding extra services or products that enhance the value of your offer.
3. **Reduce the scope:** Evaluate whether parts of the deal can be removed, like services or products the other party can handle themselves, or find simpler solutions to lower costs.
4. **Develop a negotiation strategy for final offers:** If the other party rejects these additional options, always ask for a counteroffer to avoid one-sided concessions. For instance, if your initial price is $118,000 and the customer offers $88,000, splitting the difference would lead to $103,000 (the customer's objective). Halving the difference again results in $110,500 (the customer's likely threshold). Position your counter at $107,500 and observe their reaction. Avoid a pattern of continuous concessions that may push you to your minimum limit.

Providing extra services or products can be strategic, as the cost to you may be much lower than the perceived value to the buyer, creating leverage. This difference between cost and value forms the essence of NegoEconomics.

Example scenario: A seller offers 10 computers bundled with software and delivery for $118,000. The buyer, considering an alternative offer, demands a price near $100,000, while the seller's lowest acceptable price is $103,000.

Alternative approach: Instead of reducing the price to meet the buyer halfway (around $110,000), the seller explores value-adding options, asking, "What can be offered to increase customer value without significant cost?"

Proposal: The seller offers training for five associates on Microsoft Office. Although the training usually costs $4,500 per participant, the seller can fill unused seats in existing courses at no extra cost. This provides substantial value to the buyer but minimal cost to the seller. The offer could be structured to allow two employees per week, capped at five participants, with a 50 percent course fee discount. If necessary, the offer can be adjusted by increasing the number of participants, deepening the discount, or adding upgraded hardware.

Outcome: If the buyer values these added services, they may recognize the asymmetric value and accept the deal. If they are focused solely on price, alternative adjustments could include:

- Letting the buyer handle software installation and pickup, saving $4,000 in labor. The seller passes $3,000 in savings to the buyer and retains $1,000.
- Offering a cash discount for upfront payment, reflecting a portion of the interest savings.

Conclusion: By shifting focus from price to value and implementing NegoEconomics, the seller maximizes negotiation flexibility and improves the likelihood of a mutually beneficial agreement. If all else fails, step 4 advises using careful haggling to reach a compromise.

Locating NegoEconomics in a Project

Projects often have numerous areas ripe for NegoEconomics. The key is to question current practices and envision alternatives throughout the project's life cycle, from the initial idea to when the product no longer provides value.

Key areas to explore:

- Financial variables and conditions
- Quality and technical specifications
- Economies of scale
- Time management
- Purchasing patterns
- Rights and responsibilities

Process review: Follow the entire process step by step, asking critical questions such as:

- *Why is this done this way?* Challenge standard practices and routines.
- *What could be done differently and what would the outcomes be?* Explore potential changes for positive impacts.

Steps to analyze:

1. **Get an overview:** Create a detailed sketch of current practices for a complete view. Use this as a baseline for comparison when exploring modifications.
2. **Investigate events step by step:** Physically follow each process stage and assess:
   - *Why are things done this way?* Avoid accepting "That's how it's always been."
   - *What happens post-need?* Consider life cycle extension, resale, or adaptability of products/services.
3. **Identify elements and their impacts:**
   - Assess how each element affects costs, risks, profits, time, reliability, and life span.
   - Define factors that negatively influence these aspects.
4. **Explore alternatives:**
   - Evaluate alternative methods and their impacts, both positive and negative.
   - Identify opportunities, risks, and potential problems compared to the current situation.
5. **Responsibility allocation:**
   - Determine the most suitable party for tasks—those who are cost-effective, experienced, or best equipped to handle risk.
   - Plan for scenarios requiring responsibility transfers, redesigns, or additional training.
6. **Technology's role:** Consider the advantages of new technology. Innovations, such as the internet, open opportunities and may disrupt traditional practices, presenting both potential and challenges in negotiation and project management.

Examples of NegoEconomics

This section discusses several examples of NegoEconomics in action.

From Public Authority to Commercial Enterprise

In the past, telephone services were monopolized, with limited, inconvenient setups. Ordering and installing a new telephone point was time-consuming and costly. The process involved multiple steps: recording the order, forwarding it to a district, scheduling appointments, and deploying a fitter equipped with expensive tools. Customers often waited at home all day, resulting in frustration when billed $195 for work that cost the company around $895 and left many unsatisfied.

Customers were prohibited from installing their own telephone points due to safety concerns, reinforcing the company's control. The company focused on phone call revenues but overlooked how easier installations could boost phone usage.

Over time, changes emerged. Customers gained access to affordable installation tools for under $15 and could set up their own phone points. A simple connecting plug allowed easy connections, and monopolies in phone sales ended, enabling multiple purchases. The transformation from a rigid public authority to a business-focused enterprise had gradual but ultimately reshaped the industry, increasing customer autonomy and satisfaction.

Buying a Table in the 1950s: A Detailed Process

This example illustrates the complex, time-consuming procedures of the 1950s, showing both the logistical and financial challenges of that era.

Visiting the furniture store:

- *Location*: All furniture stores were centralized in city centers.
- *Advantages*: Easy for customers to access and compare products across different stores.
- *Disadvantages*: High rental costs forced stores to maintain higher prices and limited stock, displaying samples rather than ready-to-buy items, which led to extended delivery times.

Placing an order:

- After selecting a table, the customer paid a deposit, and the store sent the order to the factory.
- *Advantages*: Down payments helped stores fund operations and reduced risks related to unsold stock.
- *Disadvantages*: Long waiting periods (at least five weeks) often resulted in frustration, especially when estimated delivery times were inaccurate, prompting back-and-forth communication with the factory.

Factory processing:

- Factories didn't produce tables one by one but waited until they could manufacture a small series.
- *Advantages*: Factories minimized investment in unsold stock and avoided overproduction.
- *Disadvantages*: Limited use of advanced machinery and craftsmanship-focused production led to higher costs and slow innovation in materials and designs.

Transportation:

- To reduce damage risk and costs, items were grouped for shipment, using protective packaging and transshipments.
- *Disadvantage*: Consolidating shipments delayed delivery. Direct shipment was faster but more expensive.

Delivery to the store and customer:

- The store confirmed the correct product had arrived and contacted the customer to schedule delivery. The store's van delivered the table, placed it in the customer's home, polished it, and removed the packaging.
- *Advantages*: High-quality service with personal delivery and setup.
- *Disadvantage*: The handling process was expensive and added to the final cost.

This traditional process showcased high service levels but was costly, slow, and involved numerous steps that contributed to inefficiencies and higher prices for customers.

Understanding the Shift in Furniture Packaging and Industry Transformation

What was really in the carton? When receiving a packaged table from the furniture factory, it's easy to assume it contained only the table. However, a major portion—approximately 90 percent—was air. Transporting and stocking products with significant airspace was costly. This realization led to rethinking how tables were designed and packaged, fundamentally altering industry practices.

Innovative design solutions: The problem was presented to furniture designers with the goal of reducing air in packaging. Historically, the concept was not new; British officers had used a collapsible "campaign table" with detachable legs for easy transport. The modern adaptation was to create tables that consumers could assemble themselves by attaching legs that were not glued or permanently affixed at the factory. The solution allowed packaging to be flat, compact, and efficient.

IKEA's revolutionary approach: IKEA embraced this idea, placing trust in innovative designers. By shifting the assembly of table legs to the end user, manufacturing costs were reduced. The customer now buys a flat-packed table for $225 and assembles it themselves without adding any labor cost to the purchase price.

Benefits and industry impact:

- **Reduced costs:** Factories saved on assembly labor, and packaging became more compact, minimizing transport and storage expenses.
- **Lower rents:** Moving stores to city outskirts reduced rental costs, making it feasible to keep stock on hand and increasing product availability.
- **Immediate customer access:** Customers could purchase and take home a table the same day, improving convenience and boosting sales volumes.
- **Self-transport:** Customers could now carry the flat-packed tables themselves, eliminating the need for costly delivery services.
- **Economies of scale:** Bulk orders (e.g., 10,000 tables at a time) optimized production efficiency, allowed better use of machinery, and reduced raw material costs.
- **Innovation and collaboration:** Factories partnered with IKEA to develop superior machines and materials, and expertise was shared across production sites.
- **Global expansion:** Established processes in Sweden allowed IKEA to scale its operations and export its model worldwide.

Disadvantages and challenges:

- **Homogeneity:** The same designs appeared in countless homes, limiting uniqueness.
- **Variable quality:** Occasional quality issues, such as missing parts, required customers to return to the store.
- **Impact on smaller manufacturers:** Smaller, high-quality, exclusive workshops struggled, though some adapted by finding niche markets.
- **Supplier dominance:** IKEA's substantial influence gave it significant control over supplier terms and operations.

IKEA's shift from traditional, bulky packaging to flat-packed, customer-assembled furniture revolutionized the industry. It decreased costs, increased convenience, and established a scalable, global business model. While some challenges emerged, the transformation demonstrated the power of rethinking conventional processes through creative design and NegoEconomics.

Lessons from the Furniture Industry's Evolution Stagnant business practices often lead to zero-sum outcomes, where one party's gain results in another's increased costs, risks, or liabilities. In the furniture industry, the chain of stakeholders includes designers, manufacturers, employees, financiers, sub-suppliers, logistics providers, packaging companies, retailers, and end customers. While not all these parties may actively negotiate, they are all impacted by and contribute to industry changes.

Similar stakeholder chains exist in other industries that have seen little change over decades. These sectors often face long production times and high costs, with inefficient distribution adding further expense. Key questions for improving efficiency include these: Should responsibility be transferred to the customer? Should products be flat-packed for lower costs? Should long production runs and changes in design be considered? The answers depend on the specific enterprise and industry knowledge within it.

This type of analysis has sparked transformations across various sectors, guiding changes that enhance efficiency and competitiveness.

Benchmarking and Applying NegoEconomics

To innovate effectively, it's crucial to learn from companies that have advanced the furthest, often due to facing significant competition. By analyzing these companies, you can find creative NegoEconomics strategies that may be applicable both internally and in your partnerships. Avoid focusing solely on your segment of the business; instead, trace the process from concept to the product's end-of-life. Ask how various parties along the chain can benefit, and identify opportunities for more efficient responsibility sharing.

Key considerations include:

- **Cost identification and allocation:** Determine where costs arise and who handles them most efficiently.
- **Risk management:** Pinpoint where risks are concentrated and who is best equipped to manage them.
- **Time efficiency:** Identify delays and explore ways to shorten timelines.
- **Value generation:** Recognize where money, expertise, and goodwill are produced and who gains most from these.

Consider whether any intermediaries are unnecessary and if solutions like e-commerce could streamline processes. Apply these reflections to various scenarios, such as selling a home, to explore alternative partners beyond standard real estate agents.

Financial Variables as NegoEconomic Opportunities

Many companies adhere to industry norms without exploring if changes in financial terms could unlock new advantages. Negotiators often have limited authority to deviate from standard conditions, which are set by individuals who may not be at the negotiation table. Empowering negotiators and reexamining standard financial practices can reveal opportunities for NegoEconomics. Financial aspects include:

- **Terms of payment:** Credits and payment plans
- **Ownership models:** Options like leasing, renting, shared ownership, or outsourcing
- **Pricing and budgeting:** Tailoring price structures to maximize tax benefits
- **Currency management:** Utilizing money, goods, or services for payment
- **Payment methods:** Exploring invoicing frequency, credit cards, or automated payment systems
- **Initial payments and royalties:** Adjusting down payments or incorporating royalties for revenue sharing

The following sections dive into each of these financial aspects in more detail.

Terms of Payment Negotiating payment terms often sees buyers rejecting advances without fully exploring the proposal's benefits. Advances should be considered in light of potential returns from the supplier. Constructive dialogue is essential, with both parties clearly stating what they want and what they can offer in return. For example, a supplier may offer discounted prices or added services if an advance is granted.

Buyers should actively explore why a seller needs an advance and assess potential value exchanges, such as longer credit terms or additional services. Openness can reveal creative financial solutions and new opportunities for NegoEconomics.

However, traditional company policies and limited negotiation skills often prevent parties from exploring flexible terms. Policies like "no advances" restrict potential gains and overlook the value that alternative payment terms can bring. Staff should be empowered with the skills and authority to negotiate effectively, while management should provide guidelines for maximizing NegoEconomics through customized payment terms.

By fostering a culture of proactive communication and negotiation, organizations can leverage payment terms for mutual benefits, reducing costs and enhancing overall efficiency.

Ownership Models When deciding whether to purchase, lease, rent, or outsource, several factors must be considered: the urgency and permanence of the need, the financial and human resources available, and whether the item is viewed as an investment. The decision to own or use depends on the specific situation—whether ownership is about investment, status, or long-term utility, or whether leasing or renting offers a more flexible, cost-effective solution.

For example, in the case of smartphone storage, users initially may not see the need for extra cloud space, but later, when their devices fill up, they are willing to pay on-demand for the storage. This reflects how urgency changes perceptions of value, with companies profiting by offering on-demand solutions at the right moment.

Past decisions—such as the choice to own a large TV and cable package—may have seemed essential based on assumptions about family time, status, or convenience. However, with the rise of streaming services, smart TVs, and changing lifestyle priorities, many people are reevaluating these choices, opting for more flexible and cost-effective alternatives.

Similarly, in business, the decision to own or rent resources often remains rigid, influenced by past norms. NegoEconomics encourages a fresh evaluation: Are the resources still needed in the same way? Can alternatives like shared ownership, leasing, or outsourcing provide a better solution with lower costs and risks?

To make rational, forward-thinking decisions, it's important to reassess current needs, priorities, and available alternatives regularly, rather than clinging to outdated choices. This shift in mindset can open opportunities for cost-saving and efficiency through more flexible, creative models of ownership and usage.

Pricing and Budgeting Pricing is a multifaceted concept that can be structured in numerous ways, such as fixed, flexible, indexed, or orientation-based prices, and even through incentive mechanisms where additional costs and profits are shared. Indexes also serve as a useful tool for price adjustments.

In many cultures, the prevalence of suggested retail prices reflects a mix of factors, including fear of conflict, an aversion to haggling, and limited bargaining skills. Price plays a pivotal role in business transactions, often serving as both a measure of success and a direct contributor to the bottom line. Its influence on profitability makes price a critical factor in negotiation dynamics.

Price is frequently where interests diverge between negotiating parties. However, this divergence need not lead to confrontation. By understanding the other party's perception of price and its significance to them, negotiators can foster a productive dialogue. This dynamic is encapsulated in the concept of NegoEconomics, which leverages asymmetric value creation to achieve mutually beneficial outcomes. Importantly, the meaning of price can vary significantly depending on perspective and context, encompassing the following dimensions:

- **Cost:** The monetary amount required to acquire a good or service.
- **Prestige:** The emotional value tied to paying a high or low price, often linked to group identity.
- **Perceived value:** Determined by budget considerations, perceived utility, available alternatives, and the effort or cost involved in production.
- **Opening offer:** Often perceived as inflated, this serves as a starting point for negotiation.
- **Accepted price:** The amount both parties agree upon, which translates to tangible outcomes like cash flow and meeting financial needs.
- **Confirmation of worth:** The accepted price reaffirms the value of the good or service.
- **Correct price:** This only becomes clear when both parties fully understand the exchange's benefits.

Approaches to Pricing

- **Fixed pricing:** Fixed pricing simplifies the buyer's decision-making, particularly when comparing alternatives or working within a set budget. However, it often includes a risk premium, which can exceed what the supplier needs to mitigate potential risks. While this approach incentivizes suppliers to optimize costs, it may not reflect actual risk-sharing.
- **Flexible pricing:** Flexible pricing accommodates uncertainty, such as in large or unpredictable projects. A rigid fixed price might result in excessively high risk premiums or disputes over unanticipated costs. Flexible agreements often involve documented costs plus an agreed-upon profit margin, common in monopoly settings or high-risk environments. To maintain transparency, these agreements can include disclosure provisions and rights to audit financial records.
- **Indexed pricing:** Linking a fixed price to an index offers a way to adjust for fluctuations in costs or timelines. This method avoids contentious

debates over forecasting and ensures fair retroactive adjustments. Both parties must agree on the index, its baseline, and the extent of its application.

- **Orientation-based pricing:** This approach ties price to shared responsibility for project costs and profits. Both parties agree to share unforeseen expenses and additional profits, fostering a collaborative focus on cost efficiency. The success of this method hinges on defining the orientation price and an equitable distribution mechanism.

- **Incentive-driven pricing:** Incentive structures align the interests of both parties by sharing financial outcomes. For instance, combining price with volume and time considerations can lead to mutually advantageous arrangements. Examples include publishers negotiating royalty rates that increase after a specified sales volume, or buyers agreeing to lock in prices for extended periods to gain internal approval.

Internal Dynamics Within organizations, buyers often need to "sell" the negotiated deal to internal stakeholders. Demonstrating cost efficiency or favorable terms, such as extending current pricing into future periods, can secure internal alignment and expedite approval processes.

In conclusion, pricing strategies should not be treated as mere figures on a spreadsheet. They represent a complex interplay of cost, value, risk, and collaboration. By embracing diverse pricing methods and fostering an understanding of the broader context, negotiators can craft agreements that satisfy both parties, paving the way for sustainable partnerships and enhanced value creation.

Pricing Based on Results This involves calculating the price retroactively, where the supplier is compensated according to the results achieved. This method, which is uncommon in Nordic countries, often faces skepticism and resistance because it can seem like the supplier might earn an unreasonable amount based on the results. Many people prefer a fixed price, fearing that it might not be fair or predictable.

For instance, when a customer is planning a direct advertising campaign and asks for an overall price, the seller might propose a price structure that the customer finds unusual. For every response leading to an order, the seller might want $44 over a period of six months. The customer, however, may resist this offer because it seems too flexible and unconventional, preferring a "normal" fixed price instead.

The customer's focus on how much the other party stands to earn can lead to missing the broader perspective: The more the other party earns, the more the customer will benefit as well. Instead of rejecting such pricing methods, it's important to recognize that measuring results with certainty could be more effective. By assessing the potential outcome realistically and negotiating a distribution model that incentivizes the supplier to put in significant effort, both parties can reach a more beneficial agreement.

> **Note:** When price is allocated across different accounts, cost types, or budgetary periods, the issue often lies in bookkeeping technicalities rather than total costs over time. Redistributing costs between accounts or periods can resolve this. The tax implications depend on the nature of the costs: Some can be written off immediately, while others need to be amortized over years, and some may be tax-deductible, while others are not.

Psychological Aspects of Price These are significant in negotiations. Many buyers are primarily concerned with the price charged to their budget, which can hold greater psychological weight for them than for the seller. Allowing the other party to feel they "won" the price negotiation can lead to valuable quid pro quo opportunities that offset the costs involved in a price reduction.

An example of this is a Volvo dealer in the United States who achieved the highest per capita sales by adopting a unique approach. Instead of lowering the trade-in value of old cars by pointing out flaws, he offered customers a good trade-in price. In return, he kept discounts on new cars low. This approach challenged traditional rigid pricing principles, showing that flexibility in pricing strategies and reframing typical negotiation norms can lead to successful outcomes for both parties. The challenge lies in overcoming fixed principles like "price must always be fixed" or "we must always have a discount," which can limit creative problem-solving in pricing negotiations.

Currency Management: Money, Goods, or Services

When determining the currency for a transaction, several factors must be considered, including the risks and opportunities associated with exchange rate fluctuations. One option is to hedge the exchange risk by shifting it to others, or alternatively, to capitalize on currency fluctuations if one is knowledgeable and willing to take on the risk.

However, price does not always need to be paid in money. Accepting payment in goods or services can offer both opportunities and risks. For example, a consultant working with a new business that lacks cash could opt for a share of future profits instead of immediate payment. Similarly, if a business receives shoddy work from a service provider, rather than accepting a small cash refund, they could negotiate compensation in services, such as free access to a mailing list, which has no cost to the service provider but holds value for the business.

In other cases, like airlines offering loyalty points instead of cash, the provider may not incur additional costs since the points are linked to unsold seats. Another example is a seller of packaging machinery who may accept payment in food products from a company with excess capacity but short on cash. By reselling the food products to supermarkets, the seller could potentially make more profit than if they had insisted on cash payment in a different currency. These examples illustrate the flexibility and creativity that can be applied in pricing strategies, offering both parties potential benefits beyond traditional monetary transactions.

The problem is that the parties have become too rigid in their ideas, and blinkers prevent them from thinking along new lines.

Initial Payments and Royalties

The frequency of invoicing and mode of payment can significantly affect transaction costs, especially for small or frequent payments. Companies like electricity providers or mobile operators may face high administrative costs for handling numerous small payments. To reduce costs, mobile companies introduced cash cards or automatic debiting, streamlining payments.

Credit cards can offer advantages like free credit or serve as a bargaining tool. For example, if you make a large purchase, you can choose a credit card that costs the store more to process. In this case, you might offer to pay with cash in exchange for a discount in goods instead of money. This benefits both parties, as the store avoids credit card fees, and you get a product (like a PS5 controller) at a favorable price. However, while the government loses out on sales tax and the credit card company loses its commission, the deal remains lawful and beneficial for both the buyer and seller.

In business negotiations, it's important to recognize opportunities beyond traditional payment methods, such as down payments, royalties, or lump sum payments. These methods are commonly used for writers, inventors, and creators who can offer both a guaranteed upfront payment and performance-based compensation. For example, a publishing house may offer a guaranteed lump sum for a book, but a writer could propose adjusting the deal to receive a higher royalty instead, depending on market success, allowing for a better long-term return.

When considering how to charge for services or products, such as developing an IT system, there are various options: a fixed price, flexible pricing based on hours worked, or performance-based pricing tied to transactions. The key is to assess the potential of the project, the costs involved, and whether payment can be postponed until the system is operational. In some cases, payments could be structured around each transaction or sale, creating an ongoing revenue stream. For example, charging a small fee for each transaction, such as a dollar per credit card payment, can generate significant long-term profit, even if the fee seems negligible to customers.

Understanding the customer's needs and what competitors might do is crucial. If the customer can pass on transaction costs to their end customers, this model might be more appealing. Additionally, considering future resale opportunities, such as royalties on products sold to other customers, can create additional streams of income and value for both parties.

Ultimately, by thinking creatively about payment structures, businesses can secure favorable deals while aligning with customer interests and reducing upfront financial risks.

A Strategic Approach to Balancing Requirements, Costs, and Negotiation

The design of a technical specification of requirements is crucial because it not only defines the quality and performance of a product or system but also influences costs, timelines, risks, and expected outcomes. It is important to assess whether the specifications are nonnegotiable demands or simply preferences. The person who has written the specifications may have a limited understanding of available alternatives, and it is essential to consider how priorities have been set, what has been deliberately excluded, and which needs have influenced the wording of the requirements.

To fully understand the intentions behind a specification of requirements, it is necessary to ask several questions. Only once we have a clear understanding of these factors can we begin to engage in an unbiased discussion about the optimal specification and identify areas where flexibility can be applied to create NegoEconomics. This approach allows for better negotiation and collaboration.

A systematic analysis of all requirements is key to understanding them thoroughly. This analysis can be organized in a matrix, where each requirement is broken down individually, allowing for a structured and clear evaluation of its significance, feasibility, and potential areas for negotiation. This process helps identify opportunities for both sides to reach a mutually beneficial agreement while considering all factors involved.

Variable	Point of Departure	Negotiation Arena	Change of Conditions
Delivery	August 1	September 1	$10,000
Price	$50,000	$40,000	$10,000

Capacity 100 pieces/hour
The daily need is 70 pieces/hour

And you want a bit excess capacity of 80–110 pieces/hour.
At 80 pieces/hour there is a risk of lack of capacity in the peak season.
Over the next couple of years you cannot use more than 90 pieces/hour.

The requirement for a capacity exceeding 100 units per hour can significantly impact both the supplier's ability to deliver on time and at an acceptable price, as well as the machine's long-term maintenance costs and life span. These considerations will dictate whether a standard machine can be used or if a special-purpose machine is necessary. If a special-purpose machine is required, the supplier would likely need to redesign the machine, which introduces additional time, costs, and risks due to the uncertainty and complexity of innovation.

In some cases, the customer's demand for higher capacity could be addressed by moving to a three-shift operation instead of redesigning the machine, which would be a far less expensive solution. However, if the higher capacity becomes a permanent need, it may be necessary to design a machine that can be easily upgraded or reconstructed in the future.

To convince the customer of this solution, both parties must understand the effects of the higher-capacity requirement on delivery times, costs, and the inherent risks of innovation. Successful negotiation in this case hinges on mutual trust, open communication, and a shared understanding of the technical alternatives, which requires both parties to have sufficient professional expertise and a comprehensive view of the options available.

Note: Quality and performance will affect costs during the different phases of the project.

The technical specification of requirements is made up of a mixture of essential requirements that must be met for the project to succeed, as well as a list of desired features or functions, some of which may be more or less valuable or interesting. For technical reasons or as bargaining chips, there may be demands that can be waived during negotiation.

The specification of requirements should not be left solely to operators and technicians. Their reasons for including or excluding certain functions may be influenced by personal preferences rather than the company's best interests. Some functions may have costs that do not align with their practical benefits for the company.

It's important to avoid the "negotiating trap" of technician-to-technician discussions, which may lead to the development of new products or systems without fully considering the costs, time loss, and risks involved. Costs, risks, time consumption, and physical effort must always be weighed against the useful effect that can be achieved during the different project phases:

- Development
- Production

- Service and maintenance
- Winding up

The specification of requirements will influence various factors, including:

- Flexibility, extensibility, and compatibility
- Possibility of selling to multiple users
- Potential to extend the product's useful life
- Reliability and environmental impact
- Overall useful life
- User friendliness and working environment

Economies of Scale

One of the primary motivations behind many mergers is the potential for economies of scale, where the parties involved can reduce their unit costs by spreading high development expenses, production overheads, and distribution costs across a larger number of units. However, the benefits of these economies must be carefully evaluated in relation to the changes that come with scaling up operations.

For example, as course providers, if we send out our course catalog to 10,000 potential customers, the costs involved in finding their addresses and the postage can be significant, with a campaign costing between $9,000 and $12,500. However, if we collaborate with a colleague who offers a complementary course, rather than a competing one, we can reduce these costs by half. By partnering with a large-scale course provider who already runs numerous courses and has its own mailing list, postal discounts, and the ability to combine multiple courses in one envelope, the costs can be reduced even further, potentially to one-tenth of the original cost.

Despite these savings, there are potential disadvantages. The message may get lost in a large batch of materials, and if the recipient does not find the first couple of courses appealing, they might discard all of the materials. If the recipient dislikes one course, there's a risk they may reject the entire offering. Additionally, collaborating with larger organizations may mean compromising on branding, format, and even price flexibility, because all partners may need to standardize their offerings to fit the collective presentation.

In short, while economies of scale can provide significant cost savings, these savings often come with trade-offs that should be carefully weighed against the benefits.

Time in Agreements

Time is a critical factor in any agreement, and the discussion around time often centers on delivery timelines. Key considerations include the cost of earlier delivery, the potential earnings from starting ahead of schedule, and the financial impact of delays. However, time also has other aspects that are often overlooked or simply handled according to established practices, without exploring alternative options.

Key time considerations in agreements:

- **Duration of the agreement:** Agreements often have default durations, typically running for one year. This is based on the annual reporting cycle of companies, budget planning, and practical convenience. However, other time periods such as 6 months, 18 months, or even 3 years could provide more optimal solutions depending on the nature of the agreement.
- **Period of notice and winding up:** The length of notice periods and the winding-up period are also crucial time elements. A shorter notice period (such as 6 months) can be valuable to a party needing flexibility, while longer periods (such as 12 months) may offer more stability but can be costly for the party needing to adjust. Shorter cancellation times may be desirable to one party but problematic for another, and this dynamic should be carefully evaluated.
- **Period of suborders:** The timing of suborders, especially in long-term agreements, can impact flexibility and cost efficiency. The timing should be assessed to determine whether the supplier's commitments align with the buyer's needs.

Other time-related considerations:

- **Renewal and renegotiation workload:** Many agreements automatically renew at year-end (e.g., starting on January 1 and ending on December 31), which creates a peak workload in November and December for those renegotiating. The rush to finalize agreements can result in suboptimal decisions because the decision-makers may not fully appreciate the terms of the agreement at the time of signing. As a protective measure, companies may add excessive risk premiums to safeguard against potential future changes.
- **Preparedness and response time:** In service agreements, especially in tech-related industries (e.g., computer system service agreements), the focus should be on practical outcomes—such as how quickly the fault is remedied, not just how quickly the technician arrives.

For example, in a computer repair service agreement, the actual repair time is more important than the time of arrival. Similarly, backup systems, such as keeping an old computer as a reserve, could save money and reduce downtime.

- **Cost of downtime:** Downtime in industries such as finance or IT can be costly. For instance, if a stockbroker's customers cannot complete their transactions due to server downtime, it could result in significant losses. Similarly, the value of having a guaranteed seat on a flight or confirmed orders can be calculated by assessing how much emergency preparedness costs in different industries.
- **Example of airline pricing:** Airlines offer pricing based on the timing of bookings. How much can a wholesaler or supplier earn by requiring advance notice for orders, or how much can they save by keeping emergency stock to prevent supply chain disruptions?

Time in agreements should be considered from all perspectives—not just from the standpoint of when the contract begins or ends, but also in terms of flexibility, cancellation, notice periods, and preparedness. Exploring different time frames and aligning them with practical business needs and risks can lead to more effective and cost-efficient agreements.

Purchasing Patterns and Modern Commerce

Purchasing patterns in businesses can be optimized for profit by outsourcing certain tasks, such as stocking supplies, managing inventories, or handling mundane tasks like stocking refrigerators and tending to coffee dispensers. While managing purchases and inventories can be costly, individuals within a company may be reluctant to take on tasks such as buying coffee beans, unless they can benefit from it financially.

Modern technology, like barcode readers, enables the efficient management and monitoring of the entire purchasing process. For instance, if a customer is unable to visit a store, the store can make deliveries directly to the customer's location. This concept extends to services such as opticians who, instead of requiring customers to visit their office, come to the customer's workplace to provide service, saving time and increasing convenience.

The rise of the internet has further transformed commerce, creating an environment where suppliers and customers are just a click away. Businesses are leveraging this connectivity to form stronger partnerships, making their operations more efficient. This shift has empowered buyers and sellers alike, intensifying competition and reshaping traditional distribution models, which are increasingly becoming obsolete.

Rights

In any contract, clearly defining rights is crucial to prevent future disputes and create opportunities for negotiation (NegoEconomics). These rights should be carefully discussed and regulated to ensure both parties are aligned on expectations.

- **Development assignments:** If a buyer funds the development of a product, key questions arise:
  - Does the seller have the right to sell the same or similar products to other customers?
  - Are there restrictions on the seller's ability to resell (e.g., specific markets, time periods, or exclusions)?
  - Should the buyer, who financed the development, be entitled to royalties?
  - Is the buyer entitled to ongoing benefits, such as free upgrades or a "most favored customer" status ensuring they always get the lowest price?
- **Intellectual property rights in publishing:** For authors or creators, agreements with publishers often involve rights that can impact future income and control. Questions to consider include:
  - What compensation should you receive for assigning rights (such as language translations or adaptations to different media)?
  - Should there be a marketing spend requirement for the publisher to promote the work?
  - Should the publisher's option to exercise rights be limited in time, and should there be penalties if they don't take action within that period?
  - Will the publisher have veto rights or influence over the content?
  - How will profits from reselling the book be split, and should you demand a guaranteed fee regardless of the publisher's success in selling the book?

In both scenarios, addressing these rights clearly in the contract can avoid misunderstandings and create opportunities for mutually beneficial terms.

Example: Tesla and Rivian Collaboration

Imagine Tesla partnering with Rivian to co-develop new electric vehicle (EV) battery technology. For Tesla, this deal isn't just about technical specifications, R&D costs, and pricing. They must also consider the long-term effects of the collaboration and ask: What happens after Rivian delivers the technology?

Rivian will likely sell the same battery systems to other EV manufacturers, some of which may compete with Tesla. Tesla needs to assess their role in the development and implementation process, including funding, testing, and scaling production.

Key questions:

- **Exclusive rights:** Can Rivian sell the technology to Tesla's competitors? Can Tesla secure exclusivity before competitors access it?
- **Customization:** Should the battery be designed for general use or optimized for Tesla first?
- **Cost sharing:** How should development costs and profits be shared between the companies?
- **Upgrades and innovation:** Will Tesla automatically gain access to future upgrades from Rivian, and at what cost?
- **Preferred customer status:** Can Tesla negotiate the lowest prices compared to other buyers?

Key negotiation points:

- **Sales and licensing:** Define terms for Rivian selling to competitors.
- **Production rights:** Clarify who owns the right to produce the batteries.
- **Ownership and user rights:** Decide on intellectual property ownership and usage.
- **Exclusivity and veto power:** Set terms for Tesla's ability to block sales to specific competitors.

This collaboration isn't just a technical agreement, but also a strategic negotiation around intellectual property, market positioning, and future competitiveness in a rapidly evolving industry.

Leveraging AI in NegoEconomics

AI can significantly enhance NegoEconomics by identifying, analyzing, and optimizing opportunities, allowing negotiators to achieve superior outcomes. AI—especially ChatGPT—is very capable of identifying variables that might create NegoEconomics. Here's how AI can help:

- **Data analysis and insights:** AI processes large volumes of data to spot trends and patterns, aiding in decision-making:
    - **Cost analysis:** AI can analyze cost structures of proposals, pinpointing areas to reduce costs or increase value.

- **Competitor benchmarking:** By evaluating market trends and competitors' strategies, AI provides insights into pricing, features, or services that offer a competitive advantage.

- **Scenario planning and simulation:** AI can simulate different negotiation scenarios, allowing for better strategic decisions:
  - **Alternative offers:** AI generates package alternatives, optimizing price, services, and delivery terms for maximum value.
  - **Risk assessment:** AI models predict the financial, operational, or strategic impact of various negotiation outcomes.

- **Dynamic value creation:** AI identifies hidden opportunities for value creation:
  - Identifying asymmetries: AI can find areas where one party's cost is lower than the other's perceived value, key in NegoEconomics.
  - Optimizing resource allocation: AI suggests ways to reallocate resources to reduce inefficiencies and enhance value.

- **Real-time support:** AI-powered negotiation assistants provide real-time support:
  - **Counteroffer suggestions:** AI suggests counteroffers based on the ongoing conversation and strategic goals.
  - **Sentiment analysis:** AI analyzes language and tone to gauge emotional responses, helping negotiators adapt their approach.

- **Customizing agreements:** AI assists in crafting tailored agreements:
  - **Personalized solutions:** AI recommends flexible deal structures (payment terms, profit-sharing models) that align with both parties' objectives.
  - **Dynamic pricing models:** AI proposes variable pricing tied to performance or volume, maximizing mutual benefits.

- **Post-agreement optimization:** AI tools ensure agreements remain beneficial throughout their life cycle:
  - **Performance monitoring:** AI tracks contract performance, ensuring compliance and identifying areas for renegotiation.
  - **Continuous learning:** AI analyzes past negotiations, offering feedback to improve future strategies.

Example: AI in Action for Tesla and Rivian

In the Tesla-Rivian scenario, AI could maximize NegoEconomics by:

- **Identifying cost asymmetries:** AI might suggest offering Rivian exclusive access to Tesla's charging network, offsetting development costs and creating mutual value.
- **Simulating licensing strategies:** AI could predict the financial impact of various licensing agreements, showing how exclusivity affects both companies.
- **Optimizing battery customization:** AI could recommend the best balance between Tesla-specific features and broader compatibility for Rivian, reducing costs and maintaining competitiveness.

By integrating AI into negotiations, companies can transform traditional win-lose dynamics into collaborative, growth-oriented partnerships, unlocking creativity, efficiency, and mutual value.

AI Prompt Examples for NegoEconomics

These AI prompts can serve as valuable tools in refining negotiation strategies, optimizing value creation, and managing risks, all crucial for successful NegoEconomics:

- **Analyzing value creation**
    Prompt: "Identify cost asymmetries between our product offering and the customer's perceived value. Suggest options to reframe the deal by adding services or removing nonessential features to increase the total value for both parties."
- **Generating alternative offers**
    Prompt: "Provide three alternative packages for our offer, each emphasizing a different value driver (e.g., speed of delivery, additional services, or lower costs). Include a cost-benefit analysis for each package."
- **Scenario planning**
    Prompt: "Simulate three negotiation scenarios based on the following inputs: (1) the customer insists on a 10 percent discount, (2) the customer is open to extended payment terms, and (3) the customer values long-term exclusivity. Provide recommendations for optimal responses in each case."

- **Benchmarking competitors**

    Prompt: "Analyze competitors' recent deals in similar industries. Highlight any terms, conditions, or unique features that contributed to their success, and suggest how we might adopt or improve upon these strategies."

- **Optimizing contract terms**

    Prompt: "What payment structures could we propose to the customer that balance their cash flow concerns while minimizing our risk exposure? Include options for milestones, royalties, and delayed payments."

- **Identifying hidden costs**

    Prompt: "Break down the cost structure of the proposed deal. Identify any hidden or overlooked costs that could be shifted, reduced, or reassigned to increase efficiency and improve margins."

- **Negotiating exclusivity**

    Prompt: "Suggest ways to negotiate an exclusivity agreement that allows us to maintain market leadership while providing the counterpart with clear benefits. Include examples of exclusivity terms used in similar industries."

- **Real-time counteroffer suggestions**

    Prompt: "Based on the counterpart's latest proposal (e.g., a 20 percent discount request), suggest counteroffers that preserve value for us. Include options for adjusting timelines, bundling services, or providing add-ons instead of a price reduction."

- **Identifying value in intellectual property**

    Prompt: "Evaluate the intellectual property implications of this deal. How can we retain ownership of key innovations while providing enough value to the counterpart to secure their buy-in?"

- **Monitoring and improving agreements**

    Prompt: "Analyze our existing contract portfolio and identify any underperforming agreements. Suggest renegotiation strategies to optimize outcomes, focusing on time, costs, and risk distribution."

- **Leveraging customer psychology**

    Prompt: "Based on the customer's priorities (e.g., speed, cost, quality), suggest psychological tactics that could help reframe our value proposition to better align with their needs."
- **Assessing risk in negotiation proposals**

    Prompt: "Perform a risk assessment for the proposed deal structure. Highlight potential risks to both parties and recommend strategies to mitigate these risks while maintaining value creation."
- **Tracking dynamic pricing**

    Prompt: "Develop a dynamic pricing model for our service based on usage volume, customer segments, or seasonal demand. Ensure the model encourages long-term customer retention."
- **Enhancing negotiation strategies**

    Prompt: "Review past negotiations where we failed to reach an agreement. Analyze what went wrong and suggest alternative approaches for similar situations in the future."
- **Trust and relationship building**

    Prompt: "Suggest strategies to build trust during negotiations, focusing on transparency, mutual benefits, and shared objectives. Include examples of successful trust-building measures in high-stakes deals."

PART II

Mastering the Art of Strategy

This section, covering Chapters 7–11, builds on the foundational principles of negotiation and dives deeper into the advanced strategies that define successful deal-making. From leveraging generosity to fostering trust, adapting negotiation styles, and utilizing AI-driven insights, these chapters provide the essential tools to elevate your negotiation capabilities.

Chapter 7 challenges the traditional view that negotiation is purely competitive. Instead, it highlights the power of generosity as a strategic tool, demonstrating how giving—when done wisely—creates *Tru$tCurrency*, strengthens relationships, and unlocks additional value.

Chapter 8 explores the importance of trust and openness in negotiations. A successful deal is not just about numbers—it's about relationships. This chapter outlines practical steps to build rapport, communicate effectively, and prevent deadlocks while fostering a collaborative mindset that benefits all parties.

Chapter 9 examines the economic value of trust and why it is a critical factor in modern business. Research shows that companies and negotiators who prioritize trust experience greater profitability, efficiency, and long-term success. This chapter introduces methods for quantifying trust, demonstrating that it is not just an abstract ideal but a measurable and valuable asset.

Chapter 10 breaks down the five key negotiation styles and explains how to adapt them to different situations. Understanding your own approach—and recognizing the styles of your counterparts—allows you to adjust strategies effectively. The chapter also introduces *DISC profiling*, a tool for building the perfect negotiation team based on behavioral traits.

Finally, Chapter 11 takes an analytical approach, uncovering what sets great negotiators apart. Based on insights from over 35,000 professionals, this chapter identifies key habits and mistakes that determine negotiation success or failure. From avoiding common pitfalls to leveraging AI-driven decision-making, this chapter provides actionable takeaways for improving negotiation performance.

Together, these five chapters provide a deep dive into the strategic elements of negotiation, equipping you with the insights, frameworks, and techniques to consistently achieve superior outcomes.

CHAPTER 7

The Power of Generosity in Negotiation

In a world where "win-lose" is often the default perception of negotiation, emerging research and modern psychology paint a contrasting picture. The traditional notion that negotiation requires assertiveness, self-interest, and even dominance is not only outdated but, as data suggests, may also limit the potential for optimal outcomes. Recent findings from thought leaders like Wharton professor Adam Grant reinforce this: High-IQ individuals, often stereotyped as rational and self-serving, actually tend toward unselfish values, greater charitable giving, and prioritization of collective, long-term success over immediate personal gains.

This chapter explores the principles behind Grant's "giver advantage" and how it aligns with the SMARTnership negotiation philosophy. At SMARTnership, we recognize that effective negotiation transcends competition and hinges on collaboration, mutual benefit, and sustainable value creation. This isn't merely an ethical choice—it's a strategic one, with measurable advantages.

Rethinking Negotiation: A "Giver" Mindset

In *Give and Take*,[1] Adam Grant categorizes people into three negotiation styles: givers, takers, and matchers. *Givers* aim to benefit others, often sacrificing short-term gains for the overall good. *Takers* focus solely on personal gain,

---

[1] Grant, Adam. *Give and Take: Why Helping Others Drives Our Success* (London: Phoenix/Orion Publishing, 2014).

while *matchers* balance their actions based on reciprocity. Grant's research reveals a profound insight: In environments requiring trust, cooperation, and long-term engagement—like complex negotiations—givers consistently outperform takers.

At SMARTnership, we refer to this as *Tru$tCurrency*, a key asset in any negotiation. When parties know they are valued beyond mere transaction terms, they are more likely to engage deeply, be transparent, and seek mutually beneficial outcomes. This dynamic supports NegoEconomics, where the asymmetrical value generated by each side creates substantial collective benefits, going beyond the simple sum of the individual parts.

Generosity as Strategic Capital

Grant's studies show that givers are not indiscriminate altruists. They are strategic about how and when they extend their support. This aligns closely with the SMARTnership philosophy, where generosity is a conscious decision rooted in mutual benefit. According to Grant, successful givers focus on high-value contributions that strengthen their negotiating position. This focus on impactful, strategic giving allows them to build a reputation for trustworthiness, competence, and resilience. They understand that generosity, when managed wisely, translates into social capital and strengthens alliances.

SMARTnership and Generosity

The SMARTnership approach encourages negotiators to use their resources and goodwill as bargaining tools, not merely for concessions but to inspire reciprocal trust. When one party takes the first step in demonstrating commitment, the counterpart is more likely to mirror that behavior. This reciprocity forms a foundation for ongoing collaboration, an essential component in SMARTnership's goal to build lasting partnerships.

Overcoming the Myth: Why Generosity Isn't a Weakness

Many professionals equate generosity with weakness in negotiation. They fear that showing vulnerability or extending goodwill might be exploited by the opposing side. However, Grant's research contradicts this assumption. In negotiation, givers often emerge as the most successful players because they build networks of allies who advocate for their interests over time. This counters the "lone wolf" strategy, which limits negotiation power to the immediate, often ignoring the long-term implications of burned bridges and fractured relationships.

The SMARTnership philosophy leverages this insight by embedding generosity into our negotiation strategies. Consider a negotiator who willingly shares market data or insights that benefit the other side. Rather than weakening their position, they position themselves as indispensable partners, enhancing trust and encouraging mutual respect. These actions cultivate a mindset where both sides seek collaborative solutions, transforming a single transaction into an enduring alliance.

Tru$tCurrency and the "Giver Advantage"

Tru$tCurrency is central to the SMARTnership model, and Grant's findings bolster this concept. Tru$tCurrency represents the value of transparency, fairness, and shared objectives within a negotiation. For givers, Tru$tCurrency is a direct return on their generosity, as their consistent display of goodwill often compels others to reciprocate. This reciprocity is not incidental; it is a predictable outcome rooted in behavioral science, demonstrating that trust-building is as much a tactical choice as it is an ethical one.

By prioritizing trust and transparency, negotiators wield Tru$tCurrency as a tangible asset. This currency has long-term value, paying dividends in repeated engagements, client loyalty, and enhanced reputation. When both parties act as "givers," the negotiation environment transforms from adversarial to collaborative, yielding outcomes far greater than either side could achieve alone.

The Giver as the Ultimate Negotiator

In essence, generosity isn't just a virtue; it's an intelligent strategy for those who seek sustainable success. Grant's insights validate what SMARTnership practitioners have known and applied: that in negotiation, the true strength lies not in outmaneuvering the opponent but in uplifting them. By shifting from adversarial tactics to collaborative strategies, negotiators can unlock unprecedented value.

> **Note:** SMARTnership equips negotiators to be "smart givers," skilled at managing when, where, and how they extend generosity. This doesn't mean being naive or neglecting self-interest. Instead, it's about

recognizing that generosity, when aligned with strategic intent, is a multiplier of success. It invites the other side to reciprocate, creates asymmetrical value through NegoEconomics, and ultimately strengthens the long-term relationship.

The power of generosity is not merely theoretical—it's substantiated by data and lived experience. Adam Grant's research confirms that the most effective negotiators are those who embrace a "giver" mindset, prioritizing the collective good and building lasting relationships. This principle aligns seamlessly with SMARTnership's mission to foster high-value, trust-based negotiations that stand the test of time.

In a world where negotiation is often misconceived as a zero-sum game, the SMARTnership approach offers a revolutionary alternative. By integrating generosity, Tru$tCurrency, and strategic collaboration, negotiators can reshape the landscape, achieving outcomes that benefit all parties and set a foundation for continued growth and success.

The Real Cost of Cheap

We all want goods and services to be cheap, and preferably very cheap, but have you considered the impact that is having on our economy? Competition is good because it forces businesses to offer consumers a fair price. But how do we know when it's been taken too far?

If you want to "win" $100 in a traditional zero-sum game, the counterpart is "losing" $100. The progress for one can only happen at the expense of the counterpart.

Every time the tough gets going and the going gets tough, many businesses are scrambling to find savings through outsourcing, layoffs, quality cuts, and reduction of redundancies. They are squeezing their suppliers by pitting them against one another, and in turn forcing their suppliers to do the same. This "race to zero" may seem like a win for cost-conscious buyers, but it comes with steep consequences.

It's time to reevaluate what we are really looking for in our products, relationships, and business partners. Do we want the cheapest provider at any cost, or do we want the best value for our money? The time is right to find a different way to negotiate—one where a win doesn't always come at the expense of the counterpart. This is where SMARTnership makes sense.

In the typical procurement process, companies have suppliers compete based almost exclusively on price and quantity. A few months later, the winning supplier, now squeezed to maintain profitability, resorts to shortcuts that harm not only the client but also the end consumer. On the other hand, suppliers who repeatedly lose contracts are forced into unsustainable pricing, creating a cycle that leads to bankruptcies, job losses, and reduced competition.

Ironically, this eventually allows surviving suppliers to dictate terms and prices—a scenario no one wants.

The ripple effects of these bankruptcies go far beyond individual companies. Entire communities suffer through job losses, declining exports, and disruptions to local economies. This vicious cycle isn't limited to manufacturing but spans industries like banking, insurance, and technology.

Negotiation as the Antidote to Price Frenzy

To escape this destructive cycle, businesses must reintroduce the human element to their relationships, reducing costs not through shortcuts or cutthroat tactics, but through trust and cooperation. Overreliance on virtual brokers and automated bidding tools has created what I call "Net-Syndrome," where decisions are reduced to spreadsheets and price tags, with no meaningful dialogue or relationship-building. We can achieve far greater results through genuine negotiation.

The SMARTnership approach challenges the outdated "winner-takes-all" mindset by focusing on mutual value creation. Over the last 20 years, I have analyzed more than 35,000 negotiations and discovered that up to 42 percent of potential value in a typical transaction is left on the table. This occurs because traditional negotiations focus solely on dividing value rather than expanding it. SMARTnership is about breaking free from this zero-sum approach and fostering an environment of collaboration.

A New Paradigm for Negotiation

The foundation of SMARTnership lies in trust and cooperation and the mathematical concept of NegoEconomics, shifting focus from just price and quantity to a broader discussion of elements like logistics, payment terms, warranties, penalties, training, and more. These elements often hold asymmetric value: What is highly valuable to one party may cost the other very little to provide.

This is the essence of a SMARTnership—a negotiation model that makes the pie bigger, allowing both parties to share in the benefits. It's not just about splitting the gains; it's about creating them together. This approach dramatically changes how we do business, enabling long-term partnerships where all sides thrive. Now is the time more than ever, since AI is able to assist us in quickly and smoothly finding variables that can generate NegoEconomics.

The time has come to move beyond the race to zero. There are no winners in that contest—only losers and collateral damage. SMARTnership offers a better path forward, where collaboration replaces conflict, and trust replaces shortcuts. By working together, we can create a future where businesses, communities, and individuals all rise to the top.

CHAPTER 8

Success Is Based on Trust and Openness

An arrangement built purely on one side's victory over the other is primitive—and it will always collapse. It only survives as long as the dominant party can force the other into submission. That's not sustainable. The only real alternative is cooperation—SMARTnership. But if a negotiator doesn't understand the theory behind SMARTnership and Nego-Economics, they won't be open to it. They'll resist the transparency and fear the risks. Real collaboration only works when both parties understand and commit to the logic behind cooperation and Tru$tCurrency.

Negotiations driven by cooperation and trust are simply more effective—they deliver better results for everyone involved. You avoid unnecessary conflict by creating a positive climate rooted in open and honest communication. That starts with taking time to connect before diving into the deal. When personal chemistry clicks, logic often takes a back seat. People make decisions based on how they feel about the other party. And when that perception is positive, they're far more inclined to favor the other side's solutions—sometimes without even realizing it.

Building a Relationship with Your Counterpart

To build real rapport, start simple—talk about the weather or the local sports team. There's ancient Chinese wisdom that says negotiations should never start on an empty stomach—and they were right. Good food and drink aren't just tradition; they trigger oxytocin in the brain, which increases trust and likability. Sharing a meal literally makes us more open to each other. I've seen it time and again: Within the first 15 minutes of interaction, I can usually predict whether the negotiation will succeed.

When negotiators first meet, they're often operating in the dark. They don't know how the other side thinks, what matters most to them, what decisions have already been made, or whether they even have a strong alternative. Without taking time to build rapport, the opening minutes often turn into a struggle for control—who speaks first, who leads. That kind of power play almost always leads to early deadlock. Instead of a constructive conversation, both sides talk past each other and the interaction becomes combative.

When there's trust and familiarity, deals can be struck in minutes. When there's none, it can take weeks. And in some cultures, skipping the relationship-building phase and jumping straight into bargaining isn't just ineffective—it's deeply disrespectful and can kill the deal before it starts.

The following sections discuss ways to build trust and openness with your fellow negotiator. Take note that many of these techniques involve how you listen and talk to others.

Two-Way Communication

One-way communication is a fast track to misunderstanding, delays, and bad outcomes. Good negotiation is built on two-way dialogue. Skilled negotiators listen actively, ask smart questions, respond meaningfully, and use what they learn to explore alternatives. They stay out of combat mode and focus instead on understanding what the other side truly needs. The best negotiators make a point of stepping into the other party's shoes.

If communication breaks down early, there's no chance of finding common ground. You won't understand the other side's intentions, and you'll start holding back, entrenching yourself in your own position. Meanwhile, they'll stop listening and refuse to engage. At that point, the negotiation deadlocks—and any potential NegoEconomic value disappears. Not because the interests aren't aligned, but because the conversation isn't.

For any negotiation to work, both parties need to share credible information. And it's not up to you to decide whether your message is believable—that's entirely in the hands of your counterpart. If they don't believe you, saying "That's their fault" won't cut it. Communication only works when the sender takes full responsibility for making sure the message is received and understood.

Participate in an Open Dialogue

Two-way communication means that, instead of just listening, you engage yourself by asking questions and summarize your understanding of what's being said. Ask questions to check that your understanding is identical with the message that the counterpart meant to send. Don't hesitate to ask a question when you miss information, do not understand, are uncertain, want more details, or want to evaluate the situation.

Summarizing, or even better, asking the other party to summarize, is a very efficient tactic to avoid misunderstandings and uncertainty. It is required:

- At the end of the negotiation
- Before a break
- After a long discussion on a topic
- When the negotiations are resumed after a long break

Openness should not be total. Transparency without strategy is just exposure, but transparency powered by NegoEconomics, Tru$tCurrency, and SMARTnership becomes a competitive advantage.

If you want better contracts, stronger relationships, and higher-performing deals, the answer isn't just to open the books. The answer is to see what's inside them—together—and understand what it's truly worth to both sides.

A negotiator who reveals everything without getting something back exposes themself to the risk of being taken advantage of. When preparing your negotiation, decide what information to share and what you want to share with the counterpart in order to identify NegoEconomics.

Listen Actively

You've got two ears and one mouth, goes the saying. To listen, you must be well prepared; if not, you will be distracted planning what you want to respond while the counterpart is talking. If you engage in what the other party is sharing, you eliminate competing signals. Don't just use your ears. Create eye contact and focus on the other party. Ask questions to show your interest, to get more information, and to clarify.

Don't overestimate your memory after a negotiation—details like who said what and when are easily lost. Instead, capture how the other party reacted to your signals, and how you felt responding to theirs. Always listen with a pen in hand and write it down.

When you actively listen and take notes on the interpersonal dynamic, your awareness of the other party's signals becomes sharper. You'll gain better control over what you absorb, what you let through, and what stays stored in your long-term memory. You'll avoid being distracted by conflicting signals—and your ability to learn and adapt improves dramatically.

Speak plainly and be open—your message is more likely to be misunderstood than you think. If what you're saying is negative, the other party may perceive it as a threat or see you as difficult to negotiate with. Their natural instinct will be self-protection, not listening. They'll start preparing for conflict, even subconsciously. That risk grows if you jump into direct confrontation too soon. Instead, take time to provide context. Lay out the background clearly. Align your perceptions of reality before delivering the negative message.

Be Clear on What You Want

If you haven't planned what to say, there is a serious risk that you will say anything that comes to mind. How do you communicate your objective? Create logical links or a thread in your presentation, because it will be easier for the counterpart to follow your thought and keep attention. The counterpart can only assume three or four pieces of information at a time. Communicate in simple terms and be precise. Too much information or too many details can sometimes damage the communication more than helping it.

Do you really know what your counterpart wants to know? They are most receptive to information that supports their needs and solves their problems. Insert yourself in the counterpart's position. What questions might they ask you!?

Negotiators without experience are sometimes hard to understand, because they are not clear on what they really want. They are scared of rejection so they communicate shallowly.

Some delegates say what they do not want instead of saying what they do want. This makes the negotiation more of a guessing game. Never assume that the counterpart is able to guess your needs or that they intuitively know what it is you are looking for. It is your responsibility and no one else to make sure your counterpart understand your needs and wishes.

What is it you want to achieve? Do you want to influence the counterpart and change their opinions or get them to reframe their ideas? Are you trying to share background information? Raise awareness about something important? Or gather insights from the other party? Whatever your goal, your first job is to capture their attention—and fast. You've got 20 to 30 seconds, max, before their focus drifts and they tune back into their own thoughts.

Say What You Mean—Clearly and Directly

Direct communication can come across as confrontational and may trigger resistance. Steer clear of language that sounds accusatory or puts the other party on the defensive. Focus on describing what you see or feel. Don't say, "You're wrong, this won't work." Say, "I'm not following—can you walk me through how this would work?" That keeps the dialogue open and productive.

EXAMPLE | Ambiguity Causes Failure

At the beginning of the year, a negotiation takes place between Laura, the manager, and Daniel, an employee. For two decades, the company has consistently shut down operations in July. Daniel walks into Laura's office to talk about taking time off.

Daniel: How do you feel about me taking some time off in September this year?
Laura: I really don't know what to say to that. We usually close the whole place in July.
Daniel: I know, that's why I wanted to check with you. By the way, have you heard if we've received the order from Germany yet?

The conversation is quickly redirected, and nothing is clarified. Fast-forward to mid-August, when they run into each other in the hallway.

Daniel: I won't be seeing you for a while—take care.
Laura: Really? What are you doing?
Daniel: Heading to Greece.
Laura: To Greece? For business?
Daniel: No, I'm on vacation for three weeks.
Laura: In September? When we're so busy? Why didn't you take it in July? You can't leave now!
Daniel: We talked earlier this year and you said it was okay!
Laura: I never approved that. You can't just leave the company like this.
Daniel: You can't go back on our agreement!
Laura: We never had one.

Now both are confused, upset, and feel justified in their reactions. The situation escalates. Rational thinking is blocked, emotions dominate, and conflict resolution becomes difficult.

So what went wrong?

Daniel used vague wording, likely out of fear of rejection. He didn't clearly state his request: a three-week vacation in September. Laura, for her part, responded with ambiguity—"I don't know what to say"—which is not a decision. It's avoidance.

Daniel should have clarified: "What does that mean exactly? Can I or can't I take vacation in September?" Then he should've confirmed: "So we agree I'll be off from [date] to [date]?"

(continued)

> **EXAMPLE** (continued)
>
> Laura should never have let him shift the subject to Germany. She could've redirected:
>
> **Laura:** Wait—before we move on. About the vacation, did we agree on anything?
> **Daniel:** Yes.
> **Laura:** Okay, what exactly did we agree on?
>
> That moment of clarification would've exposed the misunderstanding early—before flights were booked and expectations locked in. Clear language, confirmation, and summary—these prevent disaster.
>
> Both sides share the blame. Both failed to confirm. Ambiguity is the enemy of agreement.

Use Open Calculations

Open calculation in negotiation are used to share cost structures and profits to build trust and focus on NegoEconomics. This enhances collaboration by reducing suspicion and identifying asymmetrical values. An open calculation can also foster the spirit of collaboration. If you are confident in the intentions of the counterpart is honorable, you don't need to fear going into a discussion concerning the open calculation. You could choose to show the counterpart your calculations in order to be able to negotiate a higher price or to improve future negotiations. However, always remember that the price you are showing is just a price, not your cost, and that nothing is finalized until a formal agreement has been reached.

The buyer requests insight into the supplier's cost structure. Their motivations may include:

- Understanding exactly what they are paying for
- Gaining clarity on the value being created and how it might be shared
- Preparing arguments for the upcoming negotiation
- Anticipating how cost fluctuations and other factors may impact future pricing
- Assessing the accuracy and fairness of your calculations—ensuring your profit margin isn't too high or too low
- Exploring ways to unbundle the contract into smaller components for separate bidding, aiming to reduce their overall costs

- If you're compelled to share your calculations, delay revealing specific numbers until you're fully prepared. Emphasize that the value lies in the overall picture—not in isolated figures. If you decide to disclose your calculations, be aware of the risks:
  - The other party may extract and misuse proprietary information about your operations.
  - The buyer gains leverage by collecting arguments to challenge your position.
  - They can identify and target components to remove in order to lower their cost.
  - They'll understand the link between your costs and your price, exposing your profit margin.

Conflict Destroys Relationships

Communication often deteriorates when the parties are in conflict. The parties become defensive and neither view the counterpart as credible. The likelihood of an open exchange of information is minimized. Both parties blame the counterpart for the conflict. Frustration increases, and as misunderstanding between the parties grows, the conflict intensifies.

Your emotions and mindset directly impact your ability to communicate and build rapport. Staying composed is essential to effective negotiation. In high-pressure settings, you may even need to mask your emotions entirely.

In highly competitive scenarios, information sharing tends to decrease, as negotiators fear weakening their position. To counter this, plan in advance what you're willing to disclose and decide how open you want to be.

When tension runs high and expectations are elevated, listening often suffers. You may focus too much on pushing your agenda and miss the other party's perspective. But they'll only truly listen to you once they feel heard themselves. You don't need to be the first to offer a solution.

If you want to move forward, focus on shared interests. Finding common ground is key to resolving conflict and continuing collaboration. But if your focus is on blame, progress will stall.

A Third Party Can Help Build Rapport

Involving a third party can help improve communication and foster rapport. Their primary role is to listen closely, identify if the parties are talking past each other, and highlight areas of agreement. Through informal engagement with both sides, they can clarify misunderstandings and uncover potential mutual gains. They may also suggest options that open the door to additional opportunities.

This third party—whether a negotiation expert, lawyer, or accountant—can adopt various roles: tough, agreeable, or neutral. They might mediate, smooth the path, or help close the deal. Tactics such as limited authority or feigned inexperience can give them flexibility. They can act informally, making moves the client might not openly support. Rather than escalating to litigation, a neutral third party can guide the process toward resolution based on commercial logic.

The mediator can be mutually agreed upon or represent one side. Their influence lies in encouraging both parties to reassess their positions realistically, understand each other more clearly, and avoid excessive demands.

The third party may be an external group that will be impacted by the negotiation's outcome. This group becomes involved in the negotiations to exert pressure on one of the parties and influence the outcome.

Informal Contacts Can Offer Valuable Insights

Informal communication can be a powerful tool. Use it to share and gather information, float offers, issue subtle threats, anchor expectations, and break potential deadlocks. These conversations often yield more honest dialogue, because people are typically more open and flexible outside the formal setting.

Without official observers or team pressure, the issue of dual loyalty fades. There's space to explore ideas freely, without immediate consequences. Focusing on shared principles rather than concrete proposals increases openness and can reveal that both sides agree on more than they realize—misunderstandings often lie in the details.

Casual, unofficial meetings before formal talks can lay the groundwork for better understanding and smoother negotiations.

Backdoor Selling

Backdoor selling occurs when a party bypasses the primary negotiator or decision-maker to influence other stakeholders within the organization. This tactic aims to gain an advantage by securing informal approvals or support before the official negotiation concludes. It often undermines the negotiation process by creating internal pressure or disrupting established authority.

Engaging with individuals outside the formal negotiation team can provide useful information. End users, maintenance staff, warehouse personnel, and administrators often have deep, firsthand knowledge of how products or systems perform, including their strengths and flaws. Some may even push for certain products to be blacklisted based on their experience.

However, these individuals may also pose a risk. They are typically candid and straightforward—sometimes too much so—especially if they haven't been trained in negotiation strategy. Without guidance on what to communicate and when, they may inadvertently reveal sensitive information or weaken your position.

A Tour of the Production Plant

During a tour of a supplier's production plant, a potential buyer casually asks the workers, "How is the overtime situation here?" The workers reply, "We don't have any overtime right now." From this response, the buyer deduces that the plant is likely running at less than 70 percent capacity.

The buyer then speaks with the service technicians, asking, "How did the spring installation of your new system go?" A technician responds, "It was chaotic. There was too much downtime, and customers had a hard time adapting. Honestly, more training is needed for operators, and the manual hasn't even been properly translated into French yet."

The buyer, who is an experienced negotiator, strategically gathers valuable information under the guise of casual conversation. This intelligence gives them an edge in the negotiation. Suppliers should be cautious about allowing unfiltered access to internal teams during facility tours.

Meanwhile, the supplier's technical expert may inadvertently become a pawn in the negotiation process. For instance, one technician privately remarks to a buyer, "Your competitors have promised to send us to a training program in the US."

These benefits are directed at the workers who will use the product, aiming to win their loyalty. Workers may be enticed by service enhancements, training offers, and gestures such as seminars, factory visits, coffee breaks, or even holiday gifts. While these costs impact the supplier, they serve to solidify relationships between the buyer and the end users, shifting leverage in favor of the buyer.

To mitigate such risks, suppliers must actively control the flow of information during plant visits and informal interactions. Here's how:

- **Limit direct access:** Restrict buyer interactions with employees who are not prepared for negotiation-related questions.
- **Train staff:** Educate employees on the importance of discretion and ensure they understand how negotiations may affect the organization.
- **Establish protocols:** Brief staff on which topics can be discussed and which must remain confidential during visits.

By taking these precautions, suppliers can avoid unintentional information leaks that could weaken their negotiating position.

Understand Your Counterpart

Negotiators often don't really try to understand the counterpart. Your own needs, problems, and interests are the center of your focus. The more successful negotiator will take into account the interests of the other party. If you are not able to see things from the point of view of the counterpart—or are uninterested—you may very well be losing potential asymmetrical value in the negotiation. AI is a great assistant, often able to think outside of the box and come up with questions you probably want to ask your counterpart. Remember, in a negotiation, you are not allowed to assume or guess about the interest of the counterpart. You'll need to know!

Imposing Your Terms Can Backfire If you dictate terms solely from your own perspective, you risk cornering the other party into a deal they can't sustain. Any short-term gain may quickly unravel. Once conditions shift in their favor, they're likely to walk away—or worse, retaliate. At best, they'll disengage and fail to meet their commitments, leaving you exposed.

Ignoring the other party's viewpoint also blinds you to critical signals and increases the risk of overcommitting or misjudging the situation. Sustainable agreements require understanding both sides.

EXAMPLE | Strategic Sale of a Factory in Cleveland

A factory owner in Cleveland, preparing for retirement, decided to sell his business. After assessing the company's value with management and the bank, they agreed that a satisfactory bid would range between $500,000 and $1 million. When bids came in, the owner was excited to see that all offers exceeded the target:

- Jordan: $1.4 million
- Taylor: $1.6 million
- Morgan: $2.1 million

At first, the owner leaned toward accepting Morgan's $2.1 million offer outright because it was significantly higher than the others. However, after reflecting, he realized he didn't fully understand each buyer's goals or the value they placed on different aspects of the business. Without this information, he couldn't ensure the deal reflected the business's true worth.

The owner invited Jordan, Taylor, and Morgan to explain their plans for the factory before negotiating specific terms. This revealed unique motivations:

- Jordan wanted the premises and machinery to start an entirely new business. Due to a tight budget, Jordan could not exceed the $1.4 million bid.
- Taylor saw the factory as an investment opportunity. Taylor intended to sell the machinery and lease the premises.
- Morgan valued the existing production line, products, and established brand. Morgan planned to move manufacturing abroad while retaining the sales rights.

These discussions revealed that the buyers weren't competing for the same assets, explaining the disparity in their bids. By identifying complementary interests, the owner created a SMARTnership solution that maximized value for everyone involved.

The deal was structured to align with each buyer's unique needs while unlocking additional value:

- Morgan purchased the production line, product rights, and brand, enabling them to retain the business's market presence without managing the physical factory.
- Taylor acquired the property and leased it to Jordan, who then bought the machinery to start the new business.

This SMARTnership approach resulted in over $3 million in total value—far surpassing the initial bids. Each party felt they gained more than they would have through a conventional negotiation:

- The factory owner received a much higher price than expected.
- Morgan secured the production rights without unnecessary overhead.
- Taylor made a profitable investment in industrial property.
- Jordan acquired the premises and machinery at a cost within budget.

Note: This example demonstrates how understanding counterpart motivations and fostering collaboration through SMARTnership can unlock hidden value. Instead of competing for the same resources, the parties worked together to create a solution that delivered substantial benefits to all involved.

> **EXAMPLE** | Understand the Demand Before You Concede
>
> A plant supervisor asks a vendor to shorten the delivery time. The vendor can do it without extra cost or risk and responds, "If it would suit you, we can have the equipment in place in three months." He makes the concession freely—without asking for anything in return and without considering what it's worth to the supervisor.
>
> But there's a reason behind the request. A faster delivery likely accelerates production and brings earlier returns on investment—real value for the manufacturer. If the vendor overlooks this, he misses the chance to share in that added value.
>
> By recognizing the benefit to the other side, the vendor could negotiate a better deal. Always ask, "Why is that important to you?" before responding to a demand. Understanding the need behind the ask creates room for smarter trades and mutual gain.

Using Alternatives to Strength Your Position

Lack of alternatives leaves you vulnerable. If you have no other buyers, suppliers, or options, the other party holds all the power and can dictate terms. Alternatives restore balance, improve decision-making, and help you identify what truly adds or subtracts value.

Creating a competitive environment is one of the most effective ways a buyer can apply pressure. The more offers you collect, the broader the spread between the highest and lowest bids. Relying on just two or three suppliers increases the risk of overpaying—especially if you keep going back to the same pool each time.

Even if you've already decided whom to buy from, always maintain other options. Make sure the supplier knows they're competing. They won't be certain what others are offering, which keeps the pressure on. Competing bids can also inspire new solutions or lead to better terms. You might even discover a supplier who challenges your original choice.

Keep all negotiations active until the final agreement is signed. Alternatives aren't just leverage—they're a source of insight, flexibility, and value, with alternative suppliers running until the very day the agreement is signed.

Use Alternatives as a Trial Balloon

Trial balloons are a useful tactic in business negotiations. You can float an idea or alternative—not as a firm proposal, but to test the other party's reaction.

For example, during technical discussions, you might leak a concept through your team or leave a document behind intentionally. This allows the other side to pick up the information, react to it, and reveal their position without a formal commitment from you.

It's a method borrowed from politics—where a minister may float an idea through the press to gauge public and political reaction before taking action.

In negotiation, introducing an alternative as a trial balloon can reveal how the other party evaluates different options. Their response gives you insight into their priorities, constraints, resources, and openness. It may also redirect their focus or open new paths for agreement—all without you having to commit.

Trial balloons do not have to be realistic. They might even be provocative, an approach that is frequently used by journalists. The other party can reject the proposal as unfeasible, at which point you can pretend not to understand their rejection. The other party attempts to make you understand why it would not work, and in doing so they unintentionally supply you with information you are looking for. If you were to ask them directly, you would not get an answer.

Handling Trial Balloons Effectively

If you're on the receiving end of a trial balloon, resist the urge to react immediately. Stay composed and shift into investigative mode. Ask questions like "How do you see that alternative playing out?" to probe its feasibility and uncover the sender's intent.

Evaluate whether the proposal is genuine or simply a tactic to test your reaction or gain leverage. Assess how realistic it is, what resources it would require, and whether it's a distraction or a serious option. The key is to stay curious, not reactive.

Preventing Negotiations from Becoming Deadlocked

Negotiation may grind to a halt or end in a stalemate and the process generates no result. Instead of finding new collaborative solutions, the parties keep repeating old arguments, and the negotiations move into verbal combat. The arguments used could be:

- The price is too high.
- The time frame available is too short.
- We want better guarantees.

The opposite party finds it difficult to assess the truth of these arguments. They have heard them many times before, and know from experience that the opponents might be bluffing.

Breaking a Deadlock in Negotiation

When talks stall, consider the following strategies:

- **Introduce new, verifiable information.** Clarify and support your demands with evidence. For example, if you're asking for better guarantees, specify what that means and back it with facts. Offering fresh data or alternatives often reopens stalled dialogue and promotes collaboration through improved two-way communication.

- **Gather more information.** Don't treat every request for details as a threat. Clarifying the full scope of the other party's needs and problems can reveal new solutions and angles for agreement.

- **Accept that cooperation isn't always possible.** Some parties will see openness as weakness and respond aggressively. You then face a choice: walk away or switch to a more competitive, zero-sum approach.

- **Offer viable alternatives.** Persuade the other side by presenting realistic options that deliver mutual value. But avoid bluffing—if you have no fallback, you risk exposure. Also note that increasing pressure often invites resistance and prolongs the deadlock.

- **Avoid concessions just to move forward.** This signals weakness and encourages a tougher stance from the other side. If you must yield on a point, make it clear it's to facilitate progress—not a shift in your position. And never give more than what's asked.

EXAMPLE | Giving in Too Soon

Luis, a supplier of electronic components, offers the buyer a service agreement guaranteeing 97 percent accessibility. Jordan, the buyer, insists on a minimum of 99 percent. Wanting to show goodwill, Luis agrees—without asking what he would receive in return. Could there have been alternative benefits to offering instead of 99 percent?

Jordan proposes an earlier delivery by two months. Luis agrees without exploring the value of that earlier delivery or checking whether it brings any real advantage. He assumes there are no extra costs and makes the concession unilaterally, ending the negotiation without gaining anything in return.

- **Consider walking away.** If you have solid alternatives and time is limited, stepping back may be a strategic move. But be cautious—threatening to walk often escalates tension. The other party may respond with stronger counterthreats, leading to confrontation or deepening the deadlock.
- **Use stalling strategically.** Pausing the negotiation allows both sides to reflect and reassess. However, delays can backfire—tensions may rise, deadlines may tighten, and cooperation may become harder to sustain.

Moving Past a Deadlock

When negotiations hit a deadlock, one party must often make a move to reopen discussions or clarify demands. For example, if the buyer says, "Your price of $10 per unit is too high," they might offer a counter like, "We can pay no more than $8.75 per unit." This gives the supplier a starting point to evaluate options.

Imagine Chris, the buyer, offers $8.75 per unit, which is $1.25 less than the supplier, Alex, initially quoted at $10 per unit for an order of 10,000 units. Alex's absolute lowest price, ensuring profitability, is $9 per unit. Alex now has three possible strategies, discussed next.

Option A: Making a Unilateral Concession
Alex lowers the price without asking for anything in return, hoping to meet Chris halfway.

Alex: I can drop the price to $9.75 per unit.
Chris: That's still too high. Can you go lower?
Alex: If you confirm the order today, I can go down another $0.25.
Chris: Let's split the difference—I'll pay $9.10 per unit.
Alex: Okay, deal.

Outcome: Alex has given up $9,000 in value without gaining anything. This approach is ineffective because the supplier gives concessions too quickly, losing valuable revenue without exploring other options. Alex ends up in a zero-sum game, where the only outcome is a reduced price.

Option B: Offering a Larger Quantity
Alex explores ways to increase the deal's overall value by proposing a larger order.

Alex: If you increase your order, we can discuss a price reduction.
Chris: How much of a discount are we talking about?
Alex: If you increase the order to 15,000 units, I can reconsider the price.
Chris: I'll check if we can handle that amount.

By linking a price reduction to a larger order, Alex signals flexibility but avoids making immediate concessions. However, Alex should avoid jumping to concessions prematurely.

Ineffective approach:

Alex: I'll drop the price to $9 per unit for 15,000 units.
Chris: I'll think about the quantity but also want free delivery.
Alex: Maybe we can make one large delivery to cut costs.
Chris: Great, I'll decide soon.

Here, Alex has made concessions on both price and delivery without securing commitment, risking further losses.

Better approach:

Alex: If you commit to 15,000 units, I'll review the price.

This way, Alex links concessions to specific commitments and avoids one-sided giveaways.

Option C: Looking for Counter-Benefits   Alex negotiates for additional benefits in exchange for a price reduction.

Alex: If you pay in cash, I can reconsider the price.
Alex: If we handle your total supply needs, we might be able to reduce costs further.
Alex: If you can adjust your quality requirements slightly, we can discuss a discount.
Alex: What can you offer to help us make this work?

By tying concessions to added value for both sides, Alex ensures the negotiation remains balanced. For instance, Chris might agree to a longer delivery timeline or pay upfront, which reduces Alex's costs and makes the reduced price viable.

Note: To break a deadlock, always link concessions to commitments or explore creative solutions that benefit both parties. Avoid giving away value without getting something in return.

Breaking the Stalemate

When negotiations stall, it's often because both sides are entrenched in positions, trading demands instead of asking questions. Don't treat this as a threat—it's an opportunity to shift the dynamic.

Take control by injecting new, specific information that clarifies your own needs, or ask the other party to do the same. When dialogue becomes focused on needs—not positions—constructive progress becomes possible.

Look past surface arguments to understand the real drivers behind their demands. For example, if they insist on a price cut, that doesn't necessarily mean cost is the true issue. It might be:

- **A need to demonstrate capability:** They want to feel in control or show their team they can negotiate well. Let them propose a solution—but don't lower the price without securing value in return.
- **A budget constraint:** If it's about fitting the deal into a quarterly cap, suggest breaking up invoicing into multiple periods.
- **A formal requirement for the lowest bid:** Internally, they may be forced to select the lowest quote, but prefer working with you. Consider shifting part of your cost to a service agreement, spare parts, or another line item to keep the base quote competitive.
- **A desire to test your limits:** They may be unsure whether your offer is final. Maintain firmness, but read their intent and respond strategically.
- **A need for time:** Instead of applying pressure, find out why. Understanding their internal process can help you anticipate their next move.
- **A belief you're earning too much:** Ask them to evaluate your price in relation to the value they'll gain. Framing your offer in terms of their benefit can help shift their perspective.

Keep the conversation rational and grounded in facts. Once it turns emotional—motivated by frustration or retaliation—you lose control. For example:

When they say: "We thought we'd get more for our money."

Do ask: "What exactly is missing?"

Don't say: "This is our standard offer. Anything extra will cost more."

When they say: "Your plant's operating costs are too high."

Do ask: "What did you expect them to be? How did you calculate that?"

Don't say: "We have a 92 percent productivity ratio—better than any competitor."

The goal is to uncover what "operating costs" mean to them—it might include things you didn't factor in, like maintenance or supervision. By clarifying, you gain new leverage.

You might offer a service contract to reduce their long-term maintenance burden—adding value without cutting price. If your offer seems expensive, find ways to reduce their cost or risk while maintaining your price. Help them see the cost is less than the return they'll gain. That's how you defuse objections and create real, asymmetrical value.

Avoiding Imbalance in the Information Flow

Negotiations often stall when the exchange of information becomes unbalanced. If one side is constantly sharing while the other stays silent, the party giving information will eventually feel exposed, manipulated, and disadvantaged. This shift in perceived power breeds resentment. Emotions rise, reactions become sharper, and the discussion grinds to a halt. The common justification? "We're not getting anywhere—they're just pumping us for answers and giving nothing in return."

What's often overlooked is that the silent party may genuinely need more data to build workable solutions. But when the flow is one-sided, it feels threatening, not collaborative.

To prevent this, establish clear ground rules from the start. Set an agenda, define the Rules of the Game, and agree on a Code of Conduct. With structure in place, both parties can see how information sharing fits within a fair process. It builds trust, prevents misinterpretation, and keeps the negotiation moving forward.

Don't Let the Counterpart Define the Playing Field

Never limit yourself to the alternatives presented by the other party. If you allow them to set the framework, you're negotiating within boundaries they control. Instead, ask targeted questions, gather more context, and introduce your own options—ones that serve your interests and shift the dynamic.

Consider this example. A buyer says to a supplier, "To make this deal work, you must lower your price by 3.5 to 5 percent. Otherwise, I can't do business with you."

Most suppliers, especially if their floor is below 3.5 percent, will simply agree to the lowest number in the range. The buyer then says, "I have authority to accept this." But now, the supplier has made a unilateral concession—lowering the price for the rest of the negotiation with nothing in return. A tough buyer will often take this as an opening and push for more.

Both buyers and sellers use this anchoring tactic.

Now contrast that with a more strategic approach. A consultant is negotiating fees for a major project. The scope is clear, but the client's budget isn't. The consultant avoids giving a fixed price and instead offers a range:

"Professional fees will be between $275,000 and $365,000." This range is stated verbally so the consultant can observe the client's reaction and adapt in real time.

Client reactions might include:

- "We only have $300,000 in our budget. Can you work within that?"
  - The consultant explores adjustments—perhaps the client handles a portion of the work, or some costs are moved to another account or fiscal year.
- "We can't go over $250,000."
  - Same strategy. Probe what's flexible and rescope where possible.
- "We need a firm number."
  - The consultant proposes a $15,000 feasibility study. It's easier for the client to approve, and it gives the consultant clarity on what the client can actually pay.
- "That's too much. None of your competitors quoted over $250,000."
  - The consultant reframes their offer—delivering a proposal at $250,000 with a different technical scope. Once the project begins, they can propose necessary additions, increasing the final fee with justification.

Key takeaway:

Use price ranges, introduce your own alternatives, and stay flexible. Don't react—guide. Let your options shape the negotiation rather than letting theirs restrict it.

Use Questions as a Negotiation Technique

Any great negotiator will tell you that the secret to getting more information is asking open questions. Many negotiators are lacking developed questioning technique. In the course of an hour's negotiation, they ask only few questions, and they answer many of the questions themselves: "What do you do when you're short of raw materials? Pause production, I assume." They don't allow the counterpart to complete the answer. They interrupt and immediately draw their own conclusions.

Questions are a powerful tool in negotiation. They open dialogue, uncover key information, and foster mutual problem-solving. Like arguments, questions should be carefully prepared in advance. Use them purposefully:

- **To gather information:** Ask open-ended questions starting with *who, what, where, why, when,* and *how.*

    Example: "When does production begin?" Avoid yes/no questions like "Do you have long delivery times?" because they're vague and often unhelpful. "Long" could mean weeks to one party and months to another.

- **To share information subtly:** Use questions to highlight facts.

    Example: "Are you aware that costs have increased 24 percent?"

- **To drive decisions:** Clarify and move the discussion forward.

    Example: "What does that mean in practical terms? Yes or no?"

Best practices when using questions:

- Avoid provocative or confrontational questions that create tension.
- Write down key questions during your prep—don't rely on memory.
- Keep questions constructive. Don't force the other party to lose face in front of others.
- Don't overload the conversation—negotiation is a dialogue, not an interrogation.
- Time your questions well. Ask critical ones when the setting is right for both sides.
- Stay aligned with your team's strategy. Avoid questions that disrupt internal tactics.
- To warm up the conversation, ask questions you already know the answer to.
- Listen carefully. If the answer is vague, rephrase or ask again. Don't hesitate to say, "I'm not sure I follow—could you clarify?"
- Once a question is asked, wait. Let the other side answer without interruption.
- Avoid leading questions like "You already have a plan in place since the company was sold, right?"

    Instead, ask, "What are your next steps now that the company has been sold?"

- Gather as much as you can informally before the formal negotiation begins—those off-the-record insights can be invaluable.

    Good questions create clarity, build trust, and often unlock the path forward.

Using Hypothetical Questions Strategically

Hypothetical questions are powerful tools to test possibilities and uncover hidden interests—without making firm commitments. They help you explore options and create openings in the negotiation:

- "What happens if we double the order?"
- "What could you offer us if we commit to buying all our annual needs from you?"
- "What do we get in return if we waive the warranty requirement?"

These questions spark movement. But *be cautious when responding*—a speculative answer may be interpreted as a binding concession. For example, if you quote a lower price for higher volume, the other side may say, "Good, I've noted that price—we'll come back to the quantity later." Suddenly, your hypothetical becomes their anchor.

Use this technique to test alternatives:

- "If we increased our purchase by 25 percent, how would that affect your pricing?"
- "If we brought the order forward by two months, what benefit would that give you?"
- "Let's say we accepted your terms—what would you offer in return?"

The beauty of hypothetical questions is that they often generate real answers—yet the questioner stays uncommitted: "I said if we can, not that we will."

If the other party uses this tactic, don't answer blindly. Probe with counter-questions:

- "How would you manage a 25 percent increase in volume?"
- "Are you saying you're ready to finalize the deal today?"

Stay alert. Hypotheticals reveal intent, test limits, and create leverage—but only when used deliberately and handled with care.

How AI Can Assist in Creating a Culture of Trust and Openness in Negotiations

AI can transform the way negotiators approach trust-building, communication, and decision-making. By leveraging data-driven insights, advanced natural language processing, and predictive analytics, AI can significantly enhance the negotiation process. The following sections explain how AI can assist with the principles outlined in this chapter.

Analyzing Human Chemistry and Compatibility

AI can assess compatibility between negotiating parties by analyzing communication styles, sentiment, and emotional cues. AI tools can:

- **Evaluate emotional tone:** Analyze video or text communications for indicators of trust, openness, and mutual respect.
- **Identify misalignment:** Flag instances where misunderstandings or conflicts may arise due to differences in communication styles or values.

    Prompt examples:

- "Analyze the emotional tone of this email thread to identify signs of mistrust or conflict."
- "Suggest strategies to improve rapport based on this negotiation transcript."

Enhancing Communication Proficiency

AI can provide real-time feedback during conversations, identifying unclear phrasing or missed opportunities for engagement. Tools like conversational AI can:

- **Detect cross-purposes dialogue:** Highlight areas where parties may be speaking at cross-purposes and suggest clarifications.
- **Improve active listening:** Summarize key points and emotional undertones to ensure both parties feel heard.

    Prompt examples:

- "Summarize this conversation and highlight points where clarity was lacking."
- "Generate a response that aligns with the other party's priorities while maintaining my position."

Facilitating Two-Way Communication

AI can simulate responses to hypothetical questions, helping negotiators anticipate how their counterparts might react. It can also model outcomes based on proposed solutions.

- **Interactive tools:** AI-powered negotiation simulations can train individuals in two-way communication dynamics.
- **Feedback loops:** Offer suggestions for reframing questions to be open-ended and constructive.

    Prompt examples:

- "Generate a list of follow-up questions to clarify the other party's goals."
- "What are potential responses to my counteroffer, and how can I prepare for them?"

Building Trust Through Open Calculations

AI can transparently analyze cost structures and provide visual representations of added value for both parties, supporting cooperative negotiation strategies.

- **Cost analysis tools:** Automatically generate "open calculations" to show how value is distributed between parties.
- **Transparency enhancements:** Use AI to suggest areas where transparency could foster trust without revealing sensitive information.

    Prompt examples:

- "Create a visualization showing the cost-benefit breakdown of our proposal compared to competitors."
- "What level of detail should I disclose to build trust without compromising my position?"

Improving Rapport Through Informal Interactions

AI-driven sentiment analysis can guide informal conversations by suggesting icebreakers or common interests, based on publicly available information about the counterpart.

- **Cultural context:** AI can provide guidance on cultural nuances to avoid breaches of protocol.
- **Dynamic adjustments:** Suggest conversational topics or tone shifts in real-time based on the counterpart's responses.

Prompt examples:

- "Suggest a conversation starter based on the counterpart's background and interests."
- "What informal questions can I ask to gauge their openness to collaboration?"

When you communicate through more than one channel—spoken words, visuals, and written content—your message becomes more engaging and memorable. People tend to retain visual information better than purely verbal input.

For complex or detailed messages, combining words with visuals increases clarity and impact. Even without a whiteboard, a simple sheet of paper and a pen can make a big difference.

Use charts, graphs, timelines, or drawings to simplify data. Visualize key points—whether that means financial figures, schedules, or comparisons. You can also paint vivid mental pictures using stories, analogies, and real-world examples that help the other party *see* what you're saying.

Make your message visual, and you make it stick.

Enhancing the Use of Visuals and Demonstrations

AI can generate tailored visuals, charts, and simulations to support complex points during negotiation.

- **Data presentation:** Create infographics or models to communicate concepts clearly and persuasively.
- **Interactive elements:** Design interactive presentations to engage counterparts and align with their priorities.

Prompt examples:

- "Generate a comparative chart showing how our offer creates added value."
- "Visualize the long-term impact of the proposed solution for both parties."

Breaking Deadlock with Data

AI can identify alternative solutions and analyze trade-offs to overcome impasses. It can also predict outcomes of various approaches based on historical data and current trends.

- **Scenario modeling:** Simulate different negotiation outcomes to evaluate the best course of action.
- **Deadlock detection:** Identify early signs of negotiation breakdown and recommend strategies to regain momentum.

Prompt examples:

- "Suggest alternative solutions based on their stated objections."
- "Simulate the impact of offering a 5 percent discount versus extending delivery timelines."

Using AI to Manage Information Flow

AI can monitor and balance the information flow between parties, ensuring equitable exchange and preventing imbalances that lead to deadlock.

- **Information management:** Flag when one party has provided significantly more information than the other.
- **Agenda support:** Generate agendas and codes of conduct to maintain fairness and transparency.

Prompt examples:

- "Evaluate whether the current information exchange is balanced and suggest adjustments."
- "Draft an agenda that ensures equal participation from both parties."

By integrating AI into negotiation processes, negotiators can enhance trust, improve communication, and create added value for all parties. AI serves as a powerful tool not only to support negotiators but also to ensure that the negotiation climate remains collaborative and constructive.

CHAPTER 9

Valuing Trust

Research shows us that approximately 15 percent of the reason people are successful is due to their formal education, experience, and intelligence. Approximately 85 percent is due to human engineering. Human engineering is how people relate to other people and how they communicate.

Businesses can realize an economic benefit if they start to focus on, and recognize, the importance of trust. I have worked on a project to be able to put a price tag on this feeling.

I am talking about trust between companies, customers, a trustworthy business management, and trust as a basic foundation for interactions and (cash) transactions in our society. It is about how trust can generate profits.

How Can You Value Trust?

About five years ago, trust was not something that could make major business leaders get excited. But things are very different today.

In recent years, I have done substantial work in trying to put a price on trust, to capitalize it, to make it sound like a bad word, because this is the way to talk to business leaders. We need to demonstrate that this is not just a soft, idealistic thought, but that it can lead to increased profits.

It varies, of course, but I dare say with certainty that if you manage to create trust-held relationships in your business, both externally and internally, you can increase profits by up to 34 percent, according to my doctorate research.

How can you do this? Imagine you have two identical products of the same quality. Two different companies offer them. Company 1 is one that you know and trust. You have no relationship with Company 2. Most people report that they would gladly pay a little extra to buy the product from the company they trust. I then make the price-difference bigger and ask the same question. At some price point, they all stop and decide that they would rather deal with the cheaper, unfamiliar company.

The point at which they decide to go with the unknown company shows where they have put a price on the value of trust. It sounds very simple, and it is. I don't believe that I have discovered something new. Trust has always been important, but very few companies today focus on, or recognize, the importance of trust.

In order to raise awareness about the importance of trust, it's essential to lay it out in terms of dollars and cents. I have studied the worldwide online auction house eBay, where you can bid on and buy new and used goods. eBay works with a so-called feedback system, where you can evaluate the trade and the selling party. eBay writes that feedback will be used as a symbol of trust toward the seller. The sellers with a high score get 8 percent more for their goods, according to my research.

Basically, it is about how extremely difficult it has become to compete on a product. Anyone can produce a super teaspoon, where the quality is virtually the same. There is always a teaspoon that is cheaper, and often it is from China. But all in all, many companies are at the same level in terms of prices and products. Therefore, I argue that the companies that are able to establish strong relationships of trust are those that will do best in the future.

Creating Trust

But how do you do it? How do you create trust? Consider the following examples.

Apple iTunes

iTunes has a feature that warns you if you are about to repurchase a track that you already have—a service that is clearly bad for profit in the short term. Why not take advantage of people's forgetfulness and let them buy the product again? I believe that the money that is lost here is recouped in the long run, because the customer feels that they have been treated fairly. It also shows that Apple will not steal your hard-earned cash, for any price.

The example also illustrates how you can create trust in a good way, through electronic interactions, which are becoming very common these days.

Amazon's "Customer Obsession" and AI Integration

Amazon has set a benchmark for trust-building through its proactive use of technology. For instance, its "Subscribe & Save" program is a feature designed to enhance customer trust. Subscribers receive regular discounts on recurring purchases like household goods or groceries. Rather than trapping users in rigid subscription plans, Amazon's AI ensures flexibility by reminding customers about upcoming deliveries and allowing them to adjust or cancel orders without penalty.

Additionally, Amazon employs AI-driven recommendations to provide personalized, relevant options, giving customers confidence in their buying choices. This transparency, combined with Amazon's liberal return policies, signals to customers that the company prioritizes fairness and long-term relationships over short-term profits.

Netflix's "Continue Watching" Feature

Netflix demonstrates trust-building through its "Continue Watching" feature, which provides a seamless user experience by reminding users where they left off in a show or movie. While it might be tempting for the platform to encourage rewatching or artificially inflate engagement metrics, Netflix prioritizes user convenience and trust over such short-term gains.

Moreover, Netflix uses AI to recommend content tailored to each viewer's preferences, signaling that the platform respects their time and interests. By combining personalization with user-centric features, Netflix reinforces the message that it values its customers' satisfaction and trust more than maximizing immediate revenue.

Mistrust Is Costly

> Trust is best created between people, and therefore (though it might sound a bit odd) I think the best thing you can do as a company is to create a trust strategy that includes the employees—a strategy that addresses what it takes to create trust. How should you behave and act?
>
> That trust begets trust, and distrust begets more distrust, is another of the points. And that distrust thrives can be seen in how companies are entering into agreements today.
>
> Agreements between corporate companies are quite enormous. What previously could be handled on a couple of standard sheets of paper now requires several binders. One of the companies I work with—a very large Danish electricity producer—spends a month negotiating an agreement and then five months to get the legal situation in place. This is enormously costly.
>
> High levels of trust provide low transaction costs and higher profits, and vice versa: Low levels of trust provide higher transaction costs and lower profits.

(continued)

Mistrust Is Costly   (*continued*)

> Although this appears to be moving away from focusing on capital, you can ask the following question: Isn't the trust strategy not just a way to exploit a human and very sympathetic instinct, to get more money out of the customers and trading partners?
>
> No, the point is not that one should exploit that trust as a way to make money. It's just that there really is a financial reward for acting in a proper and trustworthy manner. So why not?
>
> So is it about being a good human being? In all respects, it is. But that one person can increase revenue, while being just one person, even because you are one person, is another side to the same story. You do not have to be smart and cunning to be a good businessperson.
>
> Don't you just end up being cheated thoroughly? Yes, possibly. And of course this can hurt. But I now believe that if one is consistent in one's creation of trust, then you can afford it. I clearly think that the large, long-term benefits outweigh the few times you will experience being cheated. And trusting does not mean that you throw your common sense overboard.
>
> Does trust exist in the *Shark Tank* between the entrepreneurs and the sharks? Yes—many of the decisions to invest are emotionally based on the impact of the presentation and the behavior of the person: Are they able to convey trust to the sharks and are the sharks able to create trust with the presenter?

How AI Can Enhance Trust in Business

AI can play a pivotal role in fostering trust within businesses and between trading partners. By using AI algorithms, companies can monitor and analyze trust indicators, such as customer feedback, transaction history, and behavior patterns, to create predictive trust scores. These scores can help businesses identify reliable partners and customers.

AI-Driven Insights for Building a Trust Strategy

AI-powered tools can be used to craft a trust strategy by analyzing communication patterns, customer preferences, and employee interactions. For example, natural language processing (NLP) algorithms can assess email correspondence and customer reviews to detect sentiment, enabling companies to proactively address trust-related issues.

Consider these concrete AI applications:

- **Customer feedback analysis:** AI can process large volumes of customer feedback to identify recurring themes and trust issues, providing actionable insights.
- **Contract analysis:** Machine learning can streamline the review of complex agreements, reducing negotiation times and fostering transparency.
- **Behavioral analytics:** AI can monitor employee and customer interactions, offering insights on trust-building opportunities or potential risks.

AI can revolutionize trust-building by providing actionable insights and automating complex tasks. For instance, businesses can use AI tools to analyze large datasets, predict outcomes, and even simulate trust dynamics in partnerships. By integrating AI, companies can make data-driven decisions that reinforce trust at every level of interaction.

AI-powered tools can refine trust strategies by identifying areas of improvement and opportunities for relationship building. NLP can analyze customer reviews, social media mentions, or internal communications to detect sentiment and flag potential issues that might erode trust. This allows businesses to act preemptively, ensuring stronger relationships.

AI trust prompting in action:

- **Customer relationship management prompt:** "Identify patterns in customer complaints over the past year and recommend changes to improve trust metrics."
- **Risk mitigation prompt:** "Analyze supplier transaction history to determine reliability scores and suggest alternative partners if risks are detected."
- **Transparency in agreements prompt:** "Summarize key terms in this contract and highlight clauses that could impact trust or increase transaction costs."
- **Employee engagement prompt:** "Evaluate internal communication logs (non-intrusively) to identify and suggest improvements in trust-building initiatives among teams."

AI applications in business trust:

- **Feedback analysis:** AI can sift through customer feedback to identify trends in trust-related concerns and recommend actionable steps.
- **Behavioral analytics:** By monitoring transaction patterns, AI can flag deviations that may indicate trust issues, enabling proactive measures.

- **Custom recommendations:** Using customer purchase data, AI can personalize offerings, creating a sense of reliability and attentiveness.
- **Contract simplification:** Machine learning can streamline contract review processes, reducing ambiguity and fostering transparency.

Why AI Matters in Trust-Building

By leveraging AI, businesses can reduce friction in interactions, enhance the customer experience, and foster long-term loyalty. AI's ability to identify, quantify, and act on trust-related variables makes it an indispensable tool for modern businesses aiming to build meaningful and profitable relationships.

CHAPTER 10

The Different Negotiation Styles

I have extensively researched and analyzed the different negotiation styles that individuals use to reach a mutually beneficial agreement. I have identified five distinct negotiation styles that people use, each with its own strengths and weaknesses.

It's vital to understand the behavior behind each style in order for you to understand the behavior and identify the traits. Second, it's also important for you to identify your own behavior. But take care—perhaps you are in for a wake-up call!

This chapter also looks into setting up the perfect negotiation team by using the DISC profiling tool. When I'm assisting corporations in their negotiations, I always use the DISC profiling tool to create the "perfect" team.

The Five Main Negotiation Styles

Let's first dive into the five main negotiation styles:

- **Combative style:** The competitive style is characterized by a focus on achieving the best possible outcome for oneself, often at the expense of the other party. Negotiators who use this style tend to be assertive, aggressive, and confrontational, and they are more likely to engage in power struggles and hard bargaining tactics. While this style can be effective in certain situations, it can also damage relationships and leave the other party feeling unsatisfied or resentful.
- **Collaborative style:** The collaborative style is focused on finding a solution that benefits both parties equally. Negotiators who use this style are typically open-minded, flexible, and creative, and they are willing to

explore a wide range of options to achieve a win-win outcome. This style can be highly effective in situations where both parties have common goals and interests, but it may not be the best approach if time is limited or if one party is less willing to compromise.

- **Compromising style:** The compromising style involves finding a middle ground between the two parties' positions. Negotiators who use this style are typically willing to make concessions and trade-offs to reach an agreement, and they are skilled at finding solutions that are acceptable to both parties. This style can be useful in situations where both parties have equal bargaining power, but it may not be effective if one party has significantly more leverage or if the issues at stake are nonnegotiable.
- **Concessional style:** The accommodating style involves prioritizing the other party's needs and interests over one's own. Negotiators who use this style are typically conciliatory, empathetic, and willing to make sacrifices to maintain good relationships. This style can be useful in situations where preserving the relationship is more important than the outcome of the negotiation, but it may not be effective if the other party is overly aggressive or takes advantage of the accommodating negotiator's willingness to concede.
- **Stalling style:** This style involves avoiding the negotiation altogether or postponing it until a later time. Negotiators who use this style are typically passive, nonconfrontational, and avoid conflict whenever possible. This style can be useful in situations where the issues at stake are relatively minor or where there is no urgency to reach an agreement, but it may not be effective in situations where timely action is necessary or where there are significant consequences for not reaching an agreement.

Each negotiation style has its own unique strengths and weaknesses, and the most effective negotiators are those who are able to adapt their style to the specific situation at hand. By understanding and practicing different negotiation styles, negotiators can increase their chances of achieving successful outcomes and building positive relationships with the other party.

DISC Styles in Negotiation: Adapting to Achieve Better Outcomes

Negotiation is as much about understanding people as it is about the terms of a deal. I often use the expression "All business is human." We have to remember that it's always people who negotiate with people, even when we deal with the use of AI.

Pursuing the "perfect" negotiator requires understanding the individual's behavior and decoding their view of the world. When I am advising organizations and their negotiation team, we often use the DISC model in a revised negotiation version to identify the strengths and weaknesses of each member of the team.

Effective negotiation requires emotional intelligence and strategic adaptability. The DISC behavioral framework offers profound insights into how individuals communicate, make decisions, and approach challenges. You can significantly enhance collaboration and achieve more favorable results by tailoring your negotiation strategy to align with the DISC styles of dominance, influence, steadiness, and compliance.

What Is DISC?

The DISC model categorizes behavior into four key styles, each reflecting a distinct approach to interaction:

- **Dominance (D):** Driven, results-oriented, and decisive. D-styles value control, efficiency, and authority and often take charge in negotiations.
- **Influence (I):** Enthusiastic, friendly, and relationship-focused, I-styles seek positive interactions and prefer engaging and uplifting discussions.
- **Steadiness (S):** Patient, consistent, and dependable. S-styles value stability and harmony and often avoid conflict.
- **Compliance (C):** Analytical, detail-oriented, and logical. C-styles focus on accuracy, data, and thorough planning.

This model was first introduced by psychologist William Moulton Marston, who sought to understand why individuals behave as they do in different contexts. DISC emphasizes behavioral preferences rather than skills or intelligence, making it a flexible and universally applicable tool in negotiation.

Understanding these styles helps negotiators identify behavioral patterns and adapt their approaches for more productive discussions. While individuals may exhibit more than one DISC style trait, a dominant trait usually guides their behavior under stress, which is critical to recognize in high-pressure negotiations.

Negotiating with the Four DISC Styles

Dominance (D): The Results-Driven Negotiator

D-styles thrive in high-energy, goal-focused negotiations. They want control and prefer efficiency over lengthy discussions. Their directness can sometimes seem intimidating, but their focus on results makes them valuable allies when channeled effectively.

Key traits: Competitive, assertive, and confident decision-makers

Challenges: May push too hard, overlook details, or disregard others' perspectives

Winning strategies:

- Be concise and results-oriented; avoid overexplaining or dwelling on minor points.
- Highlight benefits that align with their goals, especially if tied to measurable outcomes.
- Show confidence and match their assertiveness without appearing aggressive.
- Offer autonomy where possible, allowing them to feel in control.

Example in practice: A D-style negotiator leads the discussion in a business acquisition deal, confidently handling tough conversations and presenting the team's most substantial offer. Their assertiveness ensures that negotiations remain focused on the desired outcomes without unnecessary distractions.

Influence (I): The Relationship-Oriented Negotiator

I-styles prioritize building connections and maintaining a positive atmosphere during negotiations. They excel at fostering rapport and creating a collaborative environment but may need help to focus on specific details or deadlines.

Key traits: Outgoing, persuasive, and optimistic communicators

Challenges: May avoid tough decisions, become distracted, or prioritize relationships over results

Winning strategies:

- Start with rapport-building to establish trust and ease tensions.
- Use engaging visuals, stories, and anecdotes to maintain their attention.
- Encourage brainstorming and collaboration to keep them actively involved.
- Maintain a friendly, upbeat tone and avoid overly critical remarks.

Example in practice: In a joint venture discussion, an I-style negotiator shares inspiring success stories to excite the counterpart, making the negotiation feel like a shared journey toward a mutual goal.

Steadiness (S): The Harmonious Negotiator

S-styles are methodical and focused on maintaining stability. They prefer calm and consistent negotiations and may need additional time to process changes or decisions.

Key traits: Loyal, empathetic, and patient

Challenges: Can be resistant to change, overly cautious, or avoid confrontation

Winning strategies:

- Build trust through open communication and reliability.
- Avoid pressuring them into quick decisions; allow time for reflection.
- Emphasize long-term benefits and stability in your proposals.
- Acknowledge their concerns and provide reassurances to ease uncertainty.

Example in Practice: An S-style negotiator reassures a supplier during contract renegotiations, framing changes as gradual adjustments that align with shared values.

Compliance (C): The Analytical Negotiator

C-styles value structure and precision, making them natural problem-solvers. They are highly data-driven and excel at evaluating complex details, but their cautious nature can lead to delays in decision-making.

Key traits: Objective, meticulous, and logical

Challenges: May overanalyze, resist ambiguity, or require extensive information before committing

Winning strategies:

- Present detailed facts, figures, and well-organized documentation.
- Respect their need for thorough evaluation without pressuring them to make quick decisions.
- Avoid emotional appeals; focus on logic and evidence-based arguments.
- Allow time for them to review and prepare responses.

Example in practice: A C-style negotiator in a financial deal carefully evaluates cost-benefit analyses and implementation plans, ensuring the agreement is airtight and risk-free.

DISC Styles in Negotiation Teams

In a team setting, leveraging DISC styles creates a powerful synergy. Within the SMARTnership framework, a negotiation team often includes three critical roles: the Head Negotiator, the Notetaker, and the Calculator. Assigning these roles based on DISC traits ensures that each team member plays to their strengths.

Dominance (D): The Natural Leader
Best role: Head Negotiator

High-D individuals thrive in leadership roles where they can take charge of the negotiation, drive results, and manage the agenda with authority.

Strengths on the team:

- Maintains control and sets the pace of discussions
- Makes bold, confident decisions under pressure
- Pushes for the best possible outcomes without unnecessary compromise

Influence (I): The Engaging Communicator
Best role: Notetaker or Head Negotiator

While the Notetaker traditionally supports an I-style person, elevate the role with their ability to track verbal exchanges and emotional dynamics.

Strengths on the team:

- Builds rapport with counterparts, fostering trust
- Tracks nonverbal cues and emotional shifts during discussions
- Keeps the atmosphere light and engaging

Steadiness (S): The Dependable Anchor   **Best role:** Notetaker or Calculator

S-styles excel in roles requiring attention to detail and long-term relationship management. Their consistency ensures all aspects of the negotiation are documented and considered.

Strengths on the team:

- Provides reassurance and a steady presence in high-pressure situations
- Ensures all parties feel heard and valued
- Focuses on creating agreements that foster trust and stability

Compliance (C): The Analytical Expert **Best role:** Calculator

C-styles are ideally suited for roles requiring analytical depth and precision. Their logical approach ensures the team makes data-driven decisions.

Strengths on the team:

- Prepares detailed financial models and risk assessments
- Identifies hidden opportunities or risks in the counterpart's proposals
- Provides clarity and structure to complex issues

Balancing DISC Styles for Success

Effective negotiation teams leverage the complementary strengths of each DISC style. For example:

- A D-style Head Negotiator drives progress, an S-style Notetaker ensures all details are captured, and a C-style Calculator verifies the financial and legal implications.
- A D-style leader benefits from an I-style team member to maintain rapport and keep the negotiation relational.

By blending DISC styles in a structured team, negotiators can confidently tackle challenges, ensuring strategic and relational success. Adaptability, empathy, and preparation are the cornerstones of effective negotiation, and DISC serves as the roadmap to achieving them.

How AI Can Assist in Leveraging Negotiation Styles and DISC Framework

Artificial intelligence can significantly enhance our understanding and application of negotiation styles and DISC behavioral traits. By leveraging AI, negotiators can improve preparation, communication, and adaptability, making every negotiation more efficient and productive. One of the latest tools is **www.crystalknows.com**, which claims to be able to create a DISC profile based on someone's LinkedIn profile. I have tried it and was impressed by the precision. It's an interesting tool to utilize prior to a negotiation with an unknown counterpart.

AI's Role in Supporting Negotiation Styles

Behavior Analysis AI can analyze communication patterns (e.g., emails, speech, or written proposals) to identify the negotiation style of your counterpart.

- **Combative style:** AI may highlight aggressive language, competitive behavior, or a focus on winning.
- **Collaborative style:** AI can recognize open-ended questions, inclusive language, and a focus on mutual benefits.
- **Compromising style:** AI might detect phrases indicating a willingness to find middle ground or make concessions.
- **Concessional style:** AI can identify language that emphasizes agreement and maintaining harmony.
- **Stalling style:** AI might flag avoidance tactics, vague responses, or delays in communication.

Prompt example: "Analyze the communication history between our team and the counterpart. Identify patterns that indicate their dominant negotiation style and suggest tailored strategies to align with their behavior."

Dynamic Strategy Recommendations AI can provide real-time recommendations during negotiations based on the detected negotiation style. For example:

- If the counterpart is combative, AI might suggest staying firm on critical points while avoiding emotional escalation.
- For collaborative counterparts, AI could recommend focusing on shared goals and presenting creative solutions.

Prompt example: "Based on the counterpart's behavior in the last meeting, suggest strategies for the next discussion to maintain a collaborative tone and achieve mutual benefits."

AI's Role in DISC-Based Negotiations

DISC Profiling AI can predict DISC traits by analyzing behavioral data, such as response times, tone, and content. This insight helps negotiators understand the counterpart's communication preferences and decision-making style.

Prompt example: "Evaluate the counterpart's emails and meeting notes to estimate their DISC profile. Suggest negotiation strategies based on their dominant trait."

Team Optimization   AI can analyze DISC profiles within a negotiation team to suggest optimal role assignments. For example:

- A Dominance (D) individual may lead negotiations, while a Compliance (C) individual ensures accuracy in data and contracts.
- AI can also detect gaps in team dynamics and suggest ways to balance strengths and weaknesses.

Prompt example: "Assess our team's DISC profiles and recommend role assignments for an upcoming negotiation to maximize effectiveness."

Simulating DISC Scenarios   AI can simulate negotiation scenarios based on DISC traits to prepare negotiators for potential challenges. For example, if negotiating with a Steadiness (S) counterpart, AI might simulate scenarios where they resist change, helping the negotiator prepare strategies to reassure and build trust.

Prompt example: "Simulate a negotiation scenario with a Steadiness (S) profile counterpart. Provide recommendations to address their concerns and maintain harmony."

Real-Time Feedback   AI tools can provide live feedback during negotiations, offering suggestions to adapt your approach. For example:

- If an Influence (I) counterpart seems disengaged, AI might recommend using stories or visuals to reengage them.
- If a Compliance (C) counterpart requests more information, AI could suggest presenting additional data or documentation.

Prompt example: "Monitor the ongoing negotiation and provide real-time suggestions to adjust our approach based on the DISC traits of the counterpart."

Additional Prompts for AI Assistance

Consider these additional AI prompts when working on negotiation styles:

- **Tailoring approaches to negotiation styles:** "What are the best strategies to handle a combative-style negotiator while maintaining a collaborative tone?"
- **Improving team synergy:** "Analyze our DISC profiles and suggest adjustments to team dynamics to enhance negotiation outcomes."
- **Balancing DISC styles in team composition:** "Recommend the ideal balance of DISC styles for our negotiation team to address both analytical and relational challenges."
- **Adapting to counterpart behavior:** "Suggest how to shift our strategy if the counterpart transitions from a collaborative style to a stalling style during the negotiation."

Benefits of Using AI for Identifying Negotiation Styles

Using AI to identify negotiation styles can be beneficial in a number of ways:

- **Enhanced preparation:** AI helps identify styles and DISC traits early, allowing negotiators to craft strategies that resonate with their counterparts.
- **Improved adaptability:** With real-time feedback, negotiators can adjust their approach dynamically.
- **Data-driven decisions:** AI reduces guesswork by analyzing communication and behavioral data to provide actionable insights.
- **Stronger team performance:** AI ensures each team member's strengths are utilized effectively, creating a cohesive and adaptable negotiation team.

By integrating AI into negotiation strategies, individuals and teams can not only navigate the complexities of different styles and DISC profiles but also achieve outcomes that are mutually beneficial and strategically sound.

CHAPTER 11

Masters of the Deal: What Sets Great Negotiators Apart

By examining a large group of negotiators, we can identify key factors that distinguish successful negotiators from those who struggle. This allows us to understand why certain issues arise and how they can be prevented or addressed. However, it's important to note that success or failure in negotiation isn't always a matter of technique. Sometimes the circumstances are simply too unfavorable for any negotiation strategy to succeed, while at other times favorable conditions make failure almost impossible.

One company manager shared his approach to recruitment: "We had over 100 applications for a new sales manager position, all from candidates who were well qualified. I threw 90 of them away, keeping only 10. The ones that stayed were the lucky ones, and we hired one of them."

Over 35,000 Negotiators Tested

The results presented here are based on studies conducted with over 35,000 negotiators who participated in simulation exercises and actual negotiations where we were involved. These negotiators came from a wide variety of sectors, company sizes, and market positions, and included project managers, buyers, finance managers, IT managers, CEOs, sales managers, and technical managers—essentially, the professionals responsible for business negotiations within their companies.

These individuals were typically well educated, with a foundation in academic training. The negotiations covered a range of scenarios, including development projects, agency agreements, joint ventures, and cross-border cooperation within organizations. Importantly, the exercises did not require specific technical, financial, or trade-related expertise. The key differentiator was the negotiators' skill level. The findings from this study align closely with our observations in similar real-life negotiations.

How Much Do All the Mistakes Cost?

Studies show that only two-thirds of negotiators successfully land a deal, and even then, they typically lose about 42 percent of the overall negotiation potential. This lost potential, often referred to as *NegoEconomics*, represents unutilized value that could have been achieved in the deal, benefiting both parties without one feeling like the loser. This is the untapped value that, for example, negotiators in boardrooms envision when calculating potential merger gains—gains that ultimately go unrealized and contribute to the failure of most major mergers.

So how much do these mistakes cost? It's impossible to give a precise answer, but we can look at a specific negotiation scenario to understand the consequences. For instance, in a negotiation where the price is $1,000,000 and the supplier gains 25 percent—a nice profit by most standards—the negotiators fail to realize a NegoEconomic opportunity of $200,000. This amount could have been achieved by adjusting factors like payment terms, delivery schedules, technical requirements, or service agreements.

However, the negotiators only manage to capture part of this $200,000 in their deal. If they were to perform at the average level observed in our study, 40 percent of the potential ($80,000) would remain unutilized. For the seller, capturing this $80,000 would increase their profit from $250,000 to $330,000—a 32 percent increase.

Moreover, over a third of negotiators in the study failed to reach an agreement at all, losing even greater potential gains. The total cost of these mistakes is not only reflected in lost profits but also in negative outcomes like environmental damage, poor working conditions, increased technical and economic risks, and the wasted time and energy spent on conflict.

Despite the high cost of these mistakes, there is a silver lining. Instead of dwelling on the failures, we should focus on the vast potential that remains untapped. For skilled negotiators, the opportunity to maximize outcomes is immense. The investment in developing negotiation skills is often far too low compared to the significant returns that could be gained, making it crucial to recognize and harness this potential for success.

The Ketchup Effect

The *ketchup effect* in negotiation illustrates how initial efforts might not yield results, but with persistence and the right adjustments, progress suddenly flows abundantly—just like shaking a stubborn ketchup bottle. It's a reminder that patience and strategic timing are essential to breaking through a negotiation deadlock.

A study reveals an interesting phenomenon in negotiations—time pressure. Out of the 120 minutes typically allocated for a negotiation, only

10 percent of negotiators are able to finish without feeling any time pressure. On the other hand, 55 percent of the negotiators only reach an agreement when they feel time running out. Under the stress of a ticking clock, they tend to force a conclusion, often settling for a compromise where both parties meet halfway—ensuring no one loses more than the other. However, in this rush, they don't have the luxury of revisiting key points or rethinking their decisions.

To explore this further, a group of negotiators who had not reached an agreement in the first two hours were given an additional 30–60 minutes. In this extended time, only 6 percent managed to come to an agreement. The rest couldn't break their unproductive patterns, showing that extra time didn't significantly improve their ability to negotiate effectively. In fact, time seemed to play a minor role in the outcome. Even with more time, 33 percent of the negotiators still failed to reach an agreement.

The small group (about 10 percent) who managed to reach an agreement without the stress of time constraints performed significantly better, utilizing up to 20 percent more of the negotiation potential. They used their time more effectively, focusing on thoughtful discussions and strategies rather than rushing to a conclusion.

What this illustrates is that it's not time itself that causes failure, but the negotiation methods employed. This is a hard truth for many to accept. During the study, we even intervened to help negotiators who had become stuck in unproductive arguments or had reached deadlock. In real life, however, such help would be unavailable.

Interestingly, in about 10 percent of the successful negotiations, one party would state, "If this had been a real negotiation, we would have ended this long ago and kicked the other party out. But since this is just an exercise, we gave them a chance." This highlights a critical risk—negotiators may not perform as well in real negotiations, where there are no safety nets. In the real world, the negotiation table is where companies can either win or lose significant amounts of money in a very short time.

Common Traits of Successful Negotiators

In our studies, we observed significant variation in negotiation behavior, but there are common traits shared by those who outperform others:

- They analyze the negotiation and variables involved.
- They prioritize important factors over less important ones.
- They assign value to soft, often intangible variables.
- They embrace AI and understand how to prompt it effectively.
- They outline the negotiation visually for a clear overview.
- They incorporate the principles of NegoEconomics.
- They take the initiative during negotiations.

- They excel in communication.
- They set high but realistic goals.
- They start negotiations promptly.
- They proactively suggest alternative solutions to avoid problems.
- They foster a positive negotiation climate.
- They actively present offers and counteroffers.
- They distribute roles within the team and maintain discipline.
- They follow a strategic approach.
- They work methodically.
- They avoid getting stuck in minor details.
- They begin bargaining early.
- They take a final break before reaching an agreement.
- They ensure they behave in a credible manner.

The following sections discuss each of these traits in more detail.

They Analyze the Negotiation and the Negotiation Variables

Successful negotiators thoroughly prepare by analyzing all potential negotiation variables—i.e., the points that could be discussed. They are aware of their own negotiation limits in each area and understand the consequences of altering any conditions. With a solid grasp of economics, they can visualize the entire deal and know how to balance costs or risks to maximize value in one area by adjusting another. They prioritize variables, showing firmness in critical areas while signaling a willingness to compromise on less important ones. Ultimately, they focus on the overall result, not just the individual components.

They Prioritize Important over Less Important Factors

They are focused on the "you win some and lose some" philosophy and early in the negotiation process focus on important NegoEconomics, creating variables instead of zero-sum variables. The 2024 Most Negotiated Terms Report by World Commerce & Contracting[1] reveals a significant disconnect between

---

[1] The 2024 Most Negotiated Terms Report by World Commerce & Contracting (WorldCC) highlights the most commonly negotiated contract terms globally, providing insights into trends, priorities, and challenges in commercial negotiations. This annual report serves as a benchmark for understanding shifts in focus areas, such as risk allocation, performance obligations, and value creation in contracts.

the terms frequently negotiated and those that truly drive business success. Despite evolving business conditions, negotiators continue to focus on traditional terms like limitation of liability, price, and indemnification. This misalignment suggests that current negotiation practices may not effectively address the factors critical to successful business outcomes.

They Make a Decision and Put a Price on the Soft Variables

Skilled negotiators recognize that many "soft" variables cannot be measured by standard economic or technical metrics. These include factors like customer loyalty, peace of mind, or emotional satisfaction. They proactively decide what they are willing to give up or compromise on in order to achieve objectives such as maintaining a regular customer, securing an agreement promptly, enjoying a desirable living situation, collaborating with respectful partners, or avoiding difficult negotiations. They assign value to these intangible factors and integrate them into their overall negotiation strategy.

They Embrace AI and Understand How to Prompt It Effectively

AI can provide negotiators with data-driven insights, predicting negotiation outcomes based on historical data, trends, and real-time analysis. By using machine learning algorithms, negotiators can simulate potential negotiation scenarios, enabling better preparation and strategy formulation.

Negotiators can utilize AI through well-crafted prompts to perform tasks such as analyzing contract language, calculating potential NegoEconomics, and suggesting counteroffers. For example:

- **Prompt:** "Analyze this contract and highlight potential areas for cost savings or risks."
- **Prompt:** "Provide alternative delivery schedules that maximize NegoEconomic benefits for both parties."

They Often Outline the Negotiation on a Board to Get an Overview

Skilled negotiators often create a visual representation of the negotiation, mapping out key points and their interconnections on a board. This overview allows them to see how various demands, such as a request for shorter delivery times, can be counterbalanced by a higher advance payment—a payment that might be more beneficial to the supplier than the costs associated with expedited production. This approach helps them assess various scenarios and be better prepared if the negotiation takes an unexpected turn. This analytical ability is particularly strong among individuals with military backgrounds, who often bring structured problem-solving skills to business negotiations.

They Incorporate the Message of NegoEconomics

Skilled negotiators understand and apply the principles of NegoEconomics. They recognize that with a combination of luck and skill, they can achieve a solution that exceeds their initial offer. They are motivated to cooperate, clearly seeing where NegoEconomics can be created and where opportunities lie. This understanding is integrated into their preparation process, where they compile a list of potential negotiation variables, ensuring that they are ready to identify and leverage opportunities for mutual benefit during the negotiation.

They Take the Initiative During Negotiations

Skilled negotiators take the initiative throughout the negotiation process. They understand that the party in control of the situation holds a key advantage in distributing the NegoEconomics. The initiative doesn't come from being overly talkative; it lies with the person who actively asks questions, listens attentively, and follows up with summaries and consequence-based questions.

They identify which variables are negotiable and whether changing conditions could create NegoEconomics. Their approach to gathering information is strategic—if they suspect that a shorter delivery time could benefit the opponent, they don't directly ask for the exact benefit but instead open the conversation on related points, such as penalties for delays. By exploring these angles, they get closer to understanding the value of a shorter delivery time without asking for a direct answer.

They are skilled at navigating these discussions and offering alternative solutions. For example, if the customer insists on day fines for delays, they may counteroffer with a bonus if delivery is earlier, thus demonstrating the value of reduced time. They don't accept a flat "no" but focus on uncovering the reasons behind it, using this insight to continue exploring potential solutions.

They Are Good at Communicating

Skilled negotiators possess highly developed communicative competence. Their presentations are marked by self-confidence and enthusiasm, which helps them effectively illustrate the advantages of their position to the other party. They are adept at listening, understanding the needs of the opponent, and utilizing a strong questioning technique to gather critical information. By actively engaging in the conversation, they maintain control and build rapport, ensuring a smoother negotiation process.

They Have High But Realistic Goals

These negotiators set ambitious goals, aiming beyond simply staying within budget or securing a slightly better deal than the next best alternative. They understand the importance of flexibility and often hold off on specifying their goals until they have a clearer understanding of the opponent's position and the strengths of both parties.

They communicate their goals clearly, which influences the opponent's own level of ambition. They know where the line is between an offer that's too low and one that's reasonable and backed by credible arguments. While they are confident in their objectives, they remain open to adjusting them if new information arises that offers a better understanding of the possibilities and limitations in the negotiation.

They Quickly Start Negotiating

Effective negotiators don't waste time on unnecessary arguments. They jump straight into the process, focusing on mapping out potential solutions and understanding each other's position. They are open with some information, realizing that in order to get something, they must also be willing to give. This openness encourages the opponent to lower their guard and mirror the same behavior. They prioritize forming a better understanding of the opponent's priorities and what adjustments will be most meaningful to them before engaging in deeper debates. Once they understand the other party's needs, they use their arguments to reinforce why their proposals benefit both sides.

They Try to Avoid Problems by Suggesting Alternatives

Rather than getting stuck in fruitless debates about whose perspective is correct, skilled negotiators use alternative solutions to bypass obstacles. They adopt the "sun and wind" method: Instead of using force or aggressive tactics, they gently suggest alternatives that allow both parties to feel positive about the outcome. This approach helps them avoid unnecessary confrontations and focus on collaboration. A typical phrase they use is the "yes, but" principle, such as "That was an interesting proposal, but how do you propose to arrange financing?"

Note: The sun and wind method is a negotiation analogy derived from an Aesop's fable, where the sun and wind compete to make a traveler remove his coat. The wind blows forcefully, but the traveler tightens his coat in resistance. The sun, however, gently shines warmth, prompting the traveler to willingly take off the coat. In negotiation, this method underscores the effectiveness of a warm, collaborative approach over a forceful or aggressive one. Building trust, showing empathy, and fostering mutual benefit often lead to better outcomes than applying pressure or creating conflict.

They Create a Positive Negotiation Climate

They cultivate a respectful, positive atmosphere in negotiations. Skilled negotiators understand the importance of maintaining a human touch and recognize that pressure leads to counterpressure, while insults provoke strong emotional reactions. They treat the opponent as an equal and are careful with their words, avoiding dismissive or disrespectful language. They listen attentively to the other party, summarizing their views to gain trust and respect. While they remain firm in their own demands, they maintain an approachable, engaging demeanor. Outside the formalities of the negotiation, they engage in casual conversation to build rapport, showing genuine interest in the other party's perspective and seeking common ground beyond the immediate business at hand.

They Actively Present Offers and Counteroffers

They are proactive in presenting both offers and counteroffers, knowing that negotiations are a back-and-forth process. While others may be hesitant or stuck, they push the conversation forward. They understand the rules of give and take and avoid one-sided concessions. They do not settle for the first offer that falls within their budget and are willing to continue bargaining. If the opponent presents an offer that deviates from what they envisioned, they reject it and instead make their own counteroffer to reset the frame of the negotiation.

They Have a Strategy

They come into negotiations with a clear strategy. This strategy allows them to maintain the initiative and drive the negotiation forward confidently. As the negotiation progresses, they adapt their tactics, becoming more assertive when discussing cost distribution, risks, and gains. They are comfortable with shifting to a zero-sum approach when necessary, ensuring they maintain control throughout the process.

They Distribute the Roles Within the Group and Are Disciplined

Before negotiations, they organize the group by assigning clear roles. One person leads the negotiations, another listens and observes, providing updates on the dynamics, and a third focuses on calculations to assess the impact of different conditions. The team remains disciplined, avoiding spontaneous disruptions. They agree on how to communicate internally (e.g., through sign language, eye contact, or small notes) and consult the team during breaks for strategic discussions.

They Work Methodically

They are methodical in their approach, using structured agendas and tools like flip charts or boards for note-taking and summaries. They avoid jumping back and forth between topics, focusing on each point until it is fully addressed. Once they finish discussing a point, they summarize to ensure mutual understanding before moving on to the next issue.

They Do Not Dig Themselves into Foxholes and Fight About Details

Instead of getting bogged down in insignificant details, they focus on the key issues. Once the main points are agreed upon, the rest will fall into place. They avoid verbal fights over minor matters and are willing to concede on less important points, but they always ensure that any concession benefits them in return, even if the opponent values the concession more.

They Start Bargaining in Good Time

They don't waste time on unnecessary arguments. Recognizing that constant counterarguments only lead to deadlock, they start bargaining early. If the opponent is unwilling to answer questions, they present their own offer, which forces the opponent to make decisions and reveal valuable information. Starting early allows time for breaks, during which they can evaluate the progress and adjust their approach.

They Take One Last Break Before Entering into an Agreement

Before agreeing to a deal, they do not rush, even if the opponent presents a final offer. They take a final break to reflect and ensure that all possibilities have been considered and the agreement is optimal. This break might extend to a day or more in real-life situations to ensure they are making the best possible decision.

They Make a Point of Behaving in a Credible Manner

Credibility is crucial in negotiations. They maintain integrity by sticking to the truth, avoiding deceit or double messages. They honor their word and avoid manipulative tactics that could undermine trust. Their credibility makes them reliable and trustworthy in the eyes of the opponent.

Common Mistakes of Failing Negotiators

People who fail in negotiations often make several critical mistakes, including:

- They only see half the negotiation.
- They aim too low.
- They do not actively search for the NegoEconomics.
- They throw themselves into traditional negotiation fights.
- The price is more important than the overall costs.
- The concept of NegoEconomics is vague to them.
- They overlook the totality.
- They do not realize that the partner also has to make money.
- They are afraid of opening up.
- They work unstructured.
- They have not distributed the roles within the group.
- They are afraid of bargaining.
- They do not set up a strategy.
- They lose the grip on the economy.
- They make insultingly low offers.
- They do not accept that the opponent makes money.

- They seek "fair" solutions.
- They are not good at listening.

The following sections dive into these mistakes in more detail.

They Only See Half the Negotiation

Many negotiators fail because they only see half of the negotiation. They focus solely on their own gains, like reducing the price, without considering how those changes may increase costs elsewhere. For example, a lower price can be offset by higher maintenance costs, which could end up making the deal more expensive overall.

These negotiators miss the point of partnership. Instead of working together to reduce risks and costs while increasing joint rewards, they become fixated on their own side of the deal. A great example of this is the Telia/Telenor merger, where national interests and egos derailed the deal, costing billions.

Take the case of a buyer who demands an earlier delivery date, believing it's a small victory worth $10,000. The supplier, however, incurs a $50,000 cost to meet this demand but doesn't communicate this to the buyer. The buyer, seeing only their own gain, doesn't realize their decision made the deal $40,000 more expensive.

The root of the problem is a lack of open communication. Many negotiators are afraid to discuss costs and risks with their counterpart, assuming it's not their job to worry about the other party's interests. However, understanding how changes affect both sides is essential to making better decisions and avoiding costly mistakes.

To succeed, negotiators need to view the situation from their opponent's perspective, asking questions like "How does this affect you?" They must understand that nothing is free—every concession comes at a cost. This dialogue and transparency are key to building a real partnership rather than a zero-sum game.

Managers play a key role in teaching their teams to look at the negotiation as a whole. Organizations should avoid suboptimizing, where small savings in one area are offset by higher costs elsewhere. Ultimately, if the strategy is too combative, it may be time to reconsider the approach.

They Aim Too Low

Negotiators often make the mistake of aiming too low from the start, never leaving room for negotiation or considering the full potential of what the deal could become. Instead, they focus solely on staying within budget or securing a deal slightly better than their next best alternative. This is especially common with buyers, who may even accept the lowest price without engaging in proper negotiation with other suppliers.

Here's a typical scenario: After receiving three offers, the buyer might look at:

- Offer A: $1,100,000
- Offer B: $1,175,000
- Offer C: $1,310,000

Offer C is immediately rejected because of its high cost, without even considering whether there could be a better deal or deeper value in it. Negotiations proceed with A, but A insists they've already made their best offer. The buyer's attitude then becomes: "We already have a supplier who meets our needs. It's not our job to push harder; it's the other suppliers who must improve their offer."

This mindset leads to a lack of motivation for actively seeking NegoEconomics—the broader value in the deal that goes beyond price. The body language speaks volumes: arms crossed, disengaged, unwilling to explore deeper options.

When B meets or falls below A's price of $1,100,000, the buyer assumes the deal is done. But this narrow thinking can miss the chance to unlock additional value.

Note: To avoid a trap like this, when B crosses the "magic line" of $1,100,000, take a moment to pause. A 10–15 minute break could provide clarity. Reflect on these questions:

- Are there additional forms of NegoEconomics that haven't been considered?
- What does the seller's calculation look like? Did they reduce their margin, or is the lower price a result of new value being created?
- Is there a better distribution of gains that benefits both parties?
- Should we accept the current offer, or continue to negotiate?
- If the seller has reduced their margin significantly to reduce costs, further negotiation may not yield more value. But if the seller has found ways to improve their position while lowering costs, it's worth exploring more.
- If the negotiation feels unbalanced, it may be worth testing the waters with a counteroffer or bringing in another supplier for a fresh round of talks.

Finally, always consider the ethical implications of your decisions. If you're using insights from one supplier (like B's proposals) to gain an advantage with another (like A), consider the long-term costs to your reputation and relationships. The negotiation is about more than just the deal at hand; it's about maintaining trust and integrity for future partnerships.

By aiming higher and broadening your perspective, you can turn a simple transaction into a true partnership that benefits all parties in the long run.

They Do Not Actively Search for the NegoEconomics

In negotiations, passivity can be the biggest obstacle. When negotiators are passive, they let the opponent steer the conversation and rarely have the necessary information to uncover the full scope of NegoEconomics. This often happens when negotiators don't understand the value of partnership, or worse, when they are inexperienced. Without insight into what is negotiable, they default to a zero-sum mindset where they believe one party must lose for the other to win. This approach prevents them from seeing how mutual benefits can be created.

If they don't actively seek out opportunities to leverage NegoEconomics—by exploring all variables and being proactive—they hand control to the other party. An experienced negotiator can then exploit these opportunities, creating value while keeping the benefits to themselves.

> **Note:** To avoid this trap, negotiators must take the initiative. It's crucial to ask the right questions, probe for details, and control the flow of the conversation. Rather than immediately making concessions or agreeing to demands, an active negotiator uses inquiries to open up the discussion and find ways to create mutual value.

A negotiator who doesn't take the initiative becomes a liability. Companies can't afford passive negotiators in the long run, because they are expensive in terms of missed opportunities and poor deals. Success in negotiations doesn't just happen—it's the result of preparation, strong communication, and a strategic mindset.

The responsibility for the outcome lies with everyone at the table. If the current team isn't up to the task, more preparation or even a change in the negotiation team may be necessary.

They Throw Themselves into Traditional Negotiation Fights

Many negotiators fall into the trap of relying on traditional, combative negotiation tactics—arguing for the sake of arguing. This approach often comes from a lack of awareness of alternative methods, and an overreliance on

CHAPTER 11   Masters of the Deal: What Sets Great Negotiators Apart

presenting a barrage of arguments to "win" the negotiation. The mindset here is simple: the more arguments they present, the more they believe they are right, and the more the opponent must accept their position.

But this method is not only unprofessional—it's also risky. Negotiators who focus solely on their arguments can easily corner themselves. They become too invested in defending their position, even when they know deep down they may be wrong. Their ego takes over, leaving them unable to back down and adapt. When this happens, they miss the opportunity to discover new, more profitable avenues for creating value—those often lie in understanding the other party's needs, not just defending your own.

One-way communication becomes the norm. Questions are rare, and listening actively is even rarer. Negotiators tend to push only for concessions, instead of actively seeking out new pieces of the puzzle that could lead to a more mutually beneficial outcome. When they don't find new information, they grow insecure and feel stuck, unable to make progress. This is the point where frustration sets in, and they fail to open up new possibilities. Without the openness and dialogue necessary to understand the other party, the process becomes stale and unproductive.

> **Note:** In order to avoid this trap, negotiators need the courage to embrace the concept of NegoEconomics and see how it can work for them. Instead of believing that dialogue is a sign of weakness, they must understand that two-way communication is a powerful tool, and that real negotiations happen through genuine interaction. Breaking free from the macho "win at all costs" mentality is essential.

Negotiators should work on creating a comprehensive view of the negotiation—what information they have, what they need, and what information could benefit the other side as well. This kind of awareness opens the door to collaboration rather than combat. Tools like timetables can be extremely helpful in framing the entire negotiation and identifying areas where mutual value can be created.

Finally, managers must take responsibility for this cultural shift. It's not enough simply to declare a new approach or write a memo. Significant investment in training and developing the team is required to move away from outdated combative methods and toward a more collaborative, value-creating strategy. A real change in behavior, not just rhetoric, is essential for success.

Price Is More Important Than the Overall Costs

Many negotiators focus narrowly on price without considering the broader, long-term costs or returns of a deal. Their understanding of the full economic picture is often vague, and they fail to analyze the key variables or anticipate how changes will affect the outcome. This lack of perspective leads them to miss opportunities to create value through NegoEconomics. Cost and profit are often siloed in different departments or budget years, making it easy to get fixated on the price alone.

For example, two suppliers offer identical products. One charges $40 per unit, while the other charges $41. The obvious choice seems to be the $40 supplier, but this ignores other hidden costs—like the $40 supplier demanding an advance payment, which could result in interest expenses on a separate budget. Many negotiators fail to account for these hidden costs, especially when interest is booked under a different account, making it difficult to compare offers accurately.

This is not just a problem for small companies. In training sessions with major Nordic corporations, procurement managers openly admitted their lack of knowledge in calculating interest and overall costs, and their reliance on the allocated budget, rather than doing the math to evaluate the true cost-effectiveness of their decisions. Some even admitted that as long as money was spent within the budget year, they didn't consider the broader financial implications.

In line with EU public tender rules, companies may choose suppliers based on the lowest price or the "most favorable offer," which includes factors like overall costs. Many buyers, however, default to choosing the lowest price, simplifying the process but limiting their ability to negotiate on the broader terms, including price and long-term costs. This makes it difficult to create NegoEconomics, as the negotiation space is restricted.

Note: To avoid this pitfall, companies should rethink their accounting systems and practices. It's crucial to revise how costs, risks, and gains are tracked throughout the project life cycle, ensuring that these elements are considered in the decision-making process. Managers must play a key role in fostering a culture that understands the full scope of costs—not just the price tag.

By documenting the negotiations and tracking the results, companies can compare the decision-making basis with actual outcomes once the project is completed. This post-project analysis can highlight how well decisions were made and serve as motivation for future negotiators. Just as financial accounts are regularly reviewed, so too should negotiations be evaluated to ensure ongoing improvements in strategy.

The Concept of NegoEconomics Is Vague to Them

For many negotiators, the concept of NegoEconomics remains unclear. They struggle to understand that an action that incurs an immediate cost can also generate multiple returns—such as reduced future costs, longer life spans, or minimized risks. This lack of awareness often stems from a fundamental gap in both economic and technical understanding, preventing negotiators from thinking in a business-oriented manner.

In some cases, negotiators resist change entirely. They may have worked in a company for years, implementing solutions that, while effective in the past, are now being challenged. For these individuals, negotiations are less about creating new value through NegoEconomics and more about defending their established ways. Any suggestion of change is seen as a direct critique of their expertise, creating a mindset that focuses more on preservation than innovation.

Note: To avoid falling into this trap, management must take responsibility for fostering a culture of competence and openness to change. In cases where training alone won't suffice, it may be necessary to reassess roles within the company. Not everyone can become an expert negotiator, and some individuals may need to transition to different roles where their skills can be better utilized. Teams must ensure they have a diverse set of competencies, allowing for more effective negotiations and project planning that can leverage the full potential of NegoEconomics.

They Overlook the Totality

One of the most common pitfalls in negotiations is when negotiators become so focused on individual details that they lose sight of the bigger picture. The result? Time and energy are wasted on trivial matters that don't impact the overall cost or risk of the deal, while the true issues that could create real value are ignored. This happens when negotiators fail to prioritize, resulting in endless debates over inconsequential points. This lack of discipline leads to verbal fights, and before long personal perceptions and prestige take over, further clouding judgment.

In one case, the Swedish-Norwegian owners in the Telia/Telenor merger spent more time arguing over the salary of the new chair of the board than on the real issues of the merger. The media seized on this, lowering their stock assessment of the company, because the owners seemed more interested in small details than in creating value for the business.

Such behavior is not uncommon among Norwegian negotiators, who often struggle with separating trivial matters from critical ones. In negotiations with the EU, Norwegian negotiators were often seen as making a fuss about everything, leaving the European counterparts bewildered about what they actually wanted. The result was a lack of clarity, which is a serious disadvantage when trying to create mutually beneficial agreements.

This focus on irrelevant details can also be seen in technicians who prefer to puzzle over each piece of the negotiation, rather than considering the broader strategic picture. It's as if they're concerned with where to place a bicycle stand, but hesitate to engage with larger, more important issues, like how to finance a significant investment.

Sometimes the strategy of starting with smaller, less important issues is employed in the hope of building rapport and trust. However, when these "small issues" become more difficult to resolve than expected, negotiators often give up, thinking, "If we can't even agree on these minor points, how can we ever agree on the big ones?"

This is where the risk lies: by focusing too narrowly on price, payment terms, or warranty conditions, negotiators may develop unrealistic expectations about what they can achieve, without realizing that concessions made on one point can be taken back in other areas. It creates a zero-sum mindset, where negotiators fail to see the value of trade-offs that could result in a better overall deal.

Note: To avoid falling into this trap, negotiators should:

- Start by forming a clear picture of the most important negotiation factors and stick to them. This clarity will guide the conversation and prevent irrelevant details from taking over.
- Create an agenda that leads toward the negotiation goal and removes distractions.
- The negotiation leader must have the authority to step in and suggest when certain questions should be deferred or handled by others.
- Appoint an observer in the group to recognize when the negotiation has stalled and suggest a short break to reassess the approach.
- Be brave enough to confront problems head-on, without allowing personal prestige or small details to cloud the judgment of the group.

Effective negotiations happen when parties focus on the total picture, not just the small pieces. When negotiators stay disciplined and keep their eyes on the bigger goal, they unlock the potential to create real value.

They Don't Understand that the Partner Also Has to Make Money

Some negotiators struggle to accept that their partner is entitled to make a profit. They focus too much on controlling or limiting the other party's earnings, often basing this on perceived costs or risks. Instead of seeking ways to add value to the deal, they fixate on the idea that the other side shouldn't profit too much. This creates a situation where both parties are negotiating from entirely different perspectives.

The issue arises when one side seeks a fair price based on the opponent's costs, while the other wants compensation based on the value they bring. This focus on fairness can prevent a cooperative agreement and lead to missed opportunities.

Note: To avoid this trap, negotiators should:

- Recognize that value conflicts are tough to resolve. Instead of focusing on fairness, aim to reach an agreement that's better than alternatives.
- Set personal value norms aside. Negotiators should not impose their own sense of fairness on the other side. Cooperation can work even if both parties disagree on how profits should be distributed.
- Evaluate alternatives. Compare propositions with second-best options rather than blocking a deal over fairness concerns.
- Understand the motivation behind profit. A partner who makes a reasonable profit will be more motivated to deliver better results.

In the end, successful negotiations are about creating value, not rigidly sticking to a sense of justice. Both sides need to profit to stay motivated and committed.

They Are Afraid of Opening Up

Many negotiators tend to rely on a strategy of waiting out the opponent, hoping that they'll blink first. This approach often stems from poor preparation and an underlying fear of revealing too much too early—afraid that doing so will give the opponent an advantage. While this can be a valid tactic when you're uncertain about the issues at play or when you're up against an impatient opponent eager to close the deal, it can also leave negotiations stagnant. Without the exchange of new information, the discussion loses momentum.

Negotiators who are unwilling to open up may find themselves stuck, failing to make any real progress. This can lead to premature concessions or agreements rushed through without sufficient time for thought. The result is often frustration, with neither party fully able to assess the value of the deal.

If both parties employ the same strategy, they end up in a stalemate, circling each other, waiting for the other to reveal their position. The danger is twofold: Either the negotiations fizzle out completely, or they devolve into arguing over trivial details, creating unnecessary conflict.

Note: To avoid this trap, you must understand that negotiation is a process of give and take. To gain something, you must be willing to give something in return. If you want the opponent to share information, consider what you can offer in exchange. Someone has to take the first step toward openness. This requires careful preparation—understand where you can afford to open up and where you must hold back. Transparency should always be strategic; revealing everything leaves you vulnerable.

For example, if you can save $10,000 by getting a delivery a month earlier, think about how to present this. You could:

- Wait to see if the opponent raises the issue.
- Bring it up as part of a broader discussion: "Let's move on to delivery times. I see the offer states November 15—do you have any comments on that?"
- Mention competitors to signal flexibility: "One of your competitors asked if an earlier delivery would be possible. Is this something we should consider?"
- Send a signal that you're considering both price and value: "Your price is a bit higher, but if you can deliver earlier, that will offset some of the cost."
- Make a concrete offer: "If you can meet the earlier delivery, we can share some of the profit with you—say, a $2,000 bonus."

Negotiation is about trust, and trust is built through open, strategic exchanges.

They Work Unstructured

Many negotiators approach negotiations without a clear structure or agenda. They skip essential steps like using joint notes or summarizing key points, which causes the process to jump around from one issue to the next without any real focus. This lack of organization—stemming from poor preparation, insecurity, or a weak negotiation technique—results in a disjointed discussion where neither side can clearly see the potential deal or the opportunities at hand. This confusion can leave the opponent uncertain about the negotiator's true intentions.

> **Note:** To avoid this trap, preparation is key. Negotiators must invest more time into planning and create a clear agenda for the discussion. Before moving on to the next topic, always summarize the current one and take joint notes to ensure everyone is on the same page. Regular breaks should be used to check if the group is staying on track and to agree on a unified approach.

Though this process may feel rigid or overly formal, this discipline is crucial. Once you master it, you can confidently improvise while still maintaining control of the negotiation.

They Have Not Distributed the Roles Within the Group

In many negotiations, the lack of clearly defined roles within the negotiating team can lead to chaos and missed opportunities. Without a structured division of responsibilities, team members can send mixed messages, confuse the opponent, and inadvertently undermine their own position. This is especially true when team members start negotiating with one another in front of the opponent or take the lead in areas outside of their expertise.

A common scenario occurs when a negotiation leader is not clearly established. Team members often assume that the highest-ranking individual should automatically lead, but negotiation leadership requires more than just authority. It requires the ability to communicate effectively, stay focused, and manage the flow of conversation. When roles aren't clearly defined, an expert might jump in with technical details that undermine the broader strategy. For example, in one case, a systems expert eagerly offered a solution to a customer's problem before the negotiation leader had the chance to formulate an appropriate response, giving away valuable insights without securing compensation.

> **Note:** To avoid these pitfalls, it's crucial to assign clear roles from the outset:
>
> - **Negotiation leader:** This person should be the one best suited for communication and strategy, not necessarily the highest-ranked person. The leader is responsible for directing the conversation, making key decisions, and ensuring that the negotiation stays on track.
> - **Listener and observer:** Appoint someone with experience in negotiations to sit slightly removed from the table, taking notes and monitoring the negotiation dynamics. This person should provide ongoing analysis of the negotiation's progress, reactions from the opponent, and suggest adjustments as needed.
> - **Economics manager:** This person is responsible for keeping track of what's being given away, what's been gained, and ensuring that the financial aspects of the deal are in line with the team's goals. They help the group maintain a clear focus on the bigger picture and prevent minor concessions from spiraling out of control.
> - **Experts:** Experts should only contribute when their specific knowledge is required. It's vital that they don't jump in prematurely or without direction because this can derail the negotiation. Internal communication protocols should be established, such as signaling the negotiation leader before anyone speaks.

- **Internal communication:** Ensure that before anyone speaks besides the negotiation leader, they receive a signal or permission to do so. This helps maintain control and consistency during the negotiation.
- **Strategic breaks:** If at any point the negotiation is hitting a wall, the team should agree to pause. A break allows for a reassessment of strategies, regrouping, and refocusing before crucial decisions are made.

By clearly defining each person's role and sticking to the agreed structure, a negotiation team can present a united front, improve communication, and ultimately increase their chances of a successful outcome.

They Are Afraid of Bargaining

Bargaining is often the Achilles' heel for many negotiators. The fear of conflict and discomfort with the bargaining phase can bring negotiations to a standstill. Instead of engaging in productive offers and counteroffers, some negotiators avoid clear decisions and fall into the trap of vague, generalized arguments. They keep repeating known points without moving forward or making any headway. This reluctance to enter the bargaining process often stems from the discomfort of having to reconcile conflicting views of what a reasonable offer looks like.

As the deadline approaches, the pressure to conclude the negotiation leads to hasty decisions. The famous "ketchup effect" occurs: Negotiations, which had been stalling, suddenly pick up speed, but the result is rushed and often unclear. The parties involved may sign an agreement without fully knowing if it falls within their authorized limits or addresses the key concerns of both sides.

Note: To avoid falling into this trap, here's what should have been done:

- **Better preparation:** Negotiators must prepare in advance, considering what an appropriate opening offer looks like and how to structure their bargaining strategy. For instance, they might say, "Presuming a significant price reduction, we can offer an advance payment." They need to clarify what they mean by a "significant" reduction, and establish their own thresholds—e.g., if they want a 9 percent return, they might start by demanding 11.5 percent, knowing they can settle for 7.5 percent if necessary.
- **Establish a timetable:** The preparation should also include a timetable that sets clear goals, defines limits, and helps assess each counteroffer effectively. This timetable is an excellent tool to guide the bargaining process and avoid rash decisions at the last minute.

- **Change their ideas about bargaining:** The fear of making an offer is often rooted in negative perceptions of bargaining as a "nasty" process. This view must be changed. Bargaining is a natural and necessary part of negotiations, and it's essential for achieving a mutually acceptable deal.
- **Start early:** Bargaining should begin as early as possible in the negotiation. Early engagement allows for more room to maneuver, making it easier to adjust and refine offers as the discussion progresses.
- **Plan for breaks:** It's important to build time for breaks into the negotiation process. During these breaks, the team can step back, evaluate the opponent's offers, and decide on their own counteroffers with a clearer mind and more strategic insight.

By embracing the process of bargaining—starting early, making offers and counteroffers, and staying well prepared—negotiators can avoid the pitfalls of fear and hesitation. This structured approach ensures a more controlled, effective negotiation process where both parties can reach a fair and workable agreement.

They Do Not Set Up a Strategy

Many negotiators fail to approach an agreement with a clear, methodical strategy. Instead, they tend to improvise, lacking a clear understanding of when to stop arguing and start exploring the negotiation possibilities. They are unsure whether to make an overall offer that covers all aspects of the agreement or to tackle each issue separately. This lack of clarity leads to unstructured negotiations, where confusion and frustration set in, preventing creative problem-solving.

One of the most common pitfalls in this situation is not distinguishing when to show openness and search for the NegoEconomics (the value exchange in negotiations) versus when to adopt a tougher stance to distribute the NegoEconomics effectively. They also fail to discuss the pros and cons of being the first to make an overall offer versus waiting for the opponent to do so. Without this strategic awareness, negotiations often devolve into verbal battles, with neither side moving closer to a win-win solution.

As tensions rise, negotiators may find themselves in a locked situation where stress and insecurity mount. At this point, they often face a choice: either make one-sided concessions (which weakens their position) or fight, turning the negotiation into a zero-sum game. Those who choose to fight, ignoring the potential for creative alternatives, fail to use NegoEconomics effectively and miss the opportunity to build a more collaborative agreement.

Note: To avoid falling into this trap, here's what should have been done:
- **Better preparation:** Negotiators need to spend more time preparing a clear, step-by-step strategy for how they can work toward an

agreement. This includes understanding the sequence of actions to take, knowing when to make offers, when to move on to new points, and when to pause for reflection. Having a roadmap in place reduces improvisation and ensures the negotiation progresses logically.
- **Develop a strategic plan:** The strategy may take various forms, depending on the nature of the negotiation and the issues at hand. For example, they could choose to make a comprehensive initial offer that sets the tone for the negotiations or opt for a more incremental approach, addressing issues one by one. Regardless of the form, it's essential that they define their approach before entering the negotiation room.
- **Recognize the value of NegoEconomics:** A successful negotiation requires flexibility—knowing when to engage in tough bargaining and when to seek creative, mutually beneficial solutions. By distinguishing between these two phases and adopting a strategic mindset, negotiators can maximize the value they gain from the negotiation.
- **Avoid the fight-or-flight response:** When stress sets in, rather than panicking and either making one-sided concessions or falling into combative tactics, take a break to regroup and re-strategize. A calm, structured approach is key to moving past locked situations and arriving at an agreement that benefits both sides.

By implementing these strategies, negotiators can avoid falling into the trap of unstructured, reactive negotiations. A well-thought-out strategy allows for greater control, more effective problem-solving, and a stronger ability to reach agreements that meet both parties' needs.

They Lose Their Grip on the Economy

One of the most critical mistakes negotiators make is losing track of the economic aspects of the deal. After an hour or so into the negotiation, they often no longer know where they stand in relation to their own pain threshold or their ultimate negotiation goal. As a result, they risk agreeing to terms that fall outside their acceptable budget, either overestimating or underestimating their position. They enter into multiple partial agreements without considering how each one impacts the overall deal. This leads to hasty decisions, which could have negative financial implications.

This happens for a variety of reasons: speed-blindness (rushing without reflecting), insecurity, or simply a lack of a clear strategy. Another common issue is the absence of a designated person within the negotiation team responsible for managing and calculating the financial aspects of the deal.

Even when teams consist of several experienced professionals, such as engineers or business graduates, the stress of the negotiation often leads them to lose track of basic calculations. The pressure to perform under time constraints can overwhelm even the most qualified individuals, making it difficult to make informed decisions.

Stress exacerbates this issue as negotiators struggle to maintain an overview of the negotiations. Without a clear picture of the deal's financial landscape, they fall into the trap of simplifying their offers to make them easily comparable. Buyers often press suppliers by insisting on comparing offers that are "apples to apples," but in doing so they ignore the broader picture of the negotiation and lose sight of the complexity of the overall deal.

Note: To avoid this trap, negotiators should implement the following practices:

- **Designate a financial overseer:** Appoint a specific individual within the team whose job it is to keep track of the financials and calculations. This person will ensure that the team has a clear understanding of how each change or concession affects the overall economy of the deal. This responsibility must not be left to chance.
- **Take breaks for reflection:** When the stress begins to mount, it is crucial to pause and step back. Take a break from the negotiations to analyze the changes and their impact on the overall deal without the pressure of the opponent's presence. This time allows the team to recalculate, reassess their position, and make decisions with clarity.
- **Utilize the timetable for structure:** Having a structured timetable will give negotiators an overview of where they are in the process and how far they've come. The timetable provides a strategic way to organize different aspects of the deal, ensuring that financial calculations are not lost in the rush of decision-making.

By staying disciplined and implementing these strategies, negotiators can regain control of the economic aspects of the deal, avoid hasty decisions, and ensure they achieve a result that is within their budget and aligned with their goals.

They Make Insultingly Low Offers

One of the most damaging negotiation tactics is to present insultingly low offers, often stemming from stinginess, poor preparation, and a lack of understanding about what a reasonable offer should look like to the other party. Some negotiators overestimate their power, thinking they can start with a low offer and then back down to a more reasonable level.

The expectation is that the other party will feel like they've "won" the negotiation by meeting halfway.

This strategy may succeed if the negotiator is inexperienced or the opponent is weak and has no alternatives. However, it usually backfires—making the other party feel disrespected and likely to walk away. Even if they stay, they're often defensive, and the negotiation loses its constructive potential. The NegoEconomics, or the exchange of value, is not achieved.

Note: To avoid this trap, negotiators should:

- **Focus on partnership:** Insultingly low offers belong in a bazaar, not in professional negotiations aimed at establishing a productive partnership. Strive to build trust and find fair, mutually beneficial terms.
- **Put yourself in their shoes:** Before making an offer, consider how you would react if you received it. This perspective helps gauge what's reasonable and fair.

By adopting a more cooperative and empathetic approach, negotiators can foster a more productive dialogue that leads to a stronger partnership.

They Do Not Accept That the Opponent Makes Money

A common mistake in negotiations is turning down advantageous propositions simply because they feel unfair or because they don't want the opponent to profit. Take the example of a company facing a potential $500,000 loss in a legal dispute. The mediator offers to settle the case for $300,000, with a contingency fee based on the savings, but the client objects, claiming it's unreasonable to pay such a high fee, even though the alternative is far worse.

This reaction is driven by the desire to avoid feeling "taken advantage of." However, the focus should not be on the opponent's profit but on the value of the outcome for both parties. By not looking at the second-best alternative—facing a potential $500,000 loss—the client fails to see the bigger picture.

Note: To avoid this trap, negotiators should:

- **Evaluate the alternatives:** Always compare the proposition at hand to your second-best option. If the current offer brings a better outcome than the alternative, it's worth considering, even if the opponent benefits.
- **Swallow your ego:** Recognize that it's okay for the opponent to make a profit, especially if it means securing a better deal for yourself. Avoid letting personal feelings of unfairness cloud your judgment.

By focusing on the overall value and not on the opponent's profit, negotiators can make better decisions that lead to more successful outcomes.

They Seek "Fair" Solutions

Failing negotiators often become obsessed with fairness, not as a principle, but as a tool to justify their demands, ignoring that true fairness emerges from collaborative value creation rather than rigid adherence to subjective or self-serving standards.

They Are Not Good at Listening

Negotiators who fail to listen often miss crucial openings and valuable information that could shape a more successful outcome. Sticking rigidly to their own plan without being open to new perspectives or feedback can lead to missed opportunities. Fear of listening can stem from insecurity or the risk of having to reconsider their approach, which feels uncomfortable.

Note: To avoid this trap, negotiators should:

- **Designate a listener:** Choose one person in the group specifically tasked with listening. This individual should master the art of truly listening—not just passively hearing, but actively absorbing what the opponent says to identify new possibilities.
- **Embrace uncertainty:** Understand that you don't have all the answers. Listening creates space for fresh insights, and new information could reveal opportunities that were previously unseen.

By prioritizing listening, negotiators can expand their view and unlock better solutions, turning uncertainty into an advantage.

Preparing to Avoid Failure

For many negotiators who struggle, the issue often lies in their approach to preparation and analysis. They must become more proactive, focusing their energy on mapping out negotiation possibilities, embracing bargaining rather than engaging in endless arguments, and improving their communicative skills. However, theoretical knowledge alone is insufficient for mastering negotiation. Practical exercises and real negotiations are essential for developing these skills.

Not everyone will naturally become a strong negotiator, and some may need others to negotiate on their behalf. There's a significant gap between theoretical understanding and practical ability, which often comes as a surprise. At the beginning of training courses, participants may agree with the advice given, unaware of the pitfalls ahead. But once they engage in their first negotiation exercise, the reality proves challenging.

Despite hours of preparation, many find themselves unprepared for the complexities at the negotiation table—technical standards, strategic choices, time pressures, and more. This highlights the disconnect between theoretical knowledge and real-world application.

The responsibility of the CEO and management is clear: The organization's structure and bookkeeping must ensure transparency and prevent manipulation. Negotiation practices should be revised, and employees must be better educated, especially in commercial matters. Unfortunately, time pressures in lean organizations often mean employees, without sufficient experience or training, are thrust into negotiations without the necessary skills. The negotiation competency of employees remains insufficient, reflecting the same gaps seen 20 years ago.

Other Common Mistakes in Negotiation

This section outlines other common mistakes to avoid, not otherwise covered in previous sections:

- The personal contact is forgotten.
- They do not understand the opponent.
- They insult the opponent.
- They forget the other interested parties.
- Cost savings within one link are eaten up by problems in another link.
- Exaggerated suspiciousness is present.
- There is a sense of stinginess.
- They guard preserves.
- Political value norms influence the situation.
- Envy impacts the process.
- Cultural differences affect the situation.
- The "we-versus-them" feeling hinders the negotiation.

The Personal Contact Is Forgotten

In many negotiations, the personal touch is often neglected, leading to misunderstandings and missed opportunities. When communication is reduced to merely exchanging offers and inquiries, key details can be lost. Suppliers might reject offers solely based on the price, while buyers may dismiss solutions that don't align with their expectations, without fully understanding the rationale behind them.

Written communication, no matter how precise, can never replace the clarity that personal contact offers. A single text, even something as straightforward as a technical specification, can be interpreted in countless ways. Take, for example, a specification that reads, "The machine capacity must be 100 pieces per minute." On the surface, it appears clear, but in reality, questions arise: Is the "must be" a firm requirement or just a preference? Does capacity refer to normal or maximum output? How was the 100-pieces-per-minute figure derived? Is it based on current capacity or future needs? These nuances can only be explored through direct conversation, not written communication.

By not engaging personally, many suppliers miss the chance to tailor their offers to the buyer's actual needs. They may never fully understand why their proposal was rejected, only to hear, "We thought the others made a better offer." But the truth is that the buyer may have already adjusted their project plans, leaving the supplier in the dark about how they could have met the buyer's real needs. This lack of personal contact limits both sides and results in missed opportunities.

They Do Not Understand the Opponent

Cultural clashes can occur even between individuals from similar backgrounds, whether it's the entrepreneur clashing with the cautious economist, or the bureaucrat butting heads with the self-employed businessperson. These misunderstandings often become apparent during high-stakes negotiations, especially when the pressure is on.

For instance, we've been called into negotiations where clients described their opponents in terms like "They just don't get what we're dealing with. We see huge potential here, but they're more focused on consolidating their positions." Or "They argue over every detail, as if it's about prestige rather than progress." These frustrations are not always about technical or economic disagreements, but about an inability to understand each other's perspectives.

Often, the root of these issues is poor communication or an incompatible personality dynamic. If the human chemistry between negotiators is off, even the most reasonable terms may fail. When we are unable to see the other side's viewpoint, misunderstandings escalate into emotional reactions, which cloud our ability to negotiate constructively.

It's crucial to separate the person from the issue at hand. A controller may question a cost estimate, but that doesn't mean they're attacking your competence—it's their job. The way we respond matters. Instead of reacting emotionally, a more thoughtful approach like "I see great potential in this project, but how can we be sure that . . ." can ease tension and keep the conversation productive.

In many cases, both sides lack the communication skills to manage the negotiation. Criticism is perceived as a personal attack, and the emotional response becomes so overwhelming that the negotiation stalls. Here, an external mediator can play a critical role by staying neutral and helping both parties focus on the facts, rather than personal grievances. Ultimately, successful negotiations are as much about understanding human dynamics as they are about the technical and economic details.

They Insult the Opponent

In many high-stakes negotiations, negotiators often inflate their own efforts, risks, and costs while downplaying those of the opponent. This often comes from a need to project strength, especially in front of employees or supporters, and it's something we see frequently in political settings. The problem arises when these inflated positions inadvertently insult the opponent.

Negotiators who operate from a position of power often don't realize how their words can come across as dismissive or insulting. For instance, phrases like "We don't see why you should have insight into our calculations; you're just a sub-supplier," or "Any of your competitors can do this, so why should we choose you?" undermine the opponent and are often delivered without thought to the emotional impact. These comments can shut down dialogue, making it difficult to move forward productively.

The key mistake here is the failure to consider how the opponent perceives the conversation. Often, the insult isn't deliberate but stems from aggressive language or an unwillingness to engage with the opponent's ideas respectfully. For example, saying, "You're wrong; this won't work" is not constructive. A more diplomatic response would be, "That's an interesting idea, but have you thought about how to address the heat generation issue?" This keeps the focus on the solution, not on criticizing the person presenting it.

The risk of insulting the opponent becomes even greater when emotions run high, as seen in the failed merger talks between Telia and Telenor, where political value norms created unnecessary conflict. In these situations, it's important to recognize that frustration and stress can lead to emotional outbursts, which only escalate tensions. Experienced negotiators know when to stay silent and avoid letting personal frustrations leak out. The goal is to manage your words and focus on finding solutions, not to let insults cloud the negotiation process.

They Forget the Other Interested Parties

In the rush to reach a deal at the negotiation table, it's easy to focus solely on the immediate parties involved. However, it's crucial to consider the broader impact on all stakeholders. While confidentiality is often necessary during negotiations, overlooking the influence of other interested parties can create significant problems down the line.

Ask yourself: How will employees, customers, suppliers, banks, owners, authorities, or even the media respond to the deal? If they view it negatively, resistance can quickly build and jeopardize the success of the agreement. For example, the Volvo/Renault merger failed partly due to strong opposition from the shareholders' national union.

To avoid this, engage these groups early. Address their concerns and bring them on board to ensure the deal not only meets its business goals but also has the necessary support for long-term success.

Cost Savings Within One Link Are Eaten Up by Problems in Another

A Swedish car manufacturer once sought to reduce production costs per car by shifting the final quality control to the customer. The idea was simple: Move the last production stage to garages, letting customers discover and report defects within the warranty period. The car was only considered fully delivered after 10,000 km, once all defects were corrected. However, the manufacturer failed to inform customers or seek their consent. The entire strategy backfired.

Customers were frustrated, and garages took advantage, inventing defects and inflating repair costs. The reputation of the brand suffered, and the quality of service was questioned. This shortsighted approach to cost-saving ultimately hurt the manufacturer more than it helped.

A similar issue is visible in the public healthcare systems of Sweden and Denmark. Politicians and bureaucrats praised economies of scale but failed to see the broader consequences. The public health service grew into a massive, inefficient system that swallowed more money while providing fewer services. The result? Not only are resources wasted, but patients suffer from delays, poor treatment, and in some cases unnecessary deaths.

By focusing solely on cost-cutting in one area, the true costs—like human suffering, burned-out staff, and greater long-term expenses—were ignored. This lack of a holistic perspective can have devastating effects, as demonstrated by both the car manufacturer's failure and the public healthcare crisis.

Exaggerated Suspiciousness Is Present

While it's important to trust your instincts in business—especially when something seems too good to be true—exaggerated suspiciousness can be just as harmful as naivety. If a proposition raises red flags, take the time to evaluate the facts carefully. It's wise to sleep on it and make sure all the details are on the table.

However, assuming that everyone is trying to deceive or cheat you is a dangerous mindset. Constantly signaling mistrust can drive away potential partners who may otherwise be honest and willing to collaborate. A healthy balance of caution and trust is key to successful negotiations and partnerships.

There Is a Sense of Stinginess

A stingy negotiator undermines the opponent's legitimate need for a fair share, often leading to frustration and feelings of being disrespected. This creates an atmosphere where the opponent no longer feels like an equal partner. It's even worse if the stingy negotiator tries to justify their approach by claiming it's a fair distribution, which only adds insult.

Successful partnerships are built on mutual understanding and consideration of both parties' interests. Negotiators must be open about their situation to foster trust and create NegoEconomics that benefit both sides. However, they also need to challenge the boundaries and avoid giving away more than necessary.

The key is balance: avoiding both naivety and stinginess. We should regularly ask ourselves, "How would the opponent react to this offer?" The time spent pushing for small concessions often doesn't lead to worthwhile gains and may ultimately drive the other party to walk away and seek new partners.

They Guard Preserves

Consider the situation where a district nurse identifies an infection in a patient's leg sore and determines that antibiotics are needed. However, instead of prescribing the medication herself, she is required to contact the doctor, who hasn't even seen the patient, to issue the prescription. This unnecessary step adds cost and delays the treatment process, despite the nurse being fully qualified to handle the situation herself.

The real issue here is not a lack of knowledge or expertise but the way responsibilities are jealously guarded within the system. Many professionals resist any redistribution of tasks or decision-making, and this "guarding of preserves" is a common barrier to more efficient and patient-centered care. The result is an organization that wastes time and resources, not because of financial constraints, but because of an unwillingness to delegate or trust others to take on responsibilities.

Ultimately, the solution is not just more funding but addressing these organizational inefficiencies and breaking down unnecessary silos of control.

Political Value Norms Influence the Situation

It's often shown that treatment at private clinics can be more cost-effective than in the public healthcare system. However, political value norms and the reluctance to challenge existing structures often prevent the public sector from becoming more efficient. While scandals, long waiting lists, and election-year pressures occasionally push for reforms, these changes are often driven by political ideals rather than practical solutions.

The real issue lies in the inability to look at the situation holistically—prioritizing patient outcomes and cost-effectiveness over entrenched political beliefs. It's crucial to accept that private practitioners can make profits while providing a more efficient service. Instead of clinging to ideological values, we need to consider what works best for patients and society as a whole.

In the private sector, outsourcing is a widely accepted practice where the best-suited party handles specific tasks. The same approach should be applied to the public sector: Focus resources on core competencies, and allow others to handle tasks that they can perform more effectively. This kind of efficiency mindset is vital for making healthcare, and businesses in general, more sustainable and effective.

Envy Impacts the Process

In many public sectors, including healthcare, envy can manifest in counterproductive ways. For instance, despite long waiting lists for treatment, employees—including highly skilled doctors and psychologists—are often tasked with nonmedical duties like making coffee, cleaning, or watering plants. This serves no productive purpose but reflects a deeper resentment: Those in positions of authority or higher expertise must occasionally "pay their dues" by taking on menial tasks.

This mindset is driven by envy, where individuals feel the need to bring others down to their level rather than focusing on the collective goal of improving patient care. In more extreme examples, such as the former Soviet Union, even highly educated professionals like professors and doctors were required to perform manual labor like bricklaying, simply because they were perceived as "privileged."

Instead of allowing envy to undermine efficiency and focus, we must recognize that each person's role—whether administrative, medical, or otherwise—should be valued for its contribution to the overall system. Rather than penalizing those with more expertise, we should empower all employees to focus on their strengths to improve the service as a whole.

Cultural Differences Affect the Situation

In negotiations involving parties from different cultural backgrounds, the risk of misunderstandings, insults, and mutual distrust rises significantly. Successful negotiators must be aware of these cultural differences and learn to navigate them. For instance, during the merger talks between Telia and Telenor, the cultural divide between Norway and Sweden—coupled with differences between businesspeople and politicians—ultimately led to the failure of the deal. Even seasoned negotiators made critical errors, triggering value norm conflicts that escalated tensions and made cooperation impossible.

Our experience from thousands of negotiations highlights a key truth: Without strong personal chemistry between the negotiators, long-term cooperation becomes nearly impossible. Instead of collaborating to achieve mutual benefits, the focus shifts to conflict, with each side trying to win at the other's expense.

We've all encountered meetings where the connection was instant, or conversely, where the atmosphere felt hostile from the start. What drives this? It's personal chemistry. When meeting someone new, we instinctively interpret nonverbal cues—our eyes, nose, and ears help us form an impression within seconds. Our past experiences, knowledge, and biases shape these impressions. However, it's important to recognize that our reactions often say more about us than about the other person. Should we trust our gut instincts, or should we challenge our preconceived opinions and allow others a fair chance? The answers to these questions are critical in determining the outcome of any negotiation.

The "We-versus-Them" Feeling Hinders the Negotiation

The "we-versus-them" feeling in negotiation fosters division and mistrust, creating an adversarial mindset that shifts the focus away from problem-solving and mutual benefit. This polarization often leads to defensive behaviors, reduced transparency, and a reluctance to explore creative solutions. By viewing the counterpart as an opponent rather than a partner, negotiators limit opportunities to build trust and uncover shared interests, ultimately jeopardizing long-term relationships and the potential for value creation. Addressing this mindset requires a shift toward collaborative frameworks, such as SMARTnership, which emphasize alignment, transparency, and joint problem-solving.

Leveraging AI for Negotiation Insights

AI has the potential to revolutionize the way negotiations are conducted by providing data-driven insights that enhance decision-making. By analyzing historical data, trends, and real-time negotiation factors, AI can predict outcomes and suggest strategies. Using machine learning algorithms, AI can simulate various negotiation scenarios, helping negotiators explore different approaches and anticipate responses. This empowers negotiators to be better prepared, optimize their strategy, and ultimately improve their chances of securing favorable deals.

AI tools can be incredibly useful for negotiators when prompted correctly. Here are a few examples of how negotiators can use AI to support their negotiations:

- **Analyzing contract language:** AI can assess contract language for ambiguous terms, identify opportunities to reduce costs, and flag potential legal or operational risks.

    Prompt: "Analyze this contract and highlight potential areas for cost savings or risks."

- **Suggesting counteroffers:** AI can evaluate delivery schedules and propose alternatives that optimize mutual benefits based on the negotiating parties' priorities and constraints.

    Prompt: "Provide alternative delivery schedules that maximize NegoEconomic benefits for both parties."

- **Simulating scenarios:** AI can provide insights into how various negotiation strategies might play out, helping negotiators understand the most likely outcomes and adjust their approach accordingly.

    Prompt: "Simulate different negotiation scenarios based on historical data and predict possible outcomes."

- **Risk assessment:** By analyzing data, AI can identify areas where the negotiation strategy might be vulnerable and recommend ways to minimize risk.

    Prompt: "Assess the potential risks in a negotiation strategy and suggest mitigation steps."

By leveraging AI in these ways, negotiators can gain a competitive edge, improve their preparation, and increase their chances of achieving successful outcomes.

PART III

The Future of Negotiation: AI, Psychology, and Advanced

This final section, covering Chapters 12–20, explores the cutting-edge transformation of negotiation, driven by artificial intelligence, cognitive biases, real-time analytics, and innovative frameworks. As negotiation moves beyond traditional human intuition into AI-assisted decision-making, this part equips you with the tools to leverage AI while maintaining human trust, strategic control, and psychological awareness.

Chapter 12 provides a practical guide to creating AI prompts tailored to negotiation. Effective prompts maximize AI's potential, allowing negotiators to streamline processes, analyze counterparty behavior, and optimize decision-making in real time.

Chapter 13 examines how AI enhances human insight without replacing the critical elements of empathy, intuition, and judgment. This chapter introduces the Four Pillars of Human-AI Synergy, ensuring that AI serves as a strategic partner rather than a substitute for relational intelligence.

Chapter 14 delves into AI as a negotiator's ally, exploring how tools like ChatGPT enhance preparation, strategy design, real-time decision-making, and emotional intelligence. AI is no longer just an analytical tool—it is an interactive assistant that supports every phase of the negotiation process.

Chapter 15 analyzes how AI is redefining contract creation and interpretation. From simplifying legal language to identifying risk and ensuring compliance, AI is transforming contract writing from a slow, cumbersome process into a dynamic and efficient strategic asset.

Chapter 16 presents findings from a major AI negotiation experiment, conducted in collaboration with Tim Cummins and World Commerce & Contracting. The results reveal how AI influences negotiation efficiency, behavioral dynamics, and strategic outcomes, showcasing the advantages and challenges of integrating AI into negotiations.

Chapter 17 explores real-time AI feedback, a game-changer in modern negotiations. AI can now analyze live conversations, assess emotional cues, and suggest tactical adjustments in real time, giving negotiators an unprecedented edge.

Chapter 18 warns of the dangers of *authority bias,* where negotiators blindly trust AI-generated recommendations without critical evaluation. This chapter provides strategies to ensure AI remains a tool for enhancement, not an unquestioned authority, emphasizing the need for balanced human judgment.

Chapter 19 focuses on the power of AI-generated prompts, showing how structured questions guide negotiations toward productive outcomes. Well-designed prompts allow AI to provide insights, strategic recommendations, and tailored responses that maximize value creation.

Chapter 20 examines AI's long-term impact on negotiation dynamics, including its role in automated deal-making, predictive analytics, and ethical concerns. While AI dramatically enhances efficiency, it also raises new challenges related to trust, fairness, and strategic transparency.

Together, these chapters provide a comprehensive roadmap for mastering AI-driven negotiation while maintaining the essential human qualities of trust, creativity, and relational intelligence. The future of negotiation is not just about technology—it is about the powerful synergy between AI and human expertise.

CHAPTER 12

Creating AI Prompts for Negotiation-Specific Tasks

We live in a time when technology can do more than assist us—it can transform how we work and negotiate. From streamlining daily tasks to uncovering new opportunities in complex discussions, AI has become an indispensable tool for professionals aiming to achieve more with less effort.

This chapter is your guide to harnessing AI, particularly tools like ChatGPT, to enhance your everyday productivity and negotiation strategies. Whether writing an email, organizing a schedule, or applying principles like NegoEconomics and Tru$tCurrency to create added value, AI can amplify your efficiency and effectiveness.

> **Note:** ChatGPT is the AI tool I have used the most. It is very knowledgeable about the SMARTnership concept. Other options include Microsoft Copilot and Meta AI.

An AI prompt is a structured or open-ended input provided to an AI system, like ChatGPT, that generates a specific response or performs a task. It acts as a starting point that guides the AI's output, enabling it to produce text, solve problems, generate ideas, or assist with complex tasks. Well-crafted prompts ensure clarity and relevance in the AI's responses.

The following table includes practical examples and tailored prompts designed to save time and improve results, helping you stay focused on what truly matters. Integrating AI into your workflow and negotiations can unlock new potential, align with the SMARTnership approach, and create outcomes that benefit everyone involved.

CHAPTER 12 Creating AI Prompts for Negotiation-Specific Tasks

Task	AI Prompt
Negotiation Strategy Outline	"Draft a negotiation strategy for this scenario: [insert scenario]. Include key goals, potential concessions, counterarguments, and tactics."
Counteroffer Preparation	"Help me prepare a counteroffer for this proposal: [insert proposal]. Suggest how to reframe the offer to achieve better terms."
Role-Playing Practice	"Act as the opposing party in this negotiation scenario: [describe scenario]. Respond to my offers and counter-arguments to simulate a real negotiation."
Concession Mapping	"Create a list of potential concessions I could make in this negotiation: [insert context]. Rank them by impact to me and perceived value to the other party."
Cultural Sensitivity Guidance	"Provide tips for negotiating with [insert country or culture]. Highlight key etiquette, communication styles, and negotiation norms."
Agenda Preparation	"Draft an agenda for an upcoming negotiation meeting on [insert topic]. Include time allocations for each key issue and space for a final agreement summary."
Mock Q&A for Negotiation	"Provide a list of potential questions the other party might ask during this negotiation: [insert topic]. Suggest strong, concise responses for each."
BATNA Analysis	"Help me evaluate my Best Alternative to a Negotiated Agreement (BATNA) for this negotiation: [insert context]. Suggest ways to strengthen it."
Scenario Planning	"Create a 'what-if' plan for this negotiation: [insert context]. Include best-case, worst-case, and most likely outcomes, with strategies for each."
Conflict Resolution Tips	"Provide a step-by-step guide for resolving potential deadlocks or conflicts in this negotiation: [insert context]. Focus on maintaining collaboration."
SMARTnership Preparation	"Assist me in preparing for a SMARTnership negotiation. Identify mutual benefits, shared goals, and strategies for creating added value."
Negotiation Style Analysis	"Analyze my counterpart's potential negotiation style based on this information: [insert context]. Suggest how I can adapt my approach to match."
NegoEconomic Value Identification	"Identify potential NegoEconomic value in this negotiation: [insert context]. Highlight cost-saving opportunities or ways to create mutual gains."

Creating AI Prompts for Negotiation-Specific Tasks

Task	AI Prompt
Message Framing for Proposals	"Draft a persuasive opening statement for this negotiation: [insert context]. Focus on framing my proposal as mutually beneficial."
Post-Negotiation Review	"Create a checklist for reviewing the outcome of a negotiation. Focus on lessons learned, unmet objectives, and opportunities for improvement."
Data Presentation for Negotiations	"Help me format this data [insert data] into a clear, visually compelling chart or table for presentation during negotiations."
Objection Handling	"List common objections I might face during this negotiation: [insert context]. Provide effective ways to address each objection."
Negotiation Notes Summary	"Summarize these negotiation notes: [insert notes]. Highlight key agreements, action items, and follow-up points."
Trial Balloon Suggestions	"Suggest hypothetical proposals or trial balloons I could introduce during this negotiation to gather insights without committing."
Win-Loss Reflection	"Guide me through a win-loss reflection for this recent negotiation: [insert context]. Identify what worked, what didn't, and how to improve next time."
Negotiation Role Assignment	"Help me assign roles for my negotiation team: [insert team details]. Match roles like lead negotiator, notetaker, and analyst based on their strengths and ensure alignment with NegoEconomic principles to maximize value asymmetry."
Scenario-Based Preparation	"Create a negotiation role-play scenario based on this context: [insert scenario]. Include how Tru$tCurrency can be leveraged to build rapport and identify opportunities for NegoEconomic value creation."
Objection Reframing	"Suggest ways to reframe these objections: [insert objections]. Highlight how to use NegoEconomics to demonstrate asymmetric value and Tru$tCurrency to reassure the counterpart."
Negotiation Playbook Creation	"Draft a negotiation playbook for this upcoming project: [insert project details]. Include sections on leveraging NegoEconomics, building Tru$tCurrency, identifying trade-offs, and maximizing mutual gains."

CHAPTER 12 Creating AI Prompts for Negotiation-Specific Tasks

Task	AI Prompt
Concession Trade-Off Mapping	"List possible trade-offs I can propose in this negotiation: [insert context]. Suggest how to present them using Tru$tCurrency to enhance credibility and NegoEconomics to emphasize mutual benefits."
Trust Building Strategy	"Suggest strategies for building Tru$tCurrency with my counterpart in this negotiation: [insert context]. Focus on transparency, shared goals, and demonstrating goodwill."
Breaking Deadlocks	"Provide specific techniques for breaking a negotiation deadlock in this scenario: [insert context]. Highlight collaborative solutions rooted in NegoEconomics and enhanced by Tru$tCurrency."
Proposal Comparison Framework	"Help me create a comparison framework for evaluating multiple proposals in this negotiation: [insert proposals]. Include metrics for Tru$tCurrency and NegoEconomic value to prioritize long-term gains."
Stress Testing Agreements	"Develop questions to stress test this draft agreement: [insert draft]. Ensure it holds up under NegoEconomic scrutiny and builds Tru$tCurrency with the counterpart."
Cost-Benefit Visualization	"Create a visual representation of the cost-benefit analysis for this negotiation: [insert details]. Highlight NegoEconomic asymmetries and Tru$tCurrency-building opportunities."
Ethical Negotiation Guidance	"Provide ethical considerations for this negotiation: [insert context]. Highlight practices that build Tru$tCurrency and preserve long-term value creation through NegoEconomics."
Cultural Adaptation Strategy	"Design a cultural adaptation strategy for negotiating with [insert culture]. Include ways to build Tru$tCurrency and tailor NegoEconomic principles to the cultural context."
Multi-Party Negotiation Plan	"Help me create a strategy for negotiating with multiple parties: [insert details]. Include coordination tips and ways to align NegoEconomic goals and Tru$tCurrency-building efforts across parties."
Time Management in Negotiations	"Suggest ways to manage time effectively during this negotiation: [insert details]. Focus on prioritizing NegoEconomic opportunities and building Tru$tCurrency efficiently."

Task	AI Prompt
Negotiation Closure Strategy	"Help me prepare a strong closing strategy for this negotiation: [insert context]. Focus on securing commitments, Tru$tCurrency, and NegoEconomic value."
Real-Time Negotiation Coaching	"Act as my real-time negotiation coach. If my counterpart says [insert statement], how should I respond to align with NegoEconomic principles and maintain Tru$tCurrency?"
Power Dynamics Assessment	"Analyze the power dynamics in this negotiation scenario: [insert details]. Suggest strategies to leverage Tru$tCurrency and NegoEconomic asymmetries."
Emotion Management Plan	"Help me manage emotions during a high-stakes negotiation: [insert context]. Provide tips for staying composed while maintaining Tru$tCurrency and focusing on NegoEconomic goals."
Feedback Request	"Draft a message asking for feedback from my counterpart after a completed negotiation: [insert details]. Emphasize Tru$tCurrency and the value of collaboration."
Contingency Planning	"Develop a contingency plan for this negotiation: [insert context]. Include fallback options that preserve Tru$tCurrency and safeguard NegoEconomic outcomes."
AI-Driven Analysis	"Analyze past negotiation transcripts: [insert text]. Identify patterns in objections, NegoEconomic opportunities, and Tru$tCurrency-building moments."
Stakeholder Alignment	"Help me align internal stakeholders before this negotiation: [insert details]. Suggest ways to ensure a unified front and alignment with NegoEconomic strategies."
SMARTnership Proposal Drafting	"Create a draft proposal emphasizing SMARTnership principles for this negotiation: [insert context]. Highlight NegoEconomic value creation and strategies for building Tru$tCurrency."
Creative Solution Ideation	"Suggest innovative solutions for resolving this negotiation impasse: [insert issue]. Focus on using NegoEconomics to add value and Tru$tCurrency to maintain goodwill."
Negotiation Audit	"Conduct an audit of this negotiation strategy: [insert strategy]. Highlight strengths, weaknesses, and areas for improvement in leveraging NegoEconomics and Tru$tCurrency."

Task	AI Prompt
NegoEconomic Value Identification	"Help me identify NegoEconomic opportunities in this negotiation: [insert details]. Focus on cost reductions and revenue enhancements that create asymmetric value."
Tru$tCurrency Monitoring	"Develop a framework for monitoring Tru$tCurrency throughout this negotiation: [insert context]. Include signals of trust erosion and ways to rebuild."
Post-Negotiation Reflection	"Guide me in a post-negotiation review: [insert outcome]. Assess how well NegoEconomic principles were applied and Tru$tCurrency was built or maintained."

CHAPTER 13

AI in Negotiation: Amplifying Human Insight for SMARTnership Success

AI generates content quickly. For example, if you prompt it, "Write an email with a counterproposal, in my negotiation with X," within seconds you'll have a draft in front of you. It's efficient, but don't let the speed fool you into thinking AI is a replacement for thoughtful communication. AI can produce text rapidly, yet much of its output may feel robotic or lack the nuanced understanding that human insight brings.

The strength of negotiation lies in the ability to relate, persuade, and understand subtleties. AI can't match you there. Instead of seeing it as a shortcut, view AI as a tool to support your natural skills. AI can write quickly, but it can't mirror the depth of empathy or judgment that a human negotiator brings to the table. The real advantage in using AI is to handle the more mechanical tasks, allowing you to focus on the aspects that truly require a human touch.

Refining AI to Reflect Your Voice in Negotiation

To use AI effectively in negotiation, it helps to shape its responses so they align with your unique style. By teaching AI to mimic your voice, the results can feel more genuine and tailored to your approach. Use these steps to teach AI to reflect your voice:

1. **Gather your work:** Collect 5–10 examples of your writing that best represent your style. This might include emails, proposals, or past negotiation summaries, with a total word count of around 1,000–2,000 words.
2. **Create a PDF:** Compile these samples into a single PDF file.
3. **Create a style guide prompt:** Ask AI to analyze the document with a prompt like "Assume you are a skilled ghostwriter focused on linguistic style. Analyze the attached text and create a style guide that captures the author's tone, structure, and phrasing."
4. **Review and define:** Once the AI generates the style guide, review it to ensure it accurately reflects your tone and remove any parts that seem off.
5. **Apply the style guide:** When asking AI to draft messages, include style instructions to ensure consistency. For example, "Please follow these guidelines: Tone: [your description], Style: [your description], Structure: [your description]."

This process will reduce the robotic tone AI sometimes generates, making its responses sound closer to how you naturally communicate.

Overcoming Challenges in Negotiation Using AI Prompts

When negotiating with small and medium-sized business procurement departments, understanding their challenges is key to framing your approach effectively. AI can provide valuable insights here, especially with prompts that encourage it to analyze common industry issues.

Example prompt: "What are the current challenges faced by procurement officers of small to medium-sized businesses in this economic climate?"

This prompt helps AI gather information about issues such as talent acquisition, regulatory pressures, and financial management. With these insights, you can tailor your negotiation strategy to align with the counterpart's realities and concerns, making your position more relevant and relatable.

Example challenges AI might identify:

- **Talent acquisition and retention:** Recruiting and retaining skilled workers can be difficult, especially in competitive job markets.

- **Regulatory compliance:** Navigating labor laws, tax requirements, and industry standards is often time-consuming and costly.
- **Cash flow management:** Managing finances to meet payroll and other obligations, especially when clients delay payments.
- **Technological adaptation:** Keeping up with technological changes to remain competitive.
- **Economic uncertainty:** Adjusting strategies amid economic downturns or fluctuations in demand.
- **Client diversification:** Reducing dependency on a small client base to avoid overexposure to risks.

By understanding these pain points, you can negotiate in a way that shows awareness of their unique position, enhancing trust and cooperation.

Leveraging Emotion-Focused Prompts in Negotiation

Effective negotiation messages often address underlying emotions, such as stress, insecurity, or hope. AI prompts designed to probe these areas can help you gain insight into your counterpart's emotional landscape, enabling you to tailor responses that resonate more deeply.

Examples of emotion-focused prompts:

- "What concerns do you have regarding this proposal/RFP/contract?"
- "What challenges are impacting your team's negotiation performance?"

With these insights, you can frame your negotiation in a way that acknowledges their challenges, creating a more empathetic connection.

Building Empathy into Negotiation Messages

Once you have an understanding of the emotional factors at play, you can respond with empathy and relevance. Consider questions like:

- What would alleviate their stress?
- How can I address their specific concerns in this negotiation?
- What tone will best reassure them and demonstrate my commitment?

By answering these questions in your messaging, you show that you're focused on their needs as much as your own, strengthening the foundation for a collaborative agreement.

Key Takeaways for Effective AI-Assisted Negotiation Writing

AI can help streamline and accelerate the negotiation preparation and messaging process, but it requires thoughtful input and human oversight. Here are some guidelines for using AI effectively in your negotiation writing:

- **Teach AI to reflect your style:** Train AI with your own written examples to make its responses sound more like you.
- **Address real challenges:** Use prompts that encourage AI to analyze and summarize the common issues and challenges faced by your counterpart's industry.
- **Acknowledge emotions:** Integrate empathy-driven prompts to ensure your messages address not only the logical but also the emotional concerns of your counterparts.

By following these practices, you can use AI as a supportive partner in negotiation, enhancing efficiency while retaining the human qualities that build trust and foster successful agreements.

The Irreplaceable Human Touch

In our rush to embrace artificial intelligence, we must remember that negotiation is fundamentally a human endeavor. While AI can process vast amounts of data and identify patterns, it cannot replicate the nuanced understanding of human emotions, cultural subtleties, and relationship dynamics that often determine negotiation success. The key lies not in choosing between human expertise and AI but in leveraging both to create what I call "Augmented Negotiation Intelligence."

The Four Pillars of Human-AI Synergy in Negotiation

This section covers the Four Pillars of Human-AI Synergy in Negotiation.

Emotional Intelligence (EQ) in the Digital Age The introduction of AI into negotiation has not diminished the importance of emotional intelligence—it has enhanced it. Consider this: while AI can analyze facial expressions and tone of voice, only humans can truly understand the context behind these signals.

Key components of modern EQ in negotiation:

- Reading micro-expressions even through digital interfaces
- Understanding emotional subtext in cross-cultural communications
- Managing emotional dynamics in hybrid (AI-assisted) negotiations
- Building rapport while using technology
- Maintaining authentic connections in data-driven discussions

Case Study: The Tehran-Stockholm Deal

In a recent negotiation between a Swedish tech company and a Malaysian manufacturer, AI analysis suggested a purely logical approach based on cost-benefit calculations. However, the human negotiator recognized that building personal trust was crucial in Malaysian business culture. By combining AI's analytical insights with cultural intelligence, they achieved a deal that was 40 percent more valuable than initially projected.

Cultural Intelligence (CQ) in a Connected World

AI can provide cultural data points, but human negotiators must transform this information into meaningful connections. The SMARTnership approach to cultural intelligence involves:

Framework for cultural navigation:

- **Surface level:** Customs, etiquette, and protocols
- **Mid-level:** Business practices and communication styles
- **Deep level:** Values, beliefs, and relationship dynamics
- **Meta level:** Integration of AI insights with cultural understanding

Practical application:

- Use AI to gather cultural data points.
- Apply human insight to interpret contextual nuances.
- Create culturally sensitive negotiation strategies.
- Build authentic cross-cultural relationships.
- Maintain cultural authenticity while leveraging technology.

Relationship Architecture in the AI Era

The term "relationship architecture" represents the deliberate design and construction of business relationships that can withstand the test of time and technology. In the age of AI, this becomes even more critical.

Components of modern relationship architecture include:

- Trust-building in digital environments
- Long-term value creation
- Strategic alliance development
- Network effect optimization
- Technology-enhanced relationship management

The trust triangle model is as follows:

- Capability trust (enhanced by AI)
- Contractual trust (verified by AI)
- Goodwill trust (uniquely human)

Creative Problem-Solving: The Human Advantage　While AI excels at analyzing existing patterns, human creativity remains unmatched in generating novel solutions. The key is to use AI as a springboard for human creativity rather than a replacement for it.

The creative negotiation process is as follows:

- **AI analysis:** Pattern recognition and data insights
- **Human interpretation:** Converting data into possibilities
- **Creative synthesis:** Generating unique solutions
- **Value innovation:** Creating new forms of value
- **Implementation design:** Making solutions work in reality

Practical Integration: The Human-AI Balance

Consider using the Human Element Scorecard assessment tool to rate your negotiation on these human elements (scale 1–5):

- Emotional connection
- Cultural resonance
- Relationship depth
- Creative solution generation
- Trust development

Implementation Framework: The 5R Model

- **Recognize** the human aspects that AI cannot replicate.
- **Retain** the essential human elements in negotiation.

- **Reinforce** human connections with AI insights.
- **Refine** the balance between human and AI inputs.
- **Renew** relationships through continuous engagement.

COMMON AI-RELATED PITFALLS AND SOLUTIONS

Pitfall	Solution
Overreliance on data	Balance quantitative insights with qualitative understanding.
Digital distance	Create meaningful connection points in virtual negotiations.
Cultural oversimplification	Use AI insights as a starting point, not an endpoint.
Trust erosion	Build "trust anchors" throughout the negotiation process.

The Future of Human-AI Collaboration in Negotiation

As AI continues to evolve, the human element in negotiation will not diminish—it will transform. The successful negotiators of tomorrow will be those who can:

- Leverage AI for enhanced understanding.
- Maintain authentic human connections.
- Create value through relationship intelligence.
- Build trust in technology-enhanced environments.
- Drive innovation through human creativity.

Try these action steps to enhance your human element:

1. **Assess** your current balance of human and AI elements.
2. **Develop** your emotional and cultural intelligence.
3. **Practice** relationship architecture principles.
4. **Integrate** AI insights with human understanding.
5. **Measure** the impact on negotiation outcomes.

Conclusion: The Human Advantage

In the age of AI, the human element is not just relevant—it's revolutionary. By combining the analytical power of AI with uniquely human capabilities, we can create a new form of negotiation that is more powerful than either human or machine alone. This is the essence of SMARTnership negotiation in the digital age: using technology to enhance, not replace, the human elements that make negotiation truly transformative.

Remember: AI can analyze a million data points, but it takes a human to understand the story behind the numbers and to build the relationships that turn good deals into great partnerships.

CHAPTER 14

AI as the Negotiator's New Ally

Negotiation is a combination of strategy, data, psychology, communication, and intuition. It requires not only preparation and planning but also the ability to adapt in real time to the dynamics of the discussion. This chapter explores how ChatGPT, a leading AI tool, can revolutionize the negotiation process at every stage.

Whether you're preparing for a high-stakes corporate deal or refining your communication with a partner, AI tools like ChatGPT empower you with insights, strategy, and adaptability.

Preparation: Building a Solid Foundation

Preparation is the backbone of successful negotiation. Without thorough groundwork, even the most skilled negotiators can falter. ChatGPT shines as a preparatory tool, offering:

- **Researching counterparts:** With just a few prompts, ChatGPT can analyze available data on your counterpart, providing insights into their priorities, constraints, and past behaviors.
- **Generating relevant questions:** Targeted questions help uncover critical details during the negotiation, ensuring you go into the conversation with clarity.

- **Market and trend analysis:** AI provides detailed summaries of industry trends, competitor activity, and economic conditions to help you frame your proposals.

Example use case: You're negotiating a long-term contract with a supplier. By asking ChatGPT, "Analyze industry trends for renewable energy suppliers over the past five years," you gain insights into what factors may influence the supplier's decision-making process.

Prompts you can use:

- "Summarize the negotiation history between [Company A] and its previous partners."
- "What are the key factors influencing the [industry] market in Q4 2024?"

Strategy: Designing Your Path to Success

Strategizing for a negotiation involves not only planning your objectives but also anticipating the moves of the other party. ChatGPT excels at helping you craft a tailored, effective strategy:

- **SWOT analysis:** It identifies your strengths and weaknesses relative to the counterpart's position and external market factors.
- **Scenario planning:** AI enables you to run simulations that model possible negotiation strategies, outcomes, and counteroffers.
- **Personality alignment:** ChatGPT can evaluate communication styles and suggest approaches that resonate with your counterpart.

Example use case: A client is resistant to your price increase, but through ChatGPT's simulation of conciliatory and assertive approaches, you discover that emphasizing shared benefits leads to the best outcome.

Prompts you can use:

- "Create a negotiation strategy for convincing a client to extend their contract by another year."
- "Based on [Company B's] values, what argument style will likely resonate best?"

During the Negotiation: Real-Time Assistance

Once the negotiation begins, it's vital to stay sharp and adaptive. ChatGPT acts as a real-time assistant by:

- **Providing tactical feedback:** Live analysis of counterpart responses can help you adjust your approach to objections or unexpected demands.
- **Clarifying complex terms:** Whether it's a financial term or legal language, ChatGPT can simplify key concepts on the spot.
- **Tracking agreements:** Use ChatGPT to maintain a dynamic summary of ongoing discussions, capturing concessions and unresolved issues.

Example use case: During a negotiation, your counterpart suggests an unfamiliar clause about intellectual property rights. ChatGPT quickly clarifies the implications, helping you decide on your response.

Prompts you can use:

- "Analyze the counterpart's latest email for tone and intent."
- "Summarize the concessions made during today's discussion."

Emotional Intelligence: Understanding and Responding

Negotiation is deeply influenced by emotional and relational dynamics. ChatGPT helps enhance emotional intelligence by:

- **Detecting sentiment:** It identifies emotional cues in written or spoken language, such as hesitation, enthusiasm, or defensiveness.
- **Crafting empathetic responses:** AI suggests language that acknowledges the counterpart's concerns while advancing your objectives.

Example use case: A counterpart expresses frustration about your timeline. ChatGPT suggests a response that empathizes while reinforcing the benefits of your proposal.

Prompts you can use:

- "Analyze this response for emotional cues and suggest adjustments for building trust."
- "How can I address concerns about delivery delays empathetically?"

Simulation: Practicing for Excellence

Rehearsing your negotiation strategy can uncover blind spots and boost confidence. ChatGPT offers:

- **Virtual roleplay:** It acts as a counterpart, simulating a wide range of negotiation scenarios and responses.
- **Outcome prediction:** AI evaluates the likely results of different approaches, helping you choose the most effective strategy.

Example use case: You practice negotiating a salary increase with ChatGPT acting as both an encouraging and a resistant manager. This prepares you for various outcomes.

Prompts you can use:

- "Simulate a negotiation with a supplier refusing to lower their prices."
- "Act as a skeptical client and challenge my proposal for a software upgrade."

Crafting Your Next Best Alternative (NBA)

A well-prepared negotiator always knows their alternatives. ChatGPT helps refine your NBA by:

- **Analyzing fallback options:** Based on market data and resources, ChatGPT identifies viable alternatives.
- **Quantifying benefits:** It calculates the financial or operational trade-offs of different options, ensuring you negotiate from a position of strength.

Example use case: You're negotiating office rental terms and need alternatives in case the landlord refuses to budge. ChatGPT suggests comparable properties in your area with their pros and cons.

Prompts you can use:

- "List alternatives if we can't secure this vendor at our desired terms."
- "Analyze the pros and cons of leasing versus buying this equipment."

Communication: Streamlining Dialogues

Clear communication drives effective negotiations. ChatGPT supports this by:

- **Structuring agendas:** It organizes your talking points and helps you prioritize key issues.
- **Drafting proposals and emails:** AI ensures your written communication is concise, professional, and persuasive.

Example use case: After a negotiation session, ChatGPT drafts a follow-up email summarizing agreements and setting the next meeting agenda.

Prompts you can use:

- "Draft an email summarizing today's discussion with the counterpart."
- "Create a one-page proposal highlighting our offer's benefits."

Review: Learning from the Process

Post-negotiation analysis is essential for growth. ChatGPT facilitates:

- **Evaluating outcomes:** It compares the final agreement with your original objectives, pinpointing successes and missed opportunities.
- **Extracting lessons:** AI identifies patterns from past negotiations to refine future strategies.

Example use case: After closing a deal, ChatGPT provides an evaluation showing how a stronger opening offer could have achieved better terms.

Prompts you can use:

- "Analyze this finalized agreement for alignment with our initial goals."
- "What lessons can I draw from this negotiation for future improvement?"

Conclusion: Your AI-Powered Negotiation Partner

ChatGPT is transforming the way negotiations are conducted. By acting as a research assistant, strategist, real-time advisor, and evaluator, it empowers negotiators to achieve superior results. While the human touch—empathy, intuition, and rapport—remains irreplaceable, ChatGPT's analytical strength and efficiency complement these traits perfectly.

By embracing this AI-driven approach, you not only enhance your capabilities but also ensure you stay ahead in the increasingly complex world of negotiation.

CHAPTER 15

AI in Contracting: Redefining How to Write and Read Contracts

Contracts are the foundation of business relationships, providing the framework for collaboration, accountability, and trust. Yet despite their importance, the traditional contracting process remains cumbersome, opaque, and often inaccessible to nonexperts. With the rise of artificial intelligence (AI), we have an unprecedented opportunity to transform how contracts are written and read—making them more efficient, understandable, and aligned with modern business needs.

This chapter delves into the revolutionary role AI plays in contract creation, review, and interpretation, illustrating its potential to enhance clarity, reduce risk, and foster mutual understanding.

The Challenges of Traditional Contracting

Before exploring AI's capabilities, it's important to understand the pain points in traditional contracting processes:

- **Complexity:** Contracts are often written in dense legal language that alienates nonlegal stakeholders. This complexity creates barriers to understanding and trust.

- **Time-intensive drafting:** Contract drafting involves repetitive tasks, from clause selection to formatting, which can slow down business operations.
- **Limited accessibility:** Traditional contracts prioritize legal precision over usability, making them difficult for nonexperts to navigate or interpret.
- **Reactive focus:** Most contracts are designed to mitigate risks and address potential disputes, rather than proactively fostering collaboration and success.

These challenges highlight the need for a paradigm shift in how contracts are created and used. This is where AI steps in.

How AI Transforms Contract Writing

AI tools, particularly generative AI like ChatGPT, are revolutionizing the way contracts are written by automating tedious tasks, improving clarity, and enabling customization. *Generative AI* refers to artificial intelligence systems that create new content—such as text, images, or even designs—by learning patterns from existing data. Unlike traditional AI, which focuses on analyzing data and providing solutions, generative AI excels at producing original output based on prompts, making it a powerful tool in creative and strategic tasks like negotiation preparation.

Automating Repetitive Tasks

AI streamlines the drafting process by automating tasks such as:

- **Clause selection:** AI can recommend appropriate clauses based on the context, reducing the time spent searching through templates.
- **Formatting and layout:** Tools like document-generation platforms ensure consistency in structure and presentation.
- **Version control:** AI tracks changes across drafts, providing a clear history of revisions and minimizing the risk of errors.

Simplifying Language

One of AI's most significant contributions is its ability to rewrite complex legalese into plain language. This makes contracts more accessible to nonlegal professionals, fostering better understanding and engagement. For instance:

- AI can provide side-by-side comparisons of a clause in both legal jargon and in plain English.
- AI can generate summaries or highlights of key terms for quick reference.

Customizing Templates

AI enables the creation of customized contract templates that align with specific business needs or industries. By analyzing historical agreements, AI can:

- Suggest tailored terms and conditions.
- Highlight clauses that have been most effective in past negotiations.

Embedding Goals and Values

AI tools can help integrate organizational goals, such as sustainability or diversity objectives, directly into contract language. For example, AI can recommend clauses that reflect environmental, social, and governance (ESG) commitments.

Enhancing Contract Reading with AI

Reading contracts is as challenging as writing them. AI significantly improves how contracts are interpreted, helping stakeholders understand critical terms, identify risks, and make informed decisions.

Simplifying Document Navigation

AI-powered tools can create interactive contracts with:

- **Searchable content:** Quickly locate specific terms or clauses using natural language queries.
- **Layered layouts:** Break down contracts into sections with summaries, hyperlinks, and visual aids.

Identifying Risk

AI tools like contract analytics software scan agreements to identify:

- **Risky clauses:** Highlighting terms such as indemnification, limitation of liability, or termination clauses that may pose potential issues.
- **Missing elements:** Identifying omissions, such as required compliance clauses or key performance indicators.

Providing Contextual Insights

AI can analyze a contract's content in the context of industry standards or regulatory requirements. For example:

- Compare payment terms to industry benchmarks.
- Flag clauses that deviate from common practices.

Providing Real-Time Explanations

With natural language processing, AI can answer questions about the contract in real time. For instance:

- "What is the payment timeline in this agreement?"
- "Does this contract include a force majeure clause, and what does it cover?"

Case Studies: AI in Action for Contracting

Case 1: Streamlining Sales Agreements

A software company used AI to generate customized sales contracts for its clients. By analyzing historical agreements, the AI tool identified common clauses and created a master template. This reduced contract drafting time by about 35 percent while ensuring compliance with company policies.

Case 2: Improving Risk Management

An energy firm implemented an AI-driven contract analytics platform to review supplier agreements. The tool identified indemnity clauses that posed excessive liability risks, enabling the firm to renegotiate terms before finalizing the deals.

The Ethical Dimension of AI in Contracting

While AI offers immense benefits, it also raises important ethical considerations:

- **Bias in algorithms:** AI must be trained on diverse datasets to avoid perpetuating biases in clause selection or risk assessment.

- **Data security:** Contracts often contain sensitive information. Organizations must ensure that AI tools comply with strict data protection standards.
- **Transparency:** It's critical to disclose when AI has been used in drafting or reviewing contracts to maintain trust between parties.

The Future of AI in Contracting

The potential applications of AI in contracting are only beginning to emerge. Future developments may include:

- **AI-generated smart contracts:** Integrating AI with blockchain (a distributed database or ledger shared across a computer network's nodes) to create self-executing agreements that automatically enforce terms
- **AI-to-AI negotiations:** Autonomous agents negotiating contract terms on behalf of their human counterparts
- **Enhanced collaboration tools:** Real-time, AI-assisted contract co-authoring platforms

Contract Writing Prompts

This section contains example AI prompts designed to assist you with contract writing and reading tasks. These prompts can be used directly with AI tools like ChatGPT to streamline contract drafting, simplify complex terms, and ensure agreements are fair and effective.

General Drafting Prompts

- "Draft a [type of contract, e.g., sales, lease, NDA] for [specific purpose]. Include standard clauses for confidentiality, termination, and liability."
- "Write a plain-language version of this clause: [paste complex clause]."
- "Generate a template for a [specific type of agreement] with customizable sections for [key details, e.g., payment terms, delivery timelines]."

Clause Suggestions

- "Suggest clauses for including sustainability goals in a vendor contract."
- "Write an indemnity clause that limits liability to [specific percentage or amount]."
- "Provide examples of force majeure clauses that cover pandemics and cyberattacks."

Formatting and Structure

- "Organize the sections of this contract into a user-friendly format with headings and summaries for each section."
- "Create a visually appealing layout for this contract with highlights for key terms."

Customization

- "Based on these details: [insert specifics], draft a customized service agreement that includes [key requirements]."
- "Generate a contract template for [industry] businesses that includes compliance with [specific regulations, e.g., GDPR]."

Scenario-Specific Drafting

- "Draft a supplier contract where payment is contingent on achieving specific milestones."
- "Write a consulting agreement where the consultant is paid a monthly retainer and a performance bonus."

Clause Summarization

- "Summarize this contract clause in plain English: [paste clause]."
- "Explain the implications of this clause: [paste clause]."

Risk Identification

- "Highlight any potential risks in this contract, such as unbalanced liability or ambiguous terms."
- "Identify missing clauses in this contract that are standard for [type of agreement, e.g., employment contracts]."

Comparison

- "Compare these two contract clauses and identify the key differences in liability terms: [paste clauses]."
- "Analyze how this contract aligns with industry benchmarks for [specific provision, e.g., payment terms]."

Regulatory Compliance

- "Check if this contract complies with [specific regulation, e.g., GDPR, HIPAA]. Highlight areas that may need adjustment."
- "Identify any clauses that could conflict with [specific legal requirements] in [region or country]."

Quick Navigation

- "Locate the section in this contract that specifies [e.g., payment terms, termination rights]."
- "List all clauses related to dispute resolution in this contract."

Rewriting and Simplification

- "Rewrite this contract to make it easier to understand for nonlegal professionals while preserving legal accuracy."
- "Simplify this sentence: [paste complex sentence]."

Executive Summaries

- "Summarize this contract into a one-page executive brief."
- "Create bullet points for the key terms of this agreement."

Creating FAQs

- "Generate a FAQ for this contract to help stakeholders understand its terms."
- "What are the three most critical takeaways from this contract for [stakeholder, e.g., the buyer]?"

Real-Time Questions

- "What does the term 'force majeure' mean in this contract, and how might it apply to [specific scenario]?"
- "Explain how the payment terms in this contract will affect cash flow for [specific situation]."

Document Improvement

- "Suggest improvements to this contract to make it more equitable for all parties."
- "Highlight opportunities to include mutual benefit clauses in this agreement."

Ethical Review

- "Analyze this contract for any ethical concerns, such as clauses that may exploit one party."
- "Suggest revisions to make this contract align with fair business practices."

SMARTnership Optimization

- "Identify opportunities in this contract to expand mutual value using SMARTnership principles."
- "Rewrite this contract to focus on collaboration and shared benefits."

Embracing AI for Better Contracts

AI is not just a tool for speeding up contract processes—it's a means of transforming them. By leveraging AI's capabilities, we can create contracts that are not only efficient but also clear, collaborative, and aligned with modern business values. As professionals in the field, it's up to us to harness this technology responsibly, ensuring that our agreements serve as bridges to success rather than barriers to understanding.

> **Note:** For further information about AI in contracting, I recommend following World Commerce & Contracting (**worldcc.com**), which is doing immensely important research in this field.

CHAPTER 16

Lessons from the Field: Harnessing Artificial Intelligence in Negotiation

The art of negotiation is undergoing a profound transformation. What once depended on intuition, experience, and interpersonal skills is now augmented by artificial intelligence (AI), offering tools that promise to enhance decision-making, streamline processes, and reveal opportunities for collaboration. This chapter explores the integration of AI into negotiation, leveraging findings from a pivotal experiment to illuminate its potential and challenges. Embedded within the broader context of this book, the discussion emphasizes the synergy between human expertise and AI's computational power.

Negotiation, a cornerstone of business and interpersonal relationships, is no stranger to innovation. From the adoption of structured frameworks to advanced behavioral analyses, negotiators have continually refined their craft. However, AI introduces a paradigm shift: the ability to process vast datasets, simulate outcomes, and propose strategies in real time. The question is no longer whether AI belongs at the negotiation table but how to use it effectively.

A Case Study in AI-Driven Negotiation

As part of a collaborative effort with Mr. Tim Cummins, president of World Commerce & Contracting, I conducted an experiment comparing traditional negotiation methods with AI-assisted approaches.

The study, published as a peer-reviewed research paper, involved 24 teams of two members each, negotiating a simulation globally against one another via Zoom. This rigorous exploration evaluated how AI influences preparation, execution, behavioral dynamics, and outcomes, shedding light on its transformative potential in the negotiation landscape.

The study evaluated three scenarios:

- Teams negotiating without AI assistance
- Teams where one party employed AI (ChatGPT) and the other did not
- Teams where both parties utilized ChatGPT

The goal was to examine the implications of AI on preparation, process efficiency, behavioral dynamics, and outcomes.

Key Details of the Experiment

Participants represented diverse industries and cultural backgrounds. Each was tasked with resolving a case involving multiple negotiable items and optional trade-offs. Time constraints heightened the pressure, mimicking real-world scenarios where swift decision-making is critical. Teams using AI received brief guidance on prompt engineering, highlighting the importance of crafting precise, goal-oriented queries.

The Results: Unpacking the Experiment's Findings

The findings are organized into three sections titled efficiency and resolution, enhanced preparation, and behavioral dynamics.

Efficiency and Resolution   AI-assisted negotiations consistently outperformed traditional ones in terms of speed and resolution quality:

- AI-enabled teams completed their tasks within 2–12 minutes, adhering to organizational expectations for rapid agreement.
- Traditional teams often exceeded time limits, with one group failing to resolve entirely.

For example, an AI-assisted team might use a prompt like this:

- "Calculate the cost implications of offering a 10 percent discount versus extending delivery timelines by 30 days."

This capability reduced deliberation time and enabled rapid alignment on mutually beneficial solutions.

Enhanced Preparation Preparation is a critical determinant of negotiation success. AI-assisted teams demonstrated structured, data-driven planning. ChatGPT's guidance ensured clarity on priorities, potential concessions, and strategies. Conversely, traditional teams often lacked cohesive approaches, resulting in fragmented discussions.

AI-equipped teams benefited from prompts like this:

- "Generate a negotiation strategy emphasizing collaboration while protecting key financial objectives."

Such tools improved preparation quality and instilled discipline in the negotiation process.

Behavioral Dynamics AI influenced the tone and dynamics of negotiations, fostering transparency and collaboration. By encouraging openness about goals and constraints, ChatGPT promoted trust and mutual understanding. In contrast, traditional teams frequently encountered emotional biases, adversarial tactics, and communication breakdowns.

For instance, an AI-assisted negotiator might leverage a prompt such as this:

- "Propose a collaborative opening statement to establish trust and set a constructive tone."

These behavioral shifts highlight AI's ability to steer negotiations toward win-win outcomes, a hallmark of SMARTnership principles.

Challenges and Lessons from Integration

This section discusses the takeaways from this experiment.

Asymmetric Usage In hybrid scenarios where only one party used AI, disparities in speed and sophistication posed challenges. AI-generated proposals often outpaced the non-AI party's ability to analyze and respond, creating friction. Moreover, integrating AI insights into team dynamics required clear communication protocols, mainly when decisions needed rapid consensus.

Learning Curve Not all participants maximized AI's potential. Those unfamiliar with generative AI struggled to craft effective prompts, treating the tool as a static search engine. This underscores the need for targeted training to unlock AI's full capabilities.

Prompting tip: To generate actionable insights, prompts should be specific and contextual. For example:

- "Based on this dataset, suggest three trade-offs that maximize value while minimizing risk."

Employing AI as a Strategic Partner

AI is redefining the role of negotiators, shifting their focus from tactical execution to strategic oversight. Negotiators can now delegate data analysis and scenario planning to AI, enabling them to concentrate on high-level decision-making and relationship management.

Standardization and Best Practices

AI's analytical consistency paves the way for standardized negotiation frameworks. By identifying patterns across datasets, AI can recommend proven strategies, reducing inefficiencies and elevating baseline performance.

Ethical Considerations

The integration of AI raises questions about fairness, confidentiality, and accountability. Organizations must navigate these challenges thoughtfully to maintain trust and equity in negotiations.

Machine-to-Machine Negotiation

As AI evolves, the prospect of fully automated negotiations looms. While promising for routine transactions, this shift may exacerbate power imbalances, especially for parties lacking access to advanced technology.

Based on this study, we recommend the following to negotiators:

- **Master prompt engineering:** Effective prompts are essential for extracting meaningful insights from AI. Negotiators should practice crafting precise, contextually rich queries.

    Example: "Draft a counterproposal emphasizing extended payment terms while preserving price integrity."

- **Establish communication protocols:** Teams using AI must align on how to incorporate AI insights seamlessly, ensuring clarity and coherence in decision-making.
- **Invest in training:** Organizations should prioritize AI literacy, equipping negotiators with the skills to leverage generative AI effectively.
- **Balance AI and human judgment:** While AI excels at data-driven analysis, human intuition and ethical reasoning remain irreplaceable.

The Future of Negotiation in an AI-Driven World

AI is not merely a tool; it is a transformative force shaping the future of negotiation. By combining computational precision with human creativity, negotiators can achieve faster, more equitable outcomes while navigating the complexities of modern agreements. The findings from this experiment underscore AI's potential to elevate negotiation strategies, aligning with the SMARTnership philosophy of collaboration and shared value creation.

Incorporating AI into negotiation processes is not about replacing human expertise but amplifying it. Negotiators who embrace this synergy will be better equipped to adapt to a rapidly evolving landscape, ensuring success in both routine and high-stakes negotiations.

A New Paradigm for Negotiation

The integration of AI marks a turning point in the history of negotiation. By offering tools that enhance preparation, streamline execution, and foster collaboration, AI is transforming how agreements are forged. Yet the human element remains central—bringing ethical oversight, emotional intelligence, and strategic vision to the table.

The future of negotiation lies in the partnership between humans and machines. Together they can achieve outcomes that are not only faster and more efficient but also more innovative and equitable. This chapter serves as a call to action for negotiators: to embrace AI as an ally, refine their skills, and lead the way in this new era of negotiation.

CHAPTER 17

Revolutionizing Negotiation with Real-Time AI Feedback

In today's fast-paced negotiation environments, leveraging AI for real-time feedback has emerged as a game-changer. Gone are the days when negotiators relied solely on instinct, memory, and fragmented notes. Now, AI tools provide immediate, actionable insights, making negotiation more strategic, informed, and adaptable. This chapter explores how AI transforms real-time negotiation dynamics, offering examples, guidance, and practical prompting strategies for integrating these tools into your negotiation practice.

The Power of Real-Time Data Analysis

One of AI's most profound contributions to negotiations is its ability to process and analyze massive amounts of data in real time. Imagine negotiating a supplier contract while the AI tool simultaneously scans historical agreements, market trends, and the supplier's track record. This capability empowers negotiators to identify patterns, risks, and opportunities that might otherwise go unnoticed.

For instance, during a high-stakes negotiation, AI can:

- Spot shifts in the counterpart's tone or responses that signal hesitation or uncertainty.
- Highlight inconsistencies between verbal statements and contractual terms.
- Identify leverage points based on live data about industry standards or competitor behavior.

You can try prompts like these:

- **Supplier contract negotiation:** "What are the most recent market trends impacting this supplier's industry?"
- **Risk assessment:** "Identify any red flags in the counterpart's terms based on historical data."

These insights allow negotiators to pivot instantly, tailoring their arguments to align with the evolving context of the discussion.

Emotion and Sentiment Analysis: The Empathy Engine

Effective negotiations are as much about understanding emotions as they are about facts. AI tools equipped with sentiment analysis can decode tone, language patterns, and even facial expressions in virtual settings. For example:

- During a video call, AI might flag signs of stress or discomfort in the counterpart's body language, suggesting a moment to pause and reassess.
- It can analyze the sentiment behind written messages, highlighting whether a proposal is being perceived as favorable or contentious.

You can try prompts like these:

- **Detecting emotional cues:** "What sentiment does the counterpart's tone suggest in their last statement?"
- **Trust building:** "Are there signs of discomfort or hesitation in their response?"

By interpreting these emotional cues, negotiators can adapt their approach to build trust, address concerns, and foster a collaborative atmosphere. This emotional intelligence, amplified by AI, bridges the gap often created by impersonal digital communications.

Tactical Assistance on the Fly

AI not only informs but also actively guides negotiators in real time. Imagine receiving strategic prompts as the conversation unfolds:

- "Ask for clarification on payment terms; the counterpart hesitated earlier when discussing timelines."
- "Reframe your proposal to emphasize mutual benefits, as the counterpart's recent responses suggest a focus on shared outcomes."

You can try prompts like these:

- **Probing questions:** "What clarification should I request to address their concerns effectively?"
- **Strategic adjustments:** "How can I reframe my proposal to align with the counterpart's focus on collaboration?"

This dynamic support can transform negotiations from reactive to proactive, helping negotiators stay ahead of the conversation rather than playing catch-up.

Simulating Scenarios for Better Outcomes

Preparation is the cornerstone of successful negotiation, and AI takes it to new heights through simulation. Before entering the negotiation room (virtual or physical), negotiators can use AI to:

- Simulate potential responses based on past behavior and negotiation styles.
- Explore various "what-if" scenarios to predict how changes in price, delivery terms, or service conditions might impact the counterpart's decision.

During negotiations, this same capability extends to real-time adjustments. For instance, AI might suggest alternate proposals or counteroffers based on live feedback from the counterpart.

You can try prompts like these:

- **Preparation:** "Simulate a response to an increased price proposal from the counterpart."
- **On-the-fly adjustments:** "If the counterpart rejects the current delivery terms, what alternative can I offer?"

Balancing Technology and Human Intuition

While AI's analytical prowess is unparalleled, it cannot replace the human touch. Successful negotiations hinge on empathy, intuition, and the ability to read between the lines—qualities unique to humans. Proper use of AI enhances these capabilities rather than replacing them. For example:

- AI provides the data; the negotiator provides the interpretation.
- AI identifies risks; the negotiator decides the trade-offs.
- AI suggests strategies; the negotiator builds rapport and trust to execute them effectively.

You can try prompts like these:

- **Data interpretation:** "What underlying risks does the flagged inconsistency in their terms suggest?"
- **Decision-making:** "Based on AI recommendations, what trade-offs might optimize mutual benefits?"

The best outcomes arise when AI augments human skills, enabling negotiators to focus on relationship-building while AI handles the data-heavy tasks.

Overcoming Challenges in AI-Driven Negotiation

Despite its benefits, integrating AI into real-time negotiations requires navigating certain challenges:

- **Maintaining the personal connection:** Overreliance on AI can make interactions feel transactional. Negotiators must ensure that technology facilitates rather than replaces genuine dialogue.
- **Managing bias in AI systems:** AI models are only as good as the data they're trained on. Using tools from reputable providers and understanding their limitations is essential to avoid perpetuating biases.
- **Adapting to rapid advances:** The technological landscape evolves quickly, and staying updated on the latest tools and features is critical to maintaining a competitive edge.

REAL-WORLD EXAMPLE: AI AT THE NEGOTIATION TABLE

Consider this scenario: A tech company is negotiating a major software procurement deal. During the discussion, AI tools flag that the supplier's repeated references to "additional development costs" suggest an area for potential cost negotiation. Simultaneously, sentiment analysis reveals that the supplier's tone becomes more positive when discussing long-term partnerships. Armed with this feedback, the negotiator pivots the conversation to emphasize shared benefits and negotiates a reduced upfront cost in exchange for a multiyear contract. The result? A win-win deal achieved with greater speed and clarity.

The Future of Real-Time AI Feedback

As AI technology continues to evolve, its role in negotiations will only expand. Future tools may integrate augmented reality (AR) to overlay insights directly in face-to-face meetings or use advanced natural language processing to predict counterpart behavior with even greater accuracy. The human-AI partnership will become an even more integral part of negotiation strategy, empowering professionals to achieve results that were once deemed unattainable.

Incorporating AI into your negotiation toolkit isn't just a choice—it's a necessity for staying competitive in the modern landscape. As you master this technology, you'll find yourself not only negotiating faster but also smarter, paving the way for long-lasting success.

CHAPTER 18

Defining Authority Bias and Mitigating the Risk

*A*uthority bias is a cognitive shortcut where individuals disproportionately favor the opinions or guidance of those perceived as authoritative, such as experts, leaders, or even advanced technologies like AI, without subjecting these views to critical scrutiny. While it can be helpful in some scenarios—such as relying on a surgeon for medical advice—it becomes a liability when the authority figure's expertise is irrelevant, biased, or outright flawed.

Origins of Authority Bias

The origins of authority bias are many, but include the following:

- **Evolutionary adaptation:** Humans evolved to rely on authority figures for survival. Trusting tribal leaders or elders often meant the difference between life and death, wiring our brains to defer to those we perceive as having superior knowledge or skills.
- **Cognitive efficiency:** Critical evaluation of every decision is mentally taxing. Authority bias acts as a mental shortcut, conserving energy by offloading judgment to someone else.
- **Cultural conditioning:** Societies often emphasize respect for authority figures, whether parents, teachers, or leaders, reinforcing the bias over time.

Modern Manifestations of Authority Bias

Authority bias can manifest in numerous settings:

- **Corporate decisions:** Blindly following a CEO's directive, even when it contradicts evidence or stakeholder feedback
- **Negotiations:** Accepting terms or advice from perceived "experts" without weighing their alignment with your interests
- **Technology:** Over-relying on AI-generated recommendations without questioning the underlying algorithms or data quality

How to Avoid Authority Bias

The following list outlines the best way to actively avoid authority bias:

- **Question the context:** Ask, "Is this person or system an expert in this specific field or decision?" Evaluate whether their expertise is relevant to the issue at hand.
- **Analyze the evidence:** Demand data or reasoning to back up claims, rather than accepting them at face value. Cross-check the information with independent sources or subject matter experts.
- **Diversify perspectives:** Consult multiple opinions, especially from those with differing viewpoints or backgrounds. Encourage a culture of constructive dissent in teams or organizations.
- **Acknowledge the emotional pull:** Be mindful of how the authority figure's status, charisma, or confidence might be influencing your perception. Separate their delivery from the actual substance of their argument.
- **Leverage Critical Thinking:** Use structured frameworks for decision-making, such as pro/con lists or SWOT analysis (strengths, weaknesses, opportunities, and threats). Employ devil's advocacy to deliberately challenge assumptions and conclusions.
- **Use technology thoughtfully:** When interacting with AI or advanced tools, remember that they reflect the biases and limitations of their programming. Treat AI as a supplementary resource, not an infallible authority.

Comparison to Anthropomorphism

Much like anthropomorphism—where we attribute humanlike qualities to nonhuman entities—authority bias can lead to misplaced trust. For example, just as someone might overestimate the "intentions" of a robot, they might uncritically accept AI outputs as objective truths. This overlap is particularly dangerous in fields like negotiation or strategy, where nuances require human judgment.

Combating authority bias requires vigilance, self-awareness, and deliberate effort to question, analyze, and diversify inputs. By implementing these safeguards, you can make more informed, balanced decisions and avoid the pitfalls of misplaced reliance on authority.

Beware of AI Solutions Searching for Problems

Generative AI is at the forefront of digital transformation, offering capabilities that once seemed like science fiction. Its potential to revolutionize data processing, decision-making, and even negotiation strategies is undeniable.

However, the mad rush to integrate AI into every corner of business has created a wave of tools that, quite frankly, are solving problems no one has. Many of these AI widgets are distractions—short-lived solutions destined to disappear within a year or two as pragmatic users move past the initial hype. As negotiators, we need to be especially discerning. Time spent on the wrong tools is time lost in honing real negotiation skills. Choose AI tools that provide genuine value, align with your goals, and have the staying power to evolve alongside your needs.

Remember, there is no "easy" button in negotiation—or in mastering AI. Like any tool, its effectiveness depends on the user. A poorly prepared negotiator relying on AI will still make poor decisions. AI won't magically turn mediocrity into excellence. What it *can* do is amplify your ability to analyze data, assess scenarios, and craft strategies—if you're willing to put in the effort to learn and integrate it meaningfully.

In negotiation, as in life, there's no substitute for preparation, practice, and critical thinking. AI is a partner, not a replacement for the skill and finesse that great negotiators bring to the table.

CHAPTER 19

The Power of Prompts in Negotiation

Using AI in negotiations is a dynamic and complex process where the right words at the right time can unlock hidden opportunities, deepen trust, and create value for all parties involved. But crafting those words often requires preparation, insight, and creativity. This is where prompts come in.

A well-designed prompt acts as a guide—a tool to steer conversations toward productive outcomes while uncovering mutual interests and building collaborative relationships. Whether you're preparing for a high-stakes corporate deal, resolving internal conflicts, or navigating cultural nuances in international negotiations, prompts provide the structure to approach each situation strategically.

This chapter is your blueprint for leveraging prompts in negotiation. It offers a collection of actionable, scenario-based questions and statements organized to address every stage of the negotiation process. Ask your AI to act as a negotiation expert. Name a specific individual (e.g., Keld Jensen).

Help the AI by uploading as many materials as possible to train it in your specific negotiations. Be aware of confidential information and, if possible, avoid uploading parts of documents that might be confidential.

- **Preparation:** Lay the groundwork by defining your goals, understanding your counterpart, and gathering critical information.
- **Relationship-building:** Establish trust and rapport as the foundation for effective communication and collaboration.
- **Strategy and execution:** Employ proven tactics and frameworks to navigate challenges and drive outcomes.

- **Objection handling:** Manage resistance and find pathways to agreement through thoughtful and respectful dialogue.
- **Closing and follow-through:** Ensure alignment on terms, commitment to outcomes, and steps for implementation.

Each prompt is designed to foster clarity, creativity, and control, helping you uncover value, align interests, and build partnerships. Whether you're negotiating with a client, colleague, or counterpart, these prompts will equip you to ask better questions, frame more persuasive arguments, and ultimately achieve smarter agreements.

Let these prompts inspire your approach, spark new ideas, and empower you to become a more confident and successful negotiator.

Prompts to Prepare for Negotiations

Consider the following prompts:

- "Describe your negotiation goals and the counterparty. What strategies can I use to achieve them?"
- "Outline potential BATNAs for this negotiation. How can I use them to strengthen my position?"
- "Identify the key issues in this negotiation. What priorities should I focus on?"
- "What data should I gather to be fully prepared for the negotiation?"
- "Suggest pre-negotiation research strategies using online tools and social media."
- "How can I use cultural, personal, or business intelligence to understand my counterpart better?"

Prompts for Building Relationships and Rapport

Consider the following prompts:

- "Craft an opening statement for a negotiation that builds trust and positions collaboration as the priority."
- "Write 10 impactful phrases to set a positive tone in a negotiation's first interaction."

Prompts for Building Relationships and Rapport

- "Provide 20 rapport-building questions designed to uncover mutual interests and create alignment."
- "Suggest techniques for leveraging emotional intelligence to connect quickly and authentically."
- "Share strategies to establish empathy and build trust with a resistant or skeptical counterpart."
- "Analyze a successful negotiation case study where relationship-building played a pivotal role."
- "Explain how to personalize negotiation approaches to fit cultural and individual preferences."
- "Discuss the role of humor in negotiations and provide examples for building trust without undermining professionalism."
- "List 10 statements to convey expertise and authority while maintaining humility in a negotiation setting."
- "Offer ways to adapt communication styles to align with the counterpart's personality and negotiation preferences."
- "Provide nonverbal negotiation techniques to project confidence and collaboration."
- "Share how social networks (e.g., LinkedIn) can be used to research and build credibility before negotiations."
- "Recommend industry-specific thought leaders to follow to gain insights relevant to counterparts' challenges."
- "Write two creative opening strategies for unengaged or uninterested negotiation partners."
- "Identify topics or icebreakers to create a relaxed atmosphere during high-stakes negotiations."
- "Outline the use of social proof and case studies to foster trust at the negotiation table."
- "Suggest language tips to maintain a constructive tone and ensure a productive negotiation atmosphere."
- "Propose a three-step framework to build trust and drive agreements in negotiations."
- "Highlight the use of testimonials and success stories to establish credibility during talks."
- "Identify methods to strengthen trust before negotiation starts."
- "How can I collaborate with the other party to find mutually beneficial outcomes?"
- "Propose steps for long-term relationship-building post-negotiation."
- "Discuss the role of storytelling in building rapport."

Prompts for Negotiation Strategies

Consider the following prompts:

- "Analyze the counterpart's position based on their public information. What elements might they prioritize?"
- "What creative strategies can I employ to achieve a win-win outcome?"
- "Which NegoEconomics principles are applicable in this situation?"
- "How can I use trust and relationship-building as part of my strategy?"
- "What roadblocks might arise, and how can I preemptively address them?"
- "Recommend ways to use framing to present my terms more persuasively."
- "What probing questions can I ask to uncover the other party's needs?"
- "How can I leverage time pressure effectively in this negotiation?"
- "Summarize successful sales negotiation stages in 10 actionable steps."
- "Develop strategies for remote negotiations that enhance trust and connection."
- "Draft an opening email designed to uncover the counterpart's priorities while demonstrating flexibility."
- "Discuss how to use anchoring to set the tone and create value in negotiations."
- "Highlight techniques for negotiating with challenging personalities while maintaining professionalism."
- "Propose ways to identify and address counterpart pain points ethically to maximize value for both sides."
- "Provide strategies for accelerating negotiation timelines without sacrificing quality outcomes."
- "Write examples of thoughtful follow-ups to reengage counterparts who delay decisions."
- "Highlight key cultural differences that may impact this negotiation."
- "What adjustments can I make for a negotiation in [specific country]?"
- "Recommend ways to build cultural rapport in an international context."
- "Suggest creative negotiation tactics that leverage co-creation with the counterpart."

Prompts for Negotiation Tactics

Consider the following prompts:

- "Suggest effective anchoring techniques for this negotiation scenario."
- "How can I use trade-offs to facilitate agreement?"
- "Recommend tactics to counteract hard bargaining techniques."
- "Suggest ways to use silence strategically during a discussion."
- "What techniques can diffuse tension in a heated negotiation?"
- "Provide negotiation tactics tailored for handling aggressive or passive-aggressive counterparts."

Prompts for Negotiation Scripts

Consider the following prompts:

- "Draft an opening statement to establish rapport and trust."
- "Write a script for handling objections effectively."
- "Create a closing script to ensure agreement on key terms."
- Develop responses to objections like "Your price is too high" or "We're happy with our current supplier."

Prompts for Risk Management

Consider the following prompts:

- "Highlight potential risks in this deal and how to mitigate them."
- "How can I identify hidden liabilities in the counterparty's offer?"
- "Suggest strategies to avoid misunderstandings during negotiation."
- "Identify proactive ways to mitigate risks associated with ambiguous terms."

Prompts for Scenario Planning

Consider the following prompts:

- "Create scenarios based on varying outcomes of the negotiation."
- "Outline contingency plans for an unexpected counterproposal."
- "What concessions can I prepare that have minimal impact on my position?"

Prompts for Advanced Techniques

Consider the following prompts:

- "How can I use body language and nonverbal cues to gain an advantage during negotiations?"
- "Suggest ways to integrate SMARTnership principles into the negotiation process."
- "What strategies can I employ to highlight asymmetric value in this negotiation?"

Prompts for Metrics and Analysis

Consider the following prompts:

- "What KPIs can I use to evaluate the success of this negotiation?"
- "Design a dashboard to track negotiation progress and outcomes."
- "Propose methods to analyze negotiation data for future improvements."

Prompts for AI and Negotiation

Consider the following prompts:

- "How can AI tools support my negotiation strategy?"
- "Recommend AI-driven insights for better decision-making."
- "Suggest ways to integrate SMARTnership principles with AI analytics."

Prompts for Training and Development

Consider the following prompts:

- "Design a workshop outline to improve negotiation skills for my team."
- "Create a role-playing exercise to simulate a high-stakes negotiation."
- "How can I train my team on recognizing counterparty tactics?"

Prompts for Sustainability in Negotiations

Consider the following prompts:

- "Propose ways to incorporate sustainability goals in this negotiation."
- "Identify standards or certifications relevant to sustainable negotiation practices."
- "Suggest arguments to position sustainability as a competitive advantage."

Prompts to Close the Deal

Consider the following prompts:

- "Draft a checklist to confirm all terms before signing an agreement."
- "How can I summarize the negotiation outcome clearly for both parties?"
- "Propose methods to ensure commitment and follow-through on agreements."

Prompts for Conflict Resolution

Consider the following prompts:

- "Suggest ways to mediate disputes during negotiations."
- "How can I reframe a contentious point to reduce resistance?"
- "What methods can deescalate conflicts during high-pressure moments?"

Prompts for Continuous Improvement

Consider the following prompts:

- "How can I analyze past negotiations to identify areas for growth?"
- "Propose a post-negotiation debriefing process for my team."
- "Design a feedback form to gather insights from the other party."

Prompts for Leveraging Tru$tCurrency

Consider the following prompts:

- "What trust-building actions can I take to enhance negotiation outcomes?"
- "How can I measure the impact of trust in this negotiation?"
- "Recommend ways to align trust with financial incentives."

Scenario-Specific Prompts

Consider the following prompts:

- "How do I negotiate price adjustments during economic uncertainty?"
- "What's the best approach for negotiating with a monopolistic supplier?"
- "How can I manage negotiations with multiple stakeholders?"

Prompts for Innovation in Negotiation

Consider the following prompts:

- "How can I incorporate co-creation into this deal to add value?"
- "Suggest unconventional negotiation tactics that suit this situation."
- "What role does storytelling play in innovative negotiation strategies?"

Prompts for Ethical Considerations

Consider the following prompts:

- "How can I uphold ethical standards in a competitive negotiation?"
- "Propose ways to handle ethically questionable tactics from the other party."
- "What are the reputational risks of aggressive negotiation?"

Prompts for Adding Final Touches

Consider the following prompts:

- "How can I ensure alignment with organizational goals in this negotiation?"
- "Propose a strategy to maintain momentum in prolonged negotiations."
- "What steps can ensure a successful transition from negotiation to implementation?"

CHAPTER 20

The Role of Artificial Intelligence in Modern Negotiation Dynamics

In the evolving landscape of negotiation, artificial intelligence (AI) has emerged as a transformative force. No longer confined to the realm of human intuition and skill, negotiation is now enhanced by AI systems that promise efficiency, reduced bias, and improved outcomes. As Horst Eidenmueller and other scholars highlight, this new era of negotiation tools reshapes how agreements are reached, decisions are made, and value is distributed. This chapter explores these advancements, their implications, and the continued importance of human expertise in the age of AI.

Efficiency: The New Paradigm

AI redefines negotiation by reducing transaction costs, optimizing processes, and identifying opportunities for value creation. Eidenmueller notes, "Smart algorithms drastically reduce information and transaction costs, improve the efficiency of negotiation processes, and identify optimal value creation options."[1] These tools allow negotiators to focus on strategic decisions while delegating repetitive tasks to machines.

From early Negotiation Support Systems (NSSs) to advanced tools like Luminance's Autopilot and Walmart's AI-powered supplier chatbots, the evolution of negotiation technology highlights its growing potential. NSSs of the 1980s laid the groundwork by incorporating game theory and decision analysis

---

[1] Eidenmueller, Horst G. M., *The Advent of the AI Negotiator: Negotiation Dynamics in the Age of Smart Algorithms* (May 15, 2024). Available at SSRN: https://ssrn.com/abstract=4828339 or http://dx.doi.org/10.2139/ssrn.4828339

into negotiation support. These early systems helped negotiators determine reservation prices and evaluate alternatives, reducing human bias and inefficiency.

Today, advanced systems take this further. Luminance's Autopilot autonomously handles straightforward negotiations, such as nondisclosure agreements, while Walmart's AI chatbots optimize supplier contracts. These systems excel in scenarios where data is abundant, and issues are clearly defined. For example, Walmart's AI achieved a 1.5 percent cost reduction on supplier contracts and extended payment terms to an average of 35 days. Such results demonstrate the tangible benefits of AI-driven negotiation.

AI also enhances transparency, ensuring that all relevant data is accounted for. Algorithms analyze interests, preferences, and scenarios to propose solutions aligned with stakeholder goals. This structured approach significantly increases the "size of the pie," creating more value for all participants.

The Power and Pitfalls of Information Asymmetry

AI's strength lies in its ability to process and leverage vast amounts of information, creating significant advantages for resource-rich entities. Eidenmueller aptly describes this phenomenon as an "information power play," where the better-informed party captures the majority of the cooperative surplus. Large corporations, equipped with proprietary datasets and advanced AI systems, dominate this dynamic.

Consider Walmart's use of AI to negotiate supplier contracts. With access to extensive market data, transaction histories, and supplier information, Walmart's AI systems dynamically adjust strategies in real time, ensuring optimal outcomes. Conversely, smaller businesses and consumers, often reliant on generic AI tools like ChatGPT, struggle to compete effectively. This disparity creates an uneven playing field, further entrenching the dominance of resource-rich organizations.

This imbalance extends beyond negotiation tables. Organizations with advanced AI systems can secure favorable terms consistently, reinforcing their market position. Smaller players, lacking the resources to invest in similar technologies, face increasing marginalization.

Challenges of AI-Driven Negotiation

Despite its benefits, AI introduces challenges that highlight its limitations. Trust, a cornerstone of successful negotiations, is difficult to replicate in

AI-driven interactions. Studies reveal that human negotiators often view AI counterparts with skepticism, offering less favorable terms. This reluctance stems from perceptions of AI as impersonal and unemotional.

Cultural nuances and emotional intelligence—critical in cross-cultural negotiations—are areas where AI struggles. For example, subtle cues like tone, body language, and cultural norms significantly influence outcomes in human-to-human interactions. While some AI systems attempt to emulate these characteristics, their effectiveness remains limited. Autonomous AI systems excel in structured, data-rich negotiations but falter in scenarios requiring empathy, rapport, or creative problem-solving.

The lack of transparency in AI decision-making, often referred to as the "black box" problem, further complicates trust. Parties may hesitate to rely on AI-generated strategies without understanding the underlying logic, particularly in high-stakes negotiations.

AI and SMARTnership: A Collaborative Approach

The SMARTnership framework emphasizes trust, transparency, and mutual value creation, offering a blueprint for integrating AI into negotiations. AI excels in technical aspects, such as data analysis, scenario planning, and process optimization. However, human negotiators remain essential for managing relational dynamics.

In negotiations involving NegoEconomics—the asymmetric value created when one party's cost becomes another's gain—AI plays a pivotal role. For instance, AI can rapidly calculate financial implications and identify areas of mutual benefit. Meanwhile, human negotiators focus on rapport building, addressing concerns, and ensuring all parties feel valued. This collaboration embodies the essence of SMARTnership.

The synergy between AI and human expertise enhances outcomes by combining precision with empathy. Negotiations become not only efficient but also aligned with long-term relational goals.

Ethical and Regulatory Considerations

The rise of AI in negotiation raises ethical and regulatory concerns. The ability of AI to profile individuals, predict preferences, and manipulate behavior poses risks of exploitation. Eidenmueller warns, "Smart algorithms allow negotiators to create net value for negotiated transactions on an unprecedented scale, but they can also claim the lion's share of the cooperative surplus."[2]

Regulatory frameworks are emerging to address these risks. The European Union's AI Act, for instance, bans applications deemed to pose "unacceptable risks," such as emotion recognition and exploitative algorithms. However, overly restrictive regulations could stifle innovation, preventing societies from fully reaping AI's benefits.

To bridge disparities, some advocate for treating advanced AI tools as public goods. Initiatives like OpenAI's efforts to democratize access are promising, though challenges persist in balancing accessibility with economic sustainability.

The Future of Negotiation

AI is reshaping the skillsets required for negotiation. Traditional competencies—emotional intelligence, active listening, and persuasive communication—must now be complemented by technological literacy. Negotiators must understand AI tools and their capabilities to harness their full potential.

Fully autonomous negotiation systems, while promising, remain a distant goal. Challenges in understanding unspoken cues, adapting to unpredictable scenarios, and fostering genuine trust limit their applicability. For now, AI's role is best viewed as complementary, enhancing human efforts rather than replacing them.

The integration of AI into negotiation represents a profound shift. By combining AI's analytical power with human adaptability, negotiators can achieve outcomes that are efficient, equitable, and sustainable.

AI has revolutionized negotiation, offering unprecedented efficiency and insights. However, its uneven distribution of benefits poses ethical and regulatory challenges. As Eidenmueller concludes, "Smart negotiation algorithms bring phenomenal wealth, but this wealth is likely to be very unequally distributed."[3] The responsibility lies with policymakers, developers, and negotiators to ensure AI serves as a tool for collaboration, not exploitation.

The future of negotiation lies at the intersection of technology and humanity. By addressing AI's challenges and fostering collaboration, negotiators can create a landscape that leverages technology to foster equitable and innovative outcomes. This partnership between man and machine embodies the next frontier in negotiation dynamics.

---

[2] Ibid.
[3] Ibid.

Implementing AI-Enhanced SMARTnership Strategies

In the rapidly evolving landscape of negotiation, the integration of AI into SMARTnership strategies offers unprecedented opportunities for value creation, efficiency, and relationship building. However, the successful implementation of these strategies requires a structured approach that addresses key challenges such as measuring return on investment (ROI), managing change, and equipping teams with the necessary skills. This chapter provides a comprehensive guide to implementing AI-enhanced SMARTnership strategies, focusing on practical frameworks and actionable insights.

Measuring ROI: Quantifying the Impact of AI-Enhanced Strategies

One of the most critical aspects of implementing AI-enhanced SMARTnership strategies is demonstrating their value. ROI measurement serves as a cornerstone for justifying investments and guiding decision-making. This section outlines a robust framework for quantifying the impact of these strategies.

Financial Metrics

Financial metrics provide a direct measure of the monetary benefits derived from AI-enhanced strategies. These include:

- **Deal value improvement:** Assessing the percentage increase in deal value achieved through AI-driven insights
- **Cost reduction:** Calculating savings from optimized resource allocation and error reduction
- **Time savings:** Monetizing the time saved through accelerated decision-making and process automation
- **Resource optimization:** Evaluating the efficiency gains from better resource utilization

Performance Metrics

Performance metrics focus on operational and quality improvements:

- **Operational efficiency:** Measuring reductions in negotiation cycle times and improvements in decision-making speed
- **Quality metrics:** Tracking agreement accuracy rates, compliance improvements, and risk identification success

Relationship Value Metrics

Beyond financial and performance metrics, the value of relationships is a critical component of ROI:

- **Partnership strength indicators:** Monitoring long-term relationship retention and partner satisfaction scores
- **Market position impact:** Evaluating gains in competitive advantage, market share, and brand value

Change Management: Navigating the Transition to AI-Enhanced Negotiation

Introducing AI into negotiation processes requires careful planning and execution to overcome resistance and ensure stakeholder buy-in. This section provides a roadmap for effective change management.

Stakeholder Analysis and Engagement

Engaging stakeholders is crucial for successful implementation. Key steps include:

- **Identification phase:** Mapping key decision-makers, analyzing influence networks, and identifying potential resistance points
- **Engagement strategy:** Developing customized communication plans, demonstrating benefits, and addressing concerns through regular feedback loops

Implementation Roadmap

A phased approach ensures a smooth transition:

- **Preparation phase:** Conducting a current state assessment, gap analysis, and resource planning
- **Rollout strategy:** Designing pilot programs, identifying quick wins, and scaling successful initiatives

Resistance Management

Resistance to change is a common challenge. Effective strategies include:

- **Education and training:** Providing comprehensive training programs to build confidence and competence
- **Demonstrating benefits:** Showcasing pilot success stories to build momentum and trust

Team Training: Building Competence in AI-Enhanced SMARTnership

Equipping teams with the skills needed to leverage AI in SMARTnership strategies is essential for long-term success. This section outlines a structured training framework.

Core Competency Development

Training programs should focus on both technical and soft skills:

- **Technical skills:** Proficiency in AI tools, data analysis, and digital platforms
- **Soft skills:** Enhancing digital emotional intelligence, cross-cultural competence, and adaptability

Training Program Structure

A tiered approach ensures comprehensive skill development:

- **Foundation level:** Covering basic AI concepts, SMARTnership principles, and digital tool fundamentals
- **Advanced level:** Addressing complex negotiation scenarios, advanced AI applications, and strategy development
- **Expert level:** Focusing on system integration, process improvement, and innovation leadership

Certification Program

Certification programs validate skills and encourage continuous learning:

- **Program components:** Including knowledge assessments, practical applications, and case study analyses
- **Assessment methods:** Utilizing online examinations, project evaluations, and peer reviews

The integration of AI into SMARTnership strategies represents a transformative opportunity for negotiators. By focusing on ROI measurement, effective change management, and comprehensive team training, organizations can unlock the full potential of AI-enhanced negotiation.

CONCLUSION

The Starting Point Is You

Every year, I engage with countless bright, insightful individuals. After presentations, I'm often asked, "How do I get my counterpart to adopt a cooperative mindset, particularly when it comes to leveraging the NegoEconomics and SMARTnership principles?"

The answer is both simple and profound: You can't directly change someone else's mindset. The only person in the room you can truly influence is yourself.

To make meaningful progress in negotiation, you must lead by example, often taking the first step. In Irish history, the Fitzgerald chieftain resolved a bitter feud by risking his own safety to extend his arm through the "Door of Reconciliation" at St. Patrick's Cathedral in Dublin. This act of trust invited his adversaries to move from conflict to collaboration. Whether you're negotiating in person or training an AI model to assist, the principle remains the same—be the first to demonstrate openness and trust.

However, trust alone isn't enough. Negotiation is fundamentally about information: exchanging, evaluating, and understanding it. Whether you're working with a human counterpart or an AI, success lies in mutual transparency: "I'll show you mine if you show me yours."

AI is revolutionizing how we negotiate. With data-driven insights and predictive modeling, AI can highlight opportunities to create value and identify risks. Yet even with advanced tools, the essential element is still human leadership. A skilled negotiator knows how to use AI to enhance, not replace, the human connection that builds trust and creates SMARTnerships.

Take a moment to evaluate your approach. What can you change in your negotiation habits to better integrate AI? How can AI help you analyze value drivers, assess trade-offs, and open discussions with more insight? Make a list:

- What issues can you approach with more openness?
- How can AI help you identify shared opportunities?
- What new tools or methods can streamline your next negotiation?

The world needs negotiators like you—bold enough to embrace innovation and transform centuries-old practices. The shift from zero-sum thinking to collaborative problem-solving is essential, whether you're partnering with people or with technology.

My mission is clear: to make negotiation smarter, partnerships more prosperous, and the world a better place. When you use AI not just to win but to create value for all parties, you elevate negotiation to a higher level—one where mutual success becomes inevitable.

In your next negotiation, consider opening with this: "I'm here to use every tool, including AI, to help us reduce costs, limit risks, and increase profits for both sides. Are you open to exploring this together?" Such a statement sets the tone for collaboration and positions you as a leader ready to leverage both human and technological intelligence.

Ultimately, transformation starts with you. By adopting a mindset of trust and collaboration—powered by human and AI insights—you'll not only change the outcome of negotiations but the way the world does business.

Acknowledgments

My deepest gratitude extends to the many individuals who have inspired, guided, and shaped my journey in negotiation since the late 1980s. Their wisdom and mentorship have been instrumental in honing my understanding of negotiation as both an art and a science.

I owe a special acknowledgment to the late Mr. Iwar Unt, whose pioneering work in Stockholm, Sweden, in 1976 laid the groundwork for the concepts I continue to develop. His mentorship remains a cornerstone of my career and a source of enduring inspiration. Mr. Unt was way ahead in describing collaborative negotiation.

The late Paige Stover, my first business agent after moving to the United States, also holds a special place in my heart. Her steadfast guidance during those early years was a beacon that helped me navigate new opportunities and challenges.

Many years ago, I met a thoughtful and inspiring gentleman, Mr. Tim Cummins, the founder and president of World Commerce & Contracting, which led to a decade-long relationship, where we meet up a couple of times every year at a WorldCC conference and co-host the video podcast *The Negotiation Room*. I have been privileged to collaborate with remarkable professionals across Europe, Asia, and the United States. Sally Guyer of World Commerce & Contracting, Lars Krull at Aalborg University, and Jurga Bendikaitė-Ursavas, director general at BMI Executive Institute stand out for their unwavering dedication to advancing the field of negotiation.

I am also deeply appreciative of the exceptional team at Wiley, especially my editor Cheryl Segura, for their invaluable role in bringing this book to life.

To my Certified Partners worldwide, especially Ms. Tine Anneberg, Professor Grazvydas Jukna, and Dr. Jason Myrowitz, for being pioneers. Thank you for tirelessly championing the principles of SMARTnership and NegoEconomics. Your commitment to fostering collaboration and creating value inspires me and amplifies the global impact of these methodologies.

I am grateful to Mr. Per Holm, CEO of BlueKolding in Denmark. His company's award-winning application of SMARTnership and NegoEconomics demonstrates the transformative power of these concepts and continues to inspire others to embrace collaborative negotiation.

To my lifelong friend Antonis, your unwavering loyalty and support through every twist and turn of life have been a constant source of strength. Similarly, my gratitude goes to Mr. Werner Valeur, a remarkable entrepreneur and dear friend, for his steadfast encouragement and invaluable insights into negotiation.

Acknowledgments

The ideas and frameworks in this book are the culmination of years of research, workshops, advisory sessions, and collaborations with thought leaders in negotiation, behavioral economics, and conflict resolution. Countless debates, breakthroughs, and lessons learned from challenging negotiations have enriched these pages.

To my wife, Keyanna, your love, patience, and encouragement have been my foundation. To my sons, Kruise and Kierland, your affection and boundless energy remind me of life's truest priorities and joys.

A special greeting to my brother, Leif, just for being my big brother!

Finally, this book is dedicated to my late mother and father, Laura and Elmo. Their love and wisdom continue to guide and inspire me every day. Their legacy lives on in all that I do, and I think of them daily.

About the Author

Dr. Keld Jensen is an internationally recognized and award-winning expert, TEDx speaker, author, and advisor on negotiation, celebrated for his profound impact in the field. In 2024, Keld added a significant milestone to his illustrious career by concluding his doctorate in negotiation, AI, and trust, further solidifying his expertise and commitment to advancing understanding in these critical areas.

He is the founder and head of the SMARTnership Negotiation Organization, a pivotal force in consulting and training for both the private sector and governmental bodies, facilitating optimized solutions to complex problems. His notable clientele includes industry giants such as Vestas, LEGO, ConocoPhillips, Novo Nordisk, Bechtel, Johnson & Johnson, and leading organizations like UNICEF and World50, as well as the governments of Canada, Denmark, and Great Britain.

Keld's extensive background in management and his role as a former CEO of PC Express AB, a publicly traded technology company, underline his leadership and strategic acumen. An associate professor, Keld teaches at top-ranked universities worldwide, including the Thunderbird School of Global Management at ASU, BMI Executive Institute in Lithuania, BMI/Louvain University in Belgium, and Denmark's Aalborg University. He is the former chair of the Centre for Negotiation at Copenhagen Business School.

With more than 200 international TV appearances, regular contributions to *Forbes* magazine, and hundreds of articles in major business publications across Europe, Asia Pacific, and the United States, Keld has established himself as a global thought leader. He is a prolific author of 27 books, which have been translated into 16 languages and have reached over three million readers worldwide. Several of these works have received awards, marking him as a significant voice in international business literature.

Keld was recognized as one of the world's 100 Top Thought Leaders in Trust in 2016 and has consistently ranked in the Global Gurus Top 30, reaching number three as a Global Guru on Negotiation worldwide in 2025. He is the creator of the world's most awarded negotiation strategy, which has received accolades from the Organization of Public Procurement Officers in Denmark and the World Commerce & Contracting Organization's Innovation and Strategic Award, and is ranked as the world's third-best negotiation training program by "Global Training." LinkedIn Training also asked Keld to design an online training program on the use of AI in negotiation, which is available on LinkedIn.

A dual citizen of the Kingdom of Denmark and the United States, Keld resides in the United States with his wonderful wife and two children, whom he humorously credits with improving his negotiation skills daily. His commitment to mentoring entrepreneurs and enhancing small and medium-sized businesses through vital negotiations has led to the creation and growth of numerous companies.

For more insights into negotiation and to access Keld's online training, visit **www.smartnershipclass.com** and **www.smartnership.org**.

Index

A

Accepted price, 69
Accessibility, 192, 228
Active listening, 95–96, 114, 228
Agendas:
  and conflict, 99
  lack of, 153
  methodical approach to, 143
  of natural leaders, 130
  for negotiation goals, 151
  preparation for, 172
  in Rules of the Game, 38, 110
  structuring, 189
  support for, 117
  working with, 44–48
Agreement customization, 80, 192
Agreement duration, 76
Agreement timing, 76–77
AI tool selection, 7–8
AI-driven negotiation, 14, 170, 200–201, 208–209, 226–227
AI-to-AI negotiations, 195
Al-Ghazal, 11
Alternative offers, 60, 80–81. *See also* Counteroffers
Alternatives:
  AI analysis of, 18, 53–54
  in conflicts, 152, 156
  counteroffers as, 159
  from counterparts, 110–111
  in deadlocks, 106–107, 116–117
  envisioning, 61
  exploring, 62
  hypothetical questions for, 113
  low offers as, 159
  negotiation support systems for, 225
  next-best, 188–189
  in ownership models, 68
  of payments, 67
  in perceived value, 69
  prompts for, 83, 138–139, 208
  as risk mitigation, 123
  SMARTnership as, 23, 90, 93–94
  suggesting, 141
  technical, 74
  as trial balloons, 104–105
Amazon, 35, 120–121
Ambiguity, 20, 97–98, 124, 129, 168, 196, 219
Analytical experts, 131. *See also* Compliance
Analytical negotiators, 129. *See also* Compliance
Anthropomorphism, 213
Apple, 38, 120
The Art of War (Sun Tzu), 11
Asymmetric discovery, 5
Asymmetric usage, 201–202
Asymmetrical value, 29, 32, 57, 88, 90, 98, 102, 110
Augmented reality (AR), 209
Authority bias, 211–213. *See also* Bias

B

Backdoor selling, 100–101
Bargaining:
  agendas for, 45
  combative style of, 125
  compromising style of, 126
  in credit card promotion, 72
  embracing, 160
  fear of, 155–157
  and generosity, 88
  limited skills of, 68
  and offers, 142
  prompts for, 219

240 INDEX

Bargaining: (*continued*)
  and requirements, 74
  in SMARTnership roadmap, 24
  in successful negotiations, 138
  timing of, 143–144
  and trust, 94
BATNA (Best Alternative
  to a Negotiated
  Agreement), 172, 216
Begin, Menachem, 33
Behavioral analysis, 5, 54, 123, 132
Behavioral dynamics, 170, 200–201
Benchmarking, 13, 47, 54, 66–71,
  80, 120, 194, 196
Best Alternative to a Negotiated
  Agreement (BATNA), 172, 216
Best practices, 112, 202
Bezos, Jeff, 35
Bias, 14, 167, 194, 201, 209, 225.
  See also Authority bias
Billpoint, 35
Biyu (fictional company), 42
Black box problem, 227
Budgeting. *See also* Pricing
  and agreements, 76
  of clients, 110–111
  constraints of, 109
  and low offers, 145
  and pricing, 67–71, 149
  realistic goals for, 141

C

Camp David Accords, 33
Cars (film), 30
Carter, Jimmy, 33
Cash flow management, 179
Change management, 230–231
ChatGPT, 79, 171, 185–190, 192,
  195, 200–201, 226
Chen, Steve, 34
Clause summarization, 196
Client diversification, 179
Collaboration agreements, 49–55
Collaboration model, 50, 52–53

Collaborative negotiating style,
  125, 132, 134
Combative negotiating style, 27,
  125, 132, 134, 145, 147–148, 157
Commercial enterprise, 63
Communication:
  and deadlocks, 44, 94, 100
  direct, 96–97
  internal, 123, 154–155
  one-way, 94, 148
  open, with counterparts, 145
  trust-building through open, 129
  two-way, 24, 94, 106, 115, 148
Communication proficiency,
  51, 53, 114
Comparison, 62, 116, 174,
  192, 196, 213
Competitor benchmarking, 80, 82.
  See also Benchmarking
Compliance (DISC), 55, 127, 129,
  131, 133. *See also* DISC
Compromise, 24, 27, 33, 34, 61, 126,
  130, 137–139
Compromising negotiating
  style, 126, 132
Concession mapping, 172, 174
Concessional negotiating style,
  27, 126, 132
Confirmation of worth, 69
Conflict:
  and active listening, 96
  from ambiguity, 97
  collaboration vs., 91
  as cost of mistakes, 136
  cultural differences as, 167
  difficulty in resolving, 152
  fear of, 68
  and insults, 163
  negotiation strategies for, 39, 93
  opening up during, 155
  prompts for, 172, 215, 233
  as relationship destroyer, 99
  resolving, 2
  S-style avoidance of, 127

in stalling negotiation style, 126
in sun and wind method of negotiation, 142
from value differences, 114
in zero-sum scenarios, 28–29
Conflict resolution, 12, 97, 172, 221, 236
Congress of Vienna, 12
Conscientiousness (DISC), 55. *See also* DISC
Contingency planning, 175
Continuous improvement, 222
Continuous learning, 6, 80, 232
Contract analysis, 123
Contract reading, 193
Copenhagen Business School, 24
Core competencies, 166, 231
Correct price, 69
Cost asymmetries, 81
Cost identification and allocation, 86
Cost sharing, 79
Cost-benefit analysis, 58, 81, 115, 129, 174, 181. *See also* Visual presentations
Counter-benefits, 108
Counteroffers. *See also* Alternative offers
active presentation of, 142
AI generation of, 19
asking for, 60
in bargaining, 155–156
prompts for, 80, 82, 115, 168, 172
in scenario planning, 186, 207
from successful negotiators, 138–140
in unbalanced negotiations, 146
Counterparts:
active listening with, 95–96
adapting to, 134
AI-to-AI negotiations with, 195
and asymmetrical values, 2
behavioral analysis of, 132, 169
clarity with, 96

code of conduct for, 40
conflicts with, 99
control from, 110
C-style negotiations with, 131, 133
data analysis on, 5, 13–14, 19
DISC profiling of, 132–133
empathy for, 206
feedback from, 209
generosity towards, 88
informal interactions with, 115–116
I-style negotiations with, 128, 130, 133
open calculation for, 98
open communication with, 145
open dialog with, 94–95
persuading, 233
prompts for dealing with, 82, 172–175, 178–180, 187, 189, 207–208, 215–219, 221
questions for, 111
relationship building with, 93–104
researching, 185
risk assessment of, 206
roleplay with, 188
skepticism over, 227
S-style negotiations with, 133
SWOT analysis of, 186
two-way communication with, 94, 115
understanding, 102–104
in we-versus-them situations, 167
in zero-sum games, 90
CQ (cultural intelligence), 181, 183
Creative problem-solving, 7, 59, 71, 156, 182–183, 227
Credit cards, 25, 67, 72
Cross-cultural negotiation, 8, 12, 14, 53, 181, 227, 231
Cross-purposes dialogue, 51, 114
crystalknows.com, 131
Cultural adaptation strategies, 174

Cultural context, 117, 174
Cultural differences, 12, 14, 50,
    161, 167, 218
Cultural intelligence (CQ), 181, 183
Cultural sensitivity, 7, 172
Cummins, Tim, 200
Currency management, 71–72
Customer feedback analysis, 123
Customization, 79, 192,
    194, 196, 230

D

Data analysis, 5–7, 20, 48, 79, 202,
    205–207, 227, 231
Data security, 195
Deadlocks:
    and bargaining, 143
    breaking, 174
    and communication, 44, 94, 100
    conflict resolution for, 172
    data breaking of, 116–117
    data in ketchup effect, 136–137
    detection of, 116
    preventing, 105–109
Demonstrations, 116
Dependable anchors, 130. *See also*
    Steadiness
Development assignments, 78
Digital divide, 7
Direct communication, 96–97
DISC, 55, 85, 126–134
Disney, 30–33
Distributive negotiations, 27.
    See also Zero-sum games
Document navigation, 193
Dominance (DISC), 55, 127–128,
    130, 133. *See also* DISC
Downtime, 77, 101
Dragons' Den (TV program), 3
Dynamic adjustments, 115
Dynamic modeling, 13
Dynamic pricing, 80, 83

E

eBay, 35, 120
Economic uncertainty, 179, 222
Economics managers, 154
Economies of scale, 61, 65, 75, 164
EdgeTech, 25
Electric vehicles (EVs), 32, 78–79
Emotion management, 175
Emotional intelligence (EQ):
    AI alignment with, 15
    ChatGPT use of, 187–188
    in cross-cultural negotiations, 227
    digital, 231
    human element of, 7, 14,
        20, 203, 228
    and human-AI synergy, 180–181
    importance of, 127
    prompts for use of, 206, 217
Emotion-focused prompts, 179
Empathy:
    AI deficiency in, 177
    in concessional negotiating
        style, 126
    in DISC styles, 131
    -driven prompts, 179–180, 217
    and emotional intelli-
        gence, 187–188
    human-AI alliance of,
        20, 190, 227
    and intuition, 208
    in S-style negotiations, 129
    for strong partnerships, 159
    in sun and wind method, 142
Empathy engine, 206
Employee engagement, 123
Engaging communicators, 130.
    See also Influence
Envy, 51, 161, 166–167
EQ, *see* Emotional intelligence
Ethics:
    AI considerations of, 14
    in AI contracts, 194–195

code of conduct for, 40
consideration of, 146, 202
and generosity, 87
and giver advantage, 89
guidelines for, 6–7
legal limitations of, 36
in Middle Ages, 11
prompts related to, 174, 198, 218, 223
regulatory considerations of, 227–228
European Union AI Act, 228
EVs (electric vehicles), 32, 78–79
Exclusivity, 79, 81–82
Experts, 154, 211, 212. *See also* Nonexperts

F
Fabius, Laurent, 34
Failure avoidance, 160–161
Feedback, real-time, 133–134, 205–209
Feedback analysis, 123
Feedback loops, 115, 230
Feige, Kevin, 35
Fight-or-flight response, 27, 157
Financial metrics, 229
Financial overseers, 158
Fisher, Roger, 1
Fixed pricing, 69
Flexible pricing, 69, 72
Follett, Mary Parker, 12
Four pillars of human-AI synergy, 180–182
Furniture industry, 66

G
Game theory, 12, 225
Generative AI, 19, 192, 202–203, 213
Generosity, 51, 54, 87–91
Getting to Yes (Fisher and Ury), 1, 4

Give and Take (Grant), 87
Giver mindset, 87–89
Google, 33–34
Grant, Adam, 87–90

H
Harmonious negotiators, 129. *See also* Steadiness
Human chemistry, 49–50, 52, 93, 114, 162, 167
Human elements, of negotiation, 7, 91, 182–184, 203
Human intuition, 13, 169, 203, 208, 225
Human-AI balance, 20, 182–183
Hurley, Chad, 34
Hypothetical questions, 113, 115

I
IBM, 33
Iger, Bob, 32
IKEA, 65–66
Implementation roadmaps, 231
Incentive-driven pricing, 70
Indexed pricing, 69–70
Influence (DISC), 55, 127, 128, 131, 133. *See also* DISC
Informal Interactions, 115–116
Information asymmetry, 226
Information flow, 110, 117
Information management, 117
Initial payments, 72–73
Intellectual property rights, 78, 187
Internal communication, 123, 154–155
Internal dynamics, 70
iTunes, 120

J
Jensen, Keld, 8, 215

K
Ketchup effect, 136–137, 155

L

Language simplification, 192
Large language models (LLMs), 19
Learning curves, 202
Lenovo, 33
Licensing, 79, 81
LinkedIn, 34, 131, 217
Listeners, 154, 160. *See also* Observers
Lone wolf strategy, 88–89
Low offers, 144, 158–159
Luminance's Autopilot, 225–226

M

Machine-to-machine negotiation, 202
Mackey, John, 35
McKinsey Global Institute, 18
Magna Carta, 11
Market intelligence, 5
Marvel Studios, 35
Matchers, 87. *See also* Giver mindset
Meta AI, 171
Microsoft, 34, 61
Microsoft Copilot, 171
Mistrust, 121–122, 165, 167
Most Negotiated Terms Report, 138–139
Multi-party negotiation plans, 174
Musk, Elon, 32, 35

N

Nadella, Satya, 34
Nash, John, 12
Nationally determined contributions (NDCs), 34
Natural language processing (NLP), 122–123
Natural leaders, 130. *See also* Dominance
NegoEconomics, 57–83
 actively seeking, 146, 147
 benchmarking and applying, 66–73
 capitalizing on potential with, 2
 defining, 25–27
 Disney and Pixar as example of, 30–31
 effective use of, 156
 examples of, 62–66
 key principles of, 57–62
 leveraging AI in, 79–83, 227
 in open calculations, 98
 prioritizing, 138–139
 in SMARTnerships, 23
 strategic approach to, 73–79
 and transparency, 95
 understanding and applying, 140, 149–150
 value of, 157
Negotiating trap, 74
Negotiation Code of Conduct, 39–40, 48
Negotiation styles, 125–134
Negotiation support systems (NSSs), 225
Negotiation variables, 2, 44, 138, 140
Netflix, 121
Net-syndrome, 91
Next best alternative (NBA), 188–189
NLP (natural language processing), 122–123
Nonexperts, 191–192. *See also* Experts
Novo Nordisk, 31
NSSs (negotiation support systems), 225
NVIDIA, 31

O

Objection handling, 173, 216
Objection reframing, 173
Objective data analysis, 5. *See also* Data analysis
Observers, 100, 151, 154. *See also* Listeners

One-way communication, 94, 148
Open calculations, 98–99, 115
Open dialogues, 93
Opening offers, 69, 155, 189
Operating costs, 109
Orientation-based pricing, 68, 70
Outcome prediction, 188
Ownership and user rights, 79
Ownership models, 68

P

Palmisano, Samuel, 33
Panasonic, 32
Paris Climate Agreement, 34
Pascal, Amy, 35
Pattern recognition, 5–6, 8, 182
Payment methods, 67, 72
PayPal, 35
Perceived value, 54, 58, 60, 69, 80, 81, 172
Performance metrics, 230
Performance monitoring, 80
Period of notice, 76
Personality alignment, 186
Pixar, 30–33
Post-agreement optimization, 80
Post-negotiation, 20, 173, 176, 189, 217, 222
Power dynamics, 175
Preferred customer status, 79
Preparedness, 76–77
Preserves, 161, 165–166
Prestige, 50, 69, 150–151, 162
Price frenzy, 91
Pricing, 67–72, 77, 80, 83, 90, 98, 113. *See also* Budgeting
   dynamic, 80, 83
   fixed, 69
   flexible, 69, 72
   incentive-driven, 70
   indexed, 69–70
   orientation-based, 68, 70
   results-based, 70–71

Process integration, 8
Production rights, 79
Prompts, 215–223
Proposal comparison, 174
Public authority, 63
Purchasing patterns, 61, 77

R

Race to zero, 90–91
R&D costs, 78
Reactive focus, 192
Reflection, 42, 67, 102, 107, 129, 144, 157–158
Regulatory compliance, 179, 197
Regulatory frameworks, 228
Relationship architecture, 181–183
Relationship building, 14
   with counterparts, 94
   human element in, 7
   human-AI alliance for, 20, 208
   in net-syndrome situations, 91
   NLP for, 123
   prompts for, 83, 215, 217–218
   SMARTnership strategies for, 229
Relationship value metrics, 230
Relationship-oriented negotiators, 128. *See also* Influence
Renegotiation workload, 76
Repetitive task automation, 14, 18, 192, 225
Resistance management, 231
Response time, 19, 76–77, 132
Results-based pricing, 70–71
Results-driven negotiators, 127–129. *See also* Dominance
Return on investment (ROI), 229–230, 232
Rights, 78–79
Risk assessment, 5, 80, 83, 131, 168, 194, 206
Risk identification, 196, 230
Risk management, 66, 194, 219
Risk mitigation, 123

Rivian, 78–79, 81
ROI (return on investment), 229–230, 232
Role distribution, 138, 144, 154
Role-playing, 172, 173, 188, 221
Royalties, 67, 70, 72–73, 78, 82
Rules of the Game, 24, 37–48, 110

S

Sadat, Anwar, 33
SALT (Strategic Arms Limitation Treaties), 12
Scalability, 14, 65
Scenario modeling, 116
Scenario planning, 19, 48, 80–81, 172, 186, 202, 220, 227
Scenario-based preparation, 173, 215
Scenario-specific drafting, 196
Scenario-specific prompts, 222
Schmidt, Eric, 34
Sentiment, 19, 52, 114, 122–123, 187, 206
Sentiment analysis, 52, 80, 115, 206, 209
Shared outcomes, 32, 207
Shark Tank (TV program), 3, 122
Simulations:
  in demonstrations, 116
  of negotiations, 115
  as practice, 188
  and scenario planning, 80, 186, 207
  studies based on, 135, 200
  uses of, 47
  in value creation phase, 6
Smart contracts, 195
Smart givers, 89. *See also* Giver mindset
Smith, Adam, 1
Soft variables, 139
Sony, 35
Speakers Gold, 17
Stakeholder analysis, 19, 230

Stalemates, 105, 108–110, 152
Stalling negotiating style, 27, 107, 126, 132, 134
Standardization, 202
Steadiness (DISC), 55, 127, 129, 130, 133. *See also* DISC
Stinginess, 158, 161, 165
Strategic Arms Limitation Treaties (SALT), 12
Strategic breaks, 155
Strategic plans, 157
Stress, 27, 43, 127, 137, 156–158, 163, 179, 206
Stress testing, 174
Style guides, 178
Suborders, 76
Sun and wind method, 141–142
Sun and wind method of negotiation, 142
Sun Tzu, 11
Suspiciousness, 161, 165
SWOT analysis, 186, 212

T

Takers, 87–88. *See also* Giver mindset
Talent acquisition and retention, 178
Team development, 8
Team training, 231–232
Technician-to-technician discussions, 74
Technological adaptation, 179
Tehran-Stockholm Deal, 181
Telia/Telenor merger, 145, 150, 163
Templates, 192–194, 196
Termination rights, 197
Terms of payment, 67–68
Tesla, 32, 78–79, 81
Thiel, Peter, 35
Third parties, 99–100
Three A's of AI-enhanced negotiation, 21
Time efficiency, 66

Time management, 63, 174
Time-intensive drafting, 192
Timetables, 145, 155, 158
Totality, 144, 150–151
Toyota, 38
Traditional negotiation fights, 144, 147–148
Transparency:
  agenda support for, 117
  from AI, 18, 201, 226
  at Amazon, 121
  and asymmetric value, 27
  in code of conduct, 40
  in contract analysis, 123
  enhancements for, 115
  and ethics, 14, 195
  in flexible pricing agreements, 69
  mutual, 233
  in open dialogues, 93, 95, 145
  prompts for, 83, 123–124, 174
  responsibility for, 161
  in Rules of the Game, 47
  SMARTnership approach to, 23–25, 31, 227
  strategic, 153
  trust-building through, 5–7, 32
  in Tru$tCurrency, 88–89
  and value creation, 8
  in we-versus-them situations, 167–168
Treaty of Versailles, 12
Trial balloons, 104–105, 173
Trust erosion, 183
Trust Factor, 23, 36
Trust paradox, 7
Trust triangle model, 182
Trust-building:
  AI assistance with, 114–115
  AI's importance in, 124
  at Amazon, 120
  in DISC scenarios, 133
  in empathy engine, 206
  and giver advantage, 89
  human element of, 20
  importance of, 32
  at Netflix, 121
  open calculation for, 98
  in partnerships, 159
  prompts for, 47, 83, 123, 217, 222
  questions for, 113
  in relationship architecture, 182
  in Rules of the Game, 38
  through open communication, 129
  through transparency, 5–6, 47
  in we-versus-them situations, 167
Trust-valuation, 119–122
Tsuga, Kazuhiro, 32
Two-way communication, 24, 94, 106, 115, 148

U

Uncertainty, 5, 27, 69, 74, 95, 129, 160, 206
Unilateral concessions, 107, 110
United Nations, 12, 39
Ury, William, 1

V

Value creation:
  AI-enhanced, 4–6, 182, 203, 227
  diverse pricing methods for, 69
  dynamic, 81
  and efficiency, 225
  in fair solutions, 160
  generation of, 66
  and generosity, 87
  as key principle of NegoEconomics, 58, 69
  mutual, 24, 29–30, 91
  new era of, 8
  opportunities for, 229
  prompts for, 80, 83, 173–175
  and trust, 23
  variables for, 47
  in we-versus-them situations, 168
Value norms, 50, 152, 161, 163, 166
Velocity, 25–26

Veto power, 78–79
Visual presentations, 38, 115–116, 128, 133, 138–139, 174, 193, 198

W

WALL-E (film), 30
Walmart, 225–226
The Wealth of Nations (Smith), 1
Wegovy, 31
Weiner, Jeff, 34
We-versus-them situations, 161, 167–168
Wharton, 87
Whitman, Meg, 35
Whole Foods, 35
Winding up period, 75, 76
Win-lose approach, 1, 4, 24, 30, 39, 59, 81, 87
Winner-takes-all mindset, 91
Win-win outcomes, 12, 58, 126, 156, 218
Win-win scenarios, 19, 29, 201, 209
World Commerce & Contracting, 57, 138, 170, 198, 200
World Economic Forum, 17

Y

"Yes, but" principle, 141
YouTube, 33–34
Yuanqing, Yang, 33

Z

Zero-sum bargaining, 9. *See also* Bargaining
Zero-sum games, 3, 8, 26–27, 29, 90, 107, 145, 156